SHAKESPEARE AND THE AUDIENCE

SHAKESPEARE AND THE AUDIENCE

A STUDY IN THE TECHNIQUE OF EXPOSITION

By

ARTHUR COLBY SPRAGUE

NEW YORK / RUSSELL & RUSSELL

1966

TO

GEORGE LYMAN KITTREDGE

Preface

AS A GLANCE at the headings of my chapters will suggest, Shakespeare's technique of exposition is a very broad subject, and I do not pretend to have treated it exhaustively at any point. Many related questions have been simplified or quite disregarded. A harsh critic might even assert, and with some reason, that I have proceeded as if the First Folio plays — and *Pericles* — were wholly the work of one man, writing at one time. There is no bibliography, and the accumulation of examples and references has, as far as possible, been avoided. On the other hand, I have not hesitated to quote freely from the plays themselves, following, for the sake of convenience, the text of the *Oxford Shakespeare*, edited by W. J. Craig.

To the writings of others, I am, of course, greatly indebted. Mr. Granville-Barker's *Prefaces* — unequalled in our day for the number of desirable qualities which they combine — Professor Stoll's *Shakespeare Studies* and his *Art and Artifice of Shakespeare*, Creizenach's *English Drama in the Age of Shakespeare*, Miss M. C. Bradbrook's *Elizabethan Stage Conditions*, Dr. Arnold's *Soliloquies of Shakespeare*, and Professor Schücking's *Character Problems in Shakespeare's Plays* are perhaps cited with especial frequency.

Three friends, Dr. Philip Child, Mr. L. H. Butterfield, and Mr. J. Fletcher Smith, have criticized parts of my manuscript. Professor Kittredge has read it all, chapter by chapter, as it was written; and my obligation to him is not to be expressed in a few polite phrases. The book is dedicated to him, and it is as the work of one of his students that I should like it to be read.

A. C. S.

Harvard University.
August 1935

Contents

CHAPTER VIII

CHAPTER IX

SHAKESPEARE AND THE
AUDIENCE

Chapter I

INTRODUCTION

Novelist and Playwright — The Bartley Principle —
Stage Action Explanatory — And Explained — Faces of
the Characters — Battles — Expository Scenes — Words
of the Witches — Shakespeare taking Pains — Good Exposition — And Bad.

THE novel needs all the form it can get. Hence
writers of novels subject themselves to limitations: Soames Forsyte thinks for us, but not Irene;
we look out on the universe from the point of view
of Mrs. Browning's dog. Fortunately, the right to
omniscience may always be resumed, and "it *is*
helpful to be able to say what you like about the
characters and their doings in the book." *

Drama is another matter. In a play, the author
is shut off from direct communication with us; he
may not, himself, tell us about anything. There
before our eyes he sets his characters. They speak
and act. The assumption is the assumption of real
life, and, as in real life, we draw our own inferences
from what is done and spoken. Even the practice
of soliloquy, by which a freegoing Elizabethan like
Shakespeare could externalize thought, is not really
an exception. For though the possibilities of real
life have momentarily been enlarged by the accept-

* Percy Lubbock, *The Craft of Fiction*, London [1921], p. 198.

ance of a convention, it is still one of the characters — Hamlet or Brutus or Macbeth — who is thinking aloud for us, not the author.

To this major difficulty of the playwright — that with the best will in the world he is forbidden to take a short cut and address us in person — are added certain disadvantages inherent in his prescribed method of imparting information — by word of mouth. We in the theatre may neither read again nor turn back. We are exposed to all the distractions of a crowded assembly. The wretch in front of us coughs, and we have lost the important word. The minor actor from whom we were to learn something of moment mumbles or speaks too fast. Is it, indeed, any wonder that we hear so often, " Yes, I enjoyed such and such a play, because I had read it first "?

Sharing these problems with later dramatists, Shakespeare had also to reckon with the special conditions of his own theatre. His audience were not furnished with programmes, and though the actual informative value of programmes is perhaps slight, it is not altogether negligible. His stage too — the stage of the Globe * — had neither scenery nor artificial lighting. In other words, whatever a playwright now consigns to his scene painter and

* Throughout, the stage I have in mind is the stage of the public theatre. Some of Shakespeare's plays were, of course, produced elsewhere.

electrician Shakespeare had somehow to do himself.
Finally, though he usually begins his stories early,
and as a result is much less troubled by preliminaries than Sophocles or Ibsen, the stories
themselves have a fullness and complexity which
necessarily affected his technique. Silences and
condensations abound. Lady Macbeth has a bare
two hundred and sixty lines.* There is some sacrifice of realism — for realism is in part a matter of
speed † — and the sum of things to be explained
mounts apace.

Planché in his *Recollections and Reflections* tells an
anecdote, so good that it has often been repeated,
of George Bartley, an actor and stage manager of the
early nineteenth century. Bartley's opinion of " the
intelligence of a British public " was not, writes
Planché, flattering:

> " Sir," he would say to me, " you must first tell them you
> are going to do so and so; you must then tell them you are doing
> it, and then that you have done it; and then, by G–d " (with a
> slap on his thigh), " *perhaps* they will understand you! " ‡

" His advice," Planché adds, " was most valuable
to young writers." At moments, Shakespeare himself might have been following it. Witness the great

* Harley Granville-Barker, *On Dramatic Method*, London, 1931,
p. 34.
† Thus, the famous temptation scene in *Othello*, or the scenes
between De Flores and Beatrice-Joanna in Middleton's *Changeling*,
gain much of their realism from a comparatively slow tempo.
‡ *Recollections and Reflections*, London, 1872, ii, 208.

Gadshill robbery. First, Poins outlines his scheme to the Prince, whose questions bring out the details. '' The virtue of this jest,'' Poins concludes,

> will be, the incomprehensible lies that this same fat rogue will tell us when we meet at supper: how thirty, at least, he fought with; what wards, what blows, what extremities he endured; and in the reproof of this lies the jest.   (*1 H. IV*, I, 2, 207)

When the action begins, each step is commented upon: the removal of the horses, the putting on of the vizards, the robbing of the true men, the robbing of the robbers.* At Eastcheap, as Falstaff adds and multiplies his '' buckram men '' and '' knaves in Kendal-green,'' the Prince keeps careful score; and at last, when he can hold out no longer, relates all that has happened. '' Mark now, how a plain tale shall put you down. . . .'' † Great in their own right, the scenes are composed with a technical expertness which is wholly unobtrusive.

That Bartley's injunction may not be disregarded without peril is illustrated by the play scene in *Hamlet*, where, curiously enough, '' the intelligence of a British public '' is not at stake. The scene is carefully prepared for, first in Hamlet's soliloquy at the end of the second act, then in his talk with Horatio just before the play begins. We in the audience, like Hamlet and Horatio on the stage, are to watch the King's face —

* II, 2, 1–3, 81–83, 102–106, 115 ff.
† II, 4, 283 ff.

> If his occulted guilt
> Do not itself unkennel in one speech,
> It is a damned ghost that we have seen.
> (III, 2, 85)

And after the play we are told, too, not only that the King did give himself away, but exactly when he did it.

Hamlet. O good Horatio! I'll take the ghost's word for a thousand pound. Didst perceive?
Horatio. Very well, my lord.
Hamlet. Upon the talk of the poisoning?
Horatio. I did very well note him.   (III, 2, 302)

Claudius, in other words, stood the preliminary test of the dumb show — hard as that test was — and held out even through the speeches of the Player King and Queen. Only one thing is wanting to satisfy Bartley's requirement. "Ha! he blenches," Hamlet might have shrieked in a melodrama, and the circle would have been completed. But though Shakespeare trusted the actor of Claudius to conform to what is practically a stage direction, and though no *audience* could possibly go wrong, Hamlet, in many a modern performance, rivets his eyes to a King who writhes, and makes damnable faces, almost from the outset. "Ha! he blenches" is evidently needed, after all.

Thus through a whole scene in *Hamlet*, the face of one of the characters is of supreme importance.

It is a truism that Shakespeare, when acted, assumes new values for us. Gesture and inflection, the groupings of figures, stage sounds and stage business, contribute to produce effects which we had not realized were there. Take for instance the scene at Gloucester's castle in the second act of *King Lear*. Goneril we know by now for what she is, but we hope against hope that Regan may be different. Lear is expostulating with her — " Who put my man i' the stocks? " Suddenly, a trumpet sounds; the action comes to a standstill. Then, after a moment, Oswald appears — the detestable Oswald, whom we now fear. Lear begins a last appeal:

> Who stock'd my servant? Regan, I have good hope
> Thou didst not know on 't.* . . .

And there stands Goneril, and Regan has crossed to meet her, has clasped her hands —

> *O Regan, wilt thou take her by the hand?*

It is a turning point in the tragedy. As compared with the novelist, writes Mr. Allardyce Nicoll, " the dramatist has to work in a series of leaps." Concentrating and suggesting, as he must do, he recognizes the value of physical action in impressing ideas upon the minds of his audience. A first reader of *Macbeth* might

miss the connection between (1) Duncan's bidding Ross to greet Macbeth as Thane of Cawdor, (2) the second prophecy of the witches, and (3) the actual greeting of Macbeth by Ross:

---

* II, 4, 191.

but in the theatre each of these is closely accompanied by action.*

Gower as Chorus informs us that Pericles has been shipwrecked; Pericles himself says so in soliloquy; but Elizabethan realism allowed, Elizabethan technique explains, the old stage direction " *Enter Pericles wette.*" †

Action, then, may enforce or clarify the impressions produced by the words of a play. But action will often itself need explaining, especially on the Elizabethan stage. Today the elaborate business of the hallucination scenes in Mr. O'Neill's *Emperor Jones* seems wholly entrusted to the producer, though in point of fact Jones does help with occasional comments — " What you all doin', white folks? What 's all dis? What you all lookin' at me fo'? What you doin' wid me, anyhow? . . . Is dis a auction? Is you sellin' me like dey uster befo' de war? " When, however, Aaron the Moor buried gold, with only the gold itself and a stage trap to aid illusion, he had to tell what he was about:

> He that had wit would think that I had none,
> To bury so much gold under a tree.‡ . . .

Yet the expository obligation is only a beginning. In Shakespeare's practice the word accompanies

---

* *The Theory of Drama*, London, etc. [1931], pp. 78–80; *cf.* G. P. Baker, *Dramatic Technique*, Boston and New York, 1919, p. 85, for an example from the first scene in *The Changeling.*

† II, 1.

‡ *Titus Andronicus*, II, 3, 1.

the deed, action is absorbed into the text, or may be inferred from it. Stage directions are few, but over and over again the lines are enough in themselves to suggest everything that is happening.

O Regan, wilt thou take her by the hand?

If our imagination is lively enough, the whole scene is there before our eyes. So, early in *Hamlet*, the Ghost passes. " It comes " — in armor, and like the dead King. " It would be spoke to " — " it is offended " — " it stalks away." And Horatio (even Horatio!) ' trembles and looks pale.' *

Shakespeare's references to action amount, in fact, to a minor characteristic of his style. In particular, the changing faces of his persons are mirrored for us in words, are commented upon and in themselves bear comment. " Look you, Cassius," Brutus says:

The angry spot doth glow on Caesar's brow,
And all the rest look like a chidden train:
Calphurnia's cheek is pale, and Cicero
Looks with such ferret and such fiery eyes
As we have seen him in the Capitol,
Being cross'd in conference by some senators.
(*Jul. C.*, I, 2, 181)

When one is tempted to think of Elizabethan acting as mere elocution or acrobatics, it might be well to

* I, I, 40 ff. For explanatory soliloquies accompanying business, see Morris Leroy Arnold, *The Soliloquies of Shakespeare*, New York, 1911, p. 74; *cf.* also E. E. Stoll, *Poets and Playwrights*, Minneapolis, 1930, pp. 118, 119.

recall those lines. Shakespeare, we know, was intimately acquainted with the players of his own company, and it is incredible that he should have called attention to their deficiencies. In the *Third Part of Henry VI*, a messenger brings letters to Margaret, Warwick, and the French King, informing them of Edward's marriage. " *They all read their letters*," and Oxford comments:

> I like it well that our fair queen and mistress
> Smiles at her news, while Warwick frowns at his.
> *Prince.* Nay, mark how Lewis stamps as he were nettled.
>
> (III, 3, 167)*

The effectiveness of the passage lies wholly in its visual suggestion. Or take, for a final instance, the scene in Gertrude's closet. The Ghost calls attention to the Queen's amazement —

> But, look! amazement on thy mother sits —

Hamlet, watching the ghost, speaks of ' how pale he glares,' of his ' piteous action ' and of his ' stealing away '; while Gertrude, watching Hamlet, says that ' at his eyes his spirits wildly peep ' and that his hair ' starts up and stands an end.' †

---

* *Cf.* Creizenach, *The English Drama in the Age of Shakespeare*, London, 1916, p. 403.

† III, 4, 111 ff. See also, for a fine example from *The Duchess of Malfi*, Rupert Brooke, *John Webster and the Elizabethan Drama*, New York, 1916, p. 128. " Why start you back and stare? " Eleazar asks, in *Lust's Dominion*, and Cole answers, " Seeing your face, we thought of hell " (ed. Brereton, Louvain, 1931, II, 3, p. 41).

Then there are the battle scenes, those " deplor-
able " battle scenes . . . I only wish I could see one!
The shouts and alarums, the miniature armies issuing from opposite doors, even the occasional storm-
ing of the upper stage with ladders — the one part
of realism to so many of suggestion — must have
been exciting enough. At any rate, as Shakespeare
contrived them, these scenes seldom need explaining afterwards. There has been a battle — and Hal
has killed Hotspur. There has been a battle — and
Macduff has killed Macbeth. We have seen them
at it, seen Hotspur die or Macbeth's severed head
brought in and raised aloft. As befits drama, things
have been kept in proper perspective, and meanwhile, if we were Elizabethan enough to care for a
lively simulation of single combat, we have had our
shilling's worth. Exceptional battles, exacting a
detailed description of what has happened, are
those in *Coriolanus* and *Cymbeline*. In the former, the
Romans attacking Corioli are beaten back. Marcius
rallies them, drives the Volsces into the city, and is
shut in as they 'clap-to their gates.' " See, they have
shut him in," cries the Third Soldier. Titus Lartius
enters, and asks for Marcius.

First Soldier. Following the fliers at the very heels,
With them he enters; who, upon the sudden,
Clapp'd-to their gates; he is himself alone,
To answer all the city.   (I, 4, 49)

In *Cymbeline*, the fighting is equally romantic and

even more complicated. Dispatched in one brief scene, it gets some fifty lines of formal narration in the next.* Shakespeare, Mr. Granville-Barker suggests, was experimenting.[†]

Entire scenes are given over to exposition. We take fright at that. The separate scenes are such tangible, such familiar things! "SCENE II. — *A Camp near Forres*"; " SCENE IV. — *Forres. A Room in the Palace.*" They appear on our pages — as becomes artistic entities — with a certain typographical pomp. Or we think of scenes in terms of the theatre of yesterday, with its lowered lights, its descending and ascending curtain, its creakings and muffled human voices (which of course we never allowed ourselves to notice), its definite pausing and beginning afresh. On the Elizabethan stage, continuity would have been virtually unbroken: the click of the completed rhyme of an exit tag was still audible, perhaps, as a new group took up the discourse.[‡] Again, even those scenes which at first glance appear inconsequential — accomplishing little or nothing toward advancing the story — on closer scrutiny may be found to have their uses. I have seen the

---

* v, 2–3.

† *Prefaces to Shakespeare*, 2nd Series, London, 1930, pp. 258, 259. In *Romeo and Juliet*, Benvolio on two occasions describes brawls of the Capulets and Montagues, which we have just witnessed (I, 1, 112 ff.; III, 1, 148 ff.)

‡ Scenes which made use of the curtained inner stage are an obvious exception. For the whole matter of scene divisions, see Granville-Barker, *Prefaces to Shakespeare*, 2nd Series, 130 ff.

storm scenes in *King Lear* played as an uninterrupted sequence, and they became quite unendurable. The breaks provided by Gloucester and Edmund (III, 3) and Cornwall and Edmund (III, 5) — justified in any case as leading up to the blinding of Gloucester — are to the audience an indispensable slackening of pace and relaxing of tension. " A play," Mr. Dobrée tells us, " is structurally composed, not of Sardoodledoms, or Ibsen hot-houses of preparation, but of carefully proportioned speeds, succeeding one another in varying length and intensity." * More purely expository is the later scene in *Lear* between Kent and a Gentleman.† Delius defends it, on the ground of economy, as doing away with " the necessity for several scenes which would else have been requisite for the plot, viz. a scene to account for the King of France's sudden return to his own land "(but why, one asks, did not the King send his general in the first place?) " a scene in which Cordelia should learn the heart-rending news of her beloved father's sorrows, and the crimes of her unnatural sisters; a scene to show us Lear in a new phase of his madness." ‡ In Eliza-

* *Histriophone: A Dialogue on Dramatic Diction,* " The Hogarth Essays," London, 1925, p. 18; see also C. E. Montague, " The Literary Play," *Essays and Studies by Members of The English Association,* II (1911), pp. 77, 78.

† IV, 3. A similar conversation between the same persons occurs at the end of IV, 7, but this is not strictly speaking a " scene " at all.

‡ " Shakspere's Use of Narration in Drama," *New Shakspere Society's Transactions,* 1875–76, p. 216.

bethan drama, it must be repeated, silences and condensations abound. Another minor scene, this time from *Antony and Cleopatra*, seems quite without purpose.* Antony in Rome talks with the Soothsayer (II, 3). Cleopatra in Egypt receives the Messenger (II, 5). But between come ten lines of ceremonious farewell, as Lepidus, Mecaenas, and Agrippa pass across the stage. It is as if a novelist had rounded off his account of Antony with, " And so they all set off for Mount Misenum. Meanwhile in Egypt. . . ." Brief as it is, the scene recalls to the spectators the general drift of the plot.†

Shakespeare's technique of exposition includes a provident emphasis on matters of essential consequence. Thus, though the exact limits of fate and human responsibility in *Macbeth* are as vaguely defined perhaps as they are in life, what is promised by the Weird Sisters on the heath is made unmistakably clear. " Stay, you imperfect speakers," Macbeth cries as the last " prophetic greeting " dies away:

> By Sinel's death I know I am thane of Glamis;
> But how of Cawdor? the Thane of Cawdor lives,
> A prosperous gentleman; and to be king
> Stands not within the prospect of belief
> No more than to be Cawdor. (I, 3, 70)

---

* *Cf.* M. W. MacCallum, *Shakespeare's Roman Plays and their Background*, London, 1910, p. 316.
† *Cf.* also *Cymbeline*, III, 7.

The Sisters vanish, and Macbeth and Banquo discuss what has been told them:

Macbeth. Your children shall be kings.
Banquo.   You shall be king.
Macbeth. And thane of Cawdor too; went it not so?
Banquo. To the self-same tune and words.   (I, 3, 86)

By the end of the scene, which contains further
repetition of the " hails," no audience could forget
them — and there is Lady Macbeth's letter still to
come. Preparations for the murder of Duncan, with
its accomplishment and discovery, take up the great
second act; but at the beginning of the third the
words of the Sisters are recalled and pondered in the
soliloquies of Banquo and Macbeth.* Equally striking is the treatment of the later prophecies. After
hearing them, Macbeth is for some time absent from
the stage. When he returns, he speaks these lines:

> Bring me no more reports; let them fly all:
> Till Birnam wood remove to Dunsinane
> I cannot taint with fear.   What's the boy Malcolm?
> Was he not born of woman?   The spirits that know
> All mortal consequences have pronounc'd me thus:
> " Fear not, Macbeth; no man that 's born of woman
> Shall e'er have power upon thee."   (v, 3, 1)

And at the end of the scene:

> I will not be afraid of death and bane
> Till Birnam forest come to Dunsinane.

Birnam forest fails him; but, as the battle begins, he
holds hard to those other, unequivocal words:

* III, 1, 1 ff., and 48 ff.

They have tied me to a stake; I cannot fly,
But bear-like I must fight the course. *What 's he*
That was not born of woman? Such a one
Am I to fear, or none.   (v, 7, 1)

And as Young Siward falls dying, Macbeth cries
exultantly:

Thou wast born of woman:
But swords I smile at, weapons laugh to scorn,
Brandish'd by man that's of a woman born.
                                   (v, 7, 11)

The symmetrical arrangement of the four quota-
tions, all of them entrance or exit speeches, is assuredly structural — not accidental.*

To catch a glimpse of Shakespeare at work, is
seldom vouchsafed us. In the Roman plays, indeed,
we may watch him turning North's fine prose into
his own poetry, or attempting to motivate — what
any dramatist would have to motivate — the betraying, and sparing, of Rome by Coriolanus. But
with all allowance made for these and other instances of the sort (as, notably, the revisions in *Love's
Labor's Lost*), it is still something to be able to see
Shakespeare taking precautions against misunder-
standing or confusion, practising in points of detail
the craft of a playwright. Thus, Octavius must not
be suspected of hypocrisy in his display of grief at

---

* Note also the parallelism of v, 5, 42 ff.; v, 7, 46 ff. That Kate
must marry before Bianca may, is fairly dinned into our ears in
the early scenes of *The Taming of the Shrew*.

the news of Antony's death. Mecaenas and Agrippa
see to this:

Agrippa.   Strange it is,
    That nature must compel us to lament
    Our most persisted deeds. . . .

    Caesar is touch'd.
Mecaenas. When such a spacious mirror's set before him,
    He needs must see himself.   (v, 1, 28)

On the other hand, the flattering speeches of the
Queen, near the beginning of *Cymbeline*, are immediately labelled, after her exit, by Imogen:

            Dissembling courtesy.   How fine this tyrant
            Can tickle where she wounds!

And to make all sure, the Queen on her reappearance contributes a sinister aside.* In *Henry V*, the
danger that Fluellen might be mistaken for a mere
eccentric is guarded against by the testimony of the
King,

            Though it appear a little out of fashion,
            There is much care and valour in this Welshman; †

and after Pistol's beating (the beating of an Englishman by a Welshman, mind!) Gower is at pains to
tell the Ancient what he thinks of him:

    Go, go; you are a counterfeit cowardly knave. Will you
    mock at an ancient tradition, begun upon an honourable re-
    spect, and worn as a memorable trophy of predeceased valour,
    and dare not avouch in your deeds any of your words?

---

* 1, 1, 84, 103.
† *Henry V*, iv, 1, 86.

. . . You thought, because he could not speak English in the
native garb, he could not therefore handle an English cudgel:
you find it otherwise; and henceforth let a Welsh correction
teach you a good English condition.   (v, 1, 73)

Shakespeare risks letting Goneril play the patriotic
Englishwoman, in *Lear* —

France spreads his banners in our noiseless land —

but Albany takes her down instantly with his " See
thyself, devil! "; and later, Cordelia makes it clear
that the war is not really a war between France and
England.* So when a character is acting strangely,
other characters may explain his behavior. In an
effectively ghastly episode, Titus exults over the de-
struction of the fly that appeared " in likeness of
a coal-black Moor," and Marcus is ready with the
comment,

Alas! poor man; grief has so wrought on him,
He takes false shadows for true substances.

(iii, 2, 79)

The impatience of Hotspur, which will not let him
hear what older and cooler heads have to propose, is
noticed by his father and uncle:

Northumberland. Imagination of some great exploit
Drives him beyond the bounds of patience. . . .

---

* iv, 2, 56; iv, 4, 23 ff. Somewhat awkwardly, the invasion is
made Albany's excuse for fighting on the wrong side (v, 1, 23).
In Tate's version of *Lear*, the French army is got rid of altogether —
which perhaps was the safest thing to do.

Worcester.   He apprehends a world of figures here,
                    But not the form of what he should attend.*

Of course, too, the person behaving ambiguously may himself explain his conduct in an aside. Edgar, Imogen, and Cordelia all, on occasion, do so.†

To insist that Shakespeare's technique was different from ours is not to imply that it was worse. I have little sympathy with the criticism which points condescendingly to the presence of primitive qualities in the work of great artists, as if that were enough to invalidate it! Granted that the Shakespearean form is less austerely dramatic than ours — that at moments, even, the distinctions between *genres* seem imperilled — still it was a form surprisingly well adapted to the expression of genius. One technical feature stands out, perhaps, above all: the direct importance of things said, whether by a character about himself or by others about him. Mellefont in Congreve's *Double-Dealer* was (we are told) accused by the critics of being a mere " gull." Defending him, Congreve admits that early in the play Mellefont is warned by his friend Careless. " Of what Nature was that Caution? Only to give the Audience some light into the Character of *Maskwell*, before his Appearance." But Careless was not aware that Maskwell was really a villain — " he was only a sort of Man which he did not like "

* *1 Henry IV*, 1, 3, 199, 209.
† See pages 82, 83, 120, 291, below.

— so that the warning goes unheeded.* As a practical playwright, Congreve recognizes that his lines are not spoken privately or for their own sake: the fourth wall is down, and the actor is addressing an audience *even while he remains in character.*

What then distinguishes good dramatic exposition from bad? Chiefly, I suppose, two things. Good exposition is introduced so naturally that it is quite inconspicuous; and it is presented with the utmost economy compatible with clearness. Though distinct, these qualities are related, for when a playwright — killing only one bird at a time — uses long passages of mere exposition, his hand shows. Sometimes, it is faulty expression that betrays the author's presence, as in these lines in *Jeronimo*:

Lazarotto. Up, Lazarotto; yonder comes thy prize;
Now lives Andrea, now Andrea dies.
[*Lazarotto kills him.*
Alcario. That villain Lazarotto has killed me,
Instead of Andrea; †

or these, by Shakespeare's godson:

Brusco. Hirco! have you appeas'd the mutiny
The General's discontents did raise
Amongst his fry of friends, our tattered camp —
Companions in the streets? ‡

---

* " Epistle Dedicatory " (Congreve's *Comedies*, ed. Bonamy Dobrée, Oxford, 1925, p. 116).
† *The First Part of Jeronimo* (Hazlitt's *Dodsley*, IV, 374).
‡ D'Avenant, *The Unfortunate Lovers*, II, 1, 1 ff. (*Dramatic Works*, ed. Maidment and Logan, iii, 28).

In both passages, the style has undergone a process of extension: proper names are supplied, as if in brackets; explanatory detail is amassed at the cost of verisimilitude. For contrast, take Sicinius in *Coriolanus*, who says simply,

> Bid them all home; he 's gone, and we 'll no further.
>
> (IV, 2, 1)

Sometimes, however, bad exposition assumes more insidious forms. Implausibly, the villain in melodrama tells us he is a villain, and joins with the hero in extolling the latter's goodness. Shakespeare, as we shall see, has been charged by some recent critics with similar lapses.*

Enough has been said, it may be, to suggest the ground to be covered. Those matters in a play which need explanation are explained by the characters. Their comments, on themselves and one another and on the events in which they are concerned, are in a sense much like the testimony of witnesses at a trial. As a rule they speak the truth, too — as a rule but not always — and frequently a witness will be found testifying against himself. On the other hand, the rules of evidence in Shakespearean drama are not precisely defined, and possibly even the best of them admit exceptions. Exposition, moreover, is, of course, not confined to verbal comment. Action, as we saw, has its explana-

* See Chapter VIII, below.

tory function. Parallelism and contrast, in both characters and episodes, are strikingly used. Thus Richard II and Henry Bolingbroke are contrasted, and Richard's feverish insistence that " heaven still guards the right " — the Divine Right of Kings — finds its instant answer in the discomforting news brought by Salisbury.* Harry Percy and Prince Hal, Antony and Octavius, Banquo and Macbeth, Timon and Apemantus, are deliberately paired. Hamlet himself perceives the resemblance between his cause and that of Laertes; and in *King Lear*, the theme of ingratitude is duplicated in plot and sub-plot. With these broader aspects of Shakespeare's technique — a subject in themselves — the present study is scarcely concerned.

* *Richard II*, III, 2, 36 ff.

Chapter II

TIME AND PLACE

Description for Scenery — Task of Good Reader —
Storm Scenes in *Lear* — Indication of Place — Dover
Cliff — Writing of Stage Letters — Condensation of
Time — Double Time — Songs — Night Scenes — *A
Midsummer Night's Dream*.

IN a solemn paper, " promist for, and taken as
read at, the 24th Meeting " of the New Shakspere Society, April 28, 1876, Professor Delius as-
cribed Shakespeare's frequent use of narration to
the absence of scenery on the Elizabethan Stage.
Mark Antony's first meeting with Cleopatra and
the triumph of Coriolanus were scenes (he said) " in
the visible representation of which modern decora-
tive art and scenic arrangements would put forth
all their power, and spare the poet the trouble of
making a minute description." So with Ophelia's
death and Hamlet's voyage:

> In both cases the then condition of the stage rendered any
> scenical representation impossible. What in the modern French
> opera, supported by all imaginable art of theatrical machinery
> and painting, might be an attractive and gratifying task for the
> manager, was impossible on Shakspere's stage.

Delius had grace given him to add that the description of Ophelia's death might yet have produced a
deeper impression on the Elizabethans than " all

modern operatic art could make on us at present";
but of course Shakespeare was Shakespeare and
could turn his very disadvantages into triumphs.*

The meetings of the New Shakspere Society and
" the theatrical machinery and painting " of the
" modern French opera" seem pretty remote today.
And meanwhile, knowledge of the Elizabethan stage
has gone steadily ahead. Mr. W. J. Lawrence's vein
of theatrical antiquarianism seems inexhaustible;
and, from his pleasant chapters, one learns more and
more exactly the degree of idealism which Shakespeare was justified in expecting of those first happy
audiences at the Globe. What is more, the Elizabethan stage is no longer an abstraction. It has been
many times reconstructed and put to use, so that
today a critic like Mr. Granville-Barker may write
of it from long experience of its ways. Our own
stage has been regaining something of Elizabethan
swiftness, something of Elizabethan suggestiveness.
With increase of knowledge, condescension has gone
out of fashion. "There was nothing," Mr. Drinkwater writes, that Shakespeare and his players
"wanted to do that they could not do"; their stage

* " Shakspere's Use of Narration in Drama," 216, 218. W. T.
Price, after observing that Shakespeare had no scenery in mind as
he composed, goes on more cheerfully: " His dramas, however,
admit of scenic luxury. To a modern audience the description of
Imogen's chamber would be risked in the absence of all correspondence with the words; Imogen was not wholly neglected — a
king's daughter — and deserves well of the stage-manager " (*The
Technique of the Drama*, New York, 1892 [1905], p. 144).

was an instrument magnificently equal to every demand that they could make upon it. . . . To see Shakespeare's stage as something crude and elementary is not to see it at all. . . . It was neither primitive nor crude; it was highly civilised, expert, given hardly at all to experiment, but carrying an established tradition to its highest perfection. *

As for Delius, he had only to recall the storm scenes in *The Tempest* and *Pericles*, the sumptuous pageantry in *Henry VIII*, to save himself from writing what is very like nonsense.

It remains true, of course, that description took the place of scenery. But such description as we get many times in Shakespeare — of the moon-flooded wood in *A Midsummer Night's Dream* or that other enchanted wood of Arden, of Macbeth's castle, so tranquil in the late twilight, or of the "dreadful summit" of Dover Cliff — is precisely of the sort a brilliantly endowed poet would have delighted in composing. The necessity, so far as it existed, was also an opportunity. At once lyrical and dramatic, the spirit of the age found expression on a stage which, in essentials, exactly served its needs. †

Description, then, whether in long, aria-like speeches or in unobtrusive, stray suggestions of time and place, is, like gesture and the play of faces,

* *Shakespeare,* "Great Lives," 1933, pp. 75, 87.
† *Cf.* J. A. Symonds, "The Lyrism of the English Romantic Drama," *In the Key of Blue,* London and New York, 1893 (1918); and D. W. Rannie, *Scenery in Shakespeare's Plays and Other Studies,* Oxford, 1926, pp. 132, 133.

an integral part of the Shakespearean text.* As
readers, our pleasure, the range of our imaginative
activity, is thereby perceptibly increased. Pater,
turning the pages of *Measure for Measure*, found that

the moated grange, with its dejected mistress, its long, listless,
discontented days, where we hear only the voice of a boy broken
off suddenly, . . . is the pleasantest of many glimpses we get here
of pleasant places — the fields without the town, Angelo's
garden-house, the consecrated fountain.†

Lamb, realizing sensibly enough that the stage of his
own time failed to satisfy his demands as a reader,
confounded it with the very different stage for which
the plays were designed.‡ At times, moreover,
Shakespeare's backgrounds, the references by his
persons to the place and hour, take on dramatic
significance. Mr. Daniel Corkery in the preface to
his fine volume, *The Yellow Bittern and Other Plays*
(1920), compares a passage like

> This castle hath a pleasant seat; the air
> Nimbly and sweetly recommends itself
> Unto our gentle senses
>
> (*Macb.*, 1, 6, 1)

---

* For the inclusiveness of the text, see Stoll, *Poets and Play-*
wrights, 57, 58; and M. C. Bradbrook, *Elizabethan Stage Conditions:*
A Study of their Place in the Interpretation of Shakespeare's Plays, Cambridge (England), 1932, p. 130.

† *Appreciations*, London and New York, 1889, pp. 182, 183.

‡ " On the Tragedies of Shakspeare, Considered with Reference to their Fitness for Stage Representation " (1811), in D. Nichol
Smith, *Shakespeare Criticism*, Oxford, etc., 1916 (1923).

with the modern stage-direction which makes " a
drama as interesting as a novel: one thinks of the
sun being brought at last to shine like the moon! "
In the lines quoted, " place and feeling are important things, but the most important thing is that it is
Duncan who speaks in this way of Macbeth's castle,
while in the passage: —

> Light thickens and the crow
> Makes wing to the rooky wood — *

the most important thing is that it is Macbeth who
speaks." Even more subtle, perhaps, is the effect
produced by Portia's simple, " It is almost morning," at the end of *The Merchant of Venice.*†

With all these advantages, the good reader finds
that much is expected of him still — a nice adjustment of imaginative effort, as well as susceptibility
to impressions. Paying little heed to the signboards
planted at the beginning of Shakespeare's scenes by
Rowe and his successors — those prosaic headings,
A Room in the Palace, Another Room, A Street, and the
like — such a reader re-creates time and place from
the lines themselves, remembering and forgetting,
disregarding even, and then observing attentively.
And this is no more than the first step. He must by
moonlight approach Portia's house in Belmont and
see for himself the little candle burning there in the
hall. But with another look he must see, quite as

* III, 2, 50.
† *Cf.* Raleigh, *Shakespeare*, London, 1907 (1926), p. 126.

distinctly, by the light of a London afternoon a bare platform with men dressed in bright colors standing about it on three sides, a practicable gallery at the back and beneath it a curtained room. Nor is this quite all. For at moments he should see, if possible, what the men in bright colors saw as the incantation of the lines worked on their imagination. *

Like the good reader whose task I have been describing, Shakespeare, too, in matters of time and place, remembers and forgets; or at any rate — for I suppose he always saw his figures against backgrounds — emphasizes and disregards. So does the novelist, and has human experience, the vagaries of our recollection, as his warrant. It is possible, however, as a reaction against the particularity of our traditional stage directions, to exaggerate uncertainty of background: to suggest, for instance, as Archer does, that "the normal state of mind of the Elizabethan audience was one of absolute vagueness and carelessness as to the particular locality the stage was supposed to represent." † The opening scenes in *Macbeth* have been analyzed from this point of view. Where is the second? *A Camp near Forres*, we are told, and the fourth is at *Forres: A Room in the Palace*; " but the scene hints at neither palace

---

* For several points in this and the succeeding paragraphs, I am indebted to Mr. Granville-Barker's *Prefaces*, 1st Series, London, 1927, pp. xix-xxiii, and 2nd Series, 130 ff.

† *The Old Drama and the New*, New York, 1926, p. 36; *cf.* Brander Matthews, *Shakspere as a Playwright*, New York, 1913, pp. 33, 34.

nor camp." The fifth is plainly at Macbeth's castle; but is Lady Macbeth as she reads the letter indoors or out? " In the first and third scenes, the witches appear. Here Shakespeare's conception is clear and indicated to readers. The scene is out of doors, it thunders and there is lightning, but nothing further of locality is suggested." * Now in method this analysis is sound enough, and much to be preferred to a docile following of Rowe's signboards supported, perhaps, by an old-fashioned engraving of Forres. But Forres *is* mentioned: Macbeth is on his way there in the third scene. In the first, one of the witches speaks of their meeting next " upon the heath "; and Macbeth asks them why " upon this blasted heath " they stop his way (I, 3, 77). One may reply, perhaps, that the Elizabethan audience would not have noticed such hints, but I am by no means convinced that they would not. They were, we should remember, inveterate playgoers — a small but devoted following — and may conceivably have been as quick in picking up clues as the frequenters of the movies today (and how quick they are!) At all events, it is characteristic of Shakespeare that the hints are there. And on the whole, he shows extraordinary tact in deciding when to give us something more than hints and when not.†

* A. H. Thorndike, *Shakespeare's Theater*, New York, 1916, pp. 104, 105.
† See Creizenach, *The English Drama in the Age of Shakespeare*, 357. For the contrasting vagueness of neo-classical tragedy, *cf.* Lessing,

The storm scenes in *Lear* show to advantage the
apparent limitations, the actual freedom, of a
dramatist working under Elizabethan conditions.
Lamb derided ' the contemptible machinery by
which,' in his time, ' they mimicked the storm.'
But not even John Dennis's thunder had yet been
invented when Shakespeare wrote. And what matter? There are still the characters whom the storm
concerns — Lear principally, but others as well —
and they give us the storm, to admiration. I have
seen a production of the play in which, for the sake
of obtaining a catchpenny curtain line, the second
act ended with the King's exit. The speeches cut
included these:

Gloucester. Alack! the night comes on, and the bleak winds
  Do sorely ruffle; for many miles about
  There's scarce a bush.

Regan. O! sir, to wilful men,
  The injuries that they themselves procure
  Must be their schoolmasters.   Shut up your doors;
  He is attended with a desperate train. . . .

Cornwall. Shut up your doors, my lord; 'tis a wild night:
  My Regan counsels well: come out o' the storm.

Consciousness of the storm pervades, likewise, the
scenes which follow. At times it is described at
length — as by the Gentleman or Kent — at times
apostrophized by Lear with something of its own

Hamburgische Dramaturgie, No. 46 (tr. Helen Zimmern, London,
1879, pp. 369, 370).

violence, its own terror. At other times its presence
is felt, rather than referred to, in phrases and interjections which seem drawn spontaneously from the
persons who utter them — " Fie on this storm! "
" What a night 's this! " " poor Tom's a-cold " * —
or it is insinuated in the scraps of song sung by the
Fool and Edgar. Nor is the storm forgotten when it
has ceased. " Poor Tom 's a-cold " is heard once
more. Lear in his raving says of flatterers: " When
the rain came to wet me once and the wind to make
me chatter, when the thunder would not peace at my
bidding, there I found 'em. . . ." And Cordelia,
just before Lear's waking, recalls the past in all its
terror:

> Was this a face
> To be expos'd against the warring winds?
> To stand against the deep dread-bolted thunder?
> In the most terrible and nimble stroke
> Of quick cross lightning? to watch — poor perdu! —
> With this thin helm?   Mine enemy's dog,
> Though he had bit me, should have stood that night
> Against my fire.†

With little to distract them, Shakespeare's audience found the storm primarily in its effect on the
characters. It is, moreover, no ordinary storm but
somehow, one feels, symbolic, the expression of great
forces which have interposed drastically in the
affairs of men. Lear himself takes it as such. His

---

* III, 1, 49; iii, 4, 151, 174.
† IV, 1, 52; iv, 6, 103–106; iv, 7, 31–38. *Cf.* also iv, 2, 39 ff.

successive appeals to the gods begin, in the curse
against Goneril, with perfect confidence. When at
Gloucester's he sees her again, an " if " — a doubt
— has crept in:

> O heavens,
> If you do love old men, if your sweet sway
> Allow obedience, if yourselves are old,
> Make it your cause; send down and take my part!
>
> (II, 4, 192)

He will not curse her now:

> Let shame come when it will, I do not call it:
> I do not bid the thunder-bearer shoot,
> Nor tell tales of thee to high-judging Jove.
>
> (line 229)

But, as the voices join against him, he appeals once
more, and his doubt is now of another sort, much
more terrible:

> You see me here, you gods, a poor old man,
> As full of grief as age; wretched in both!
> *If it be you that stir these daughters' hearts*
> *Against their father,* fool me not so much
> To bear it tamely; touch me with noble anger,
> And let not women's weapons, water-drops,
> Stain my man's cheeks! (line 275)

Wildly he threatens vengeance, and while he still
threatens the storm begins. The gods are against
him — against righteousness — and on the heath
Lear knows it. Why should they favor him, any-
way? *

* He addresses, indeed, the elements: the thunder, not the
'thunder-bearer.'

I tax not you, you elements, with unkindness;
I never gave you kingdom, call'd you children,
You owe me no subscription: then let fall
Your horrible pleasure. . . .

But yet I call you servile ministers,
That have with two pernicious daughters join'd
Your high-engender'd battles 'gainst a head
So old and white as this. O! O! 'tis foul.

(III, 2, 16)

Capable as it was of producing effects like these, the Elizabethan method may seem at its simplest almost pitifully *naïve*. Sidney at any rate thought so, writing that " the player, when he cometh in, must ever begin with telling where he is." * Sometimes, the appropriate information is given in response to a question. " What is this forest call'd," asks the Archbishop of York? And Hastings replies:

'Tis Gaultree Forest, an't shall please your Grace.

Yet a similar interrogation, " What wood is this before us? " is answered in words that instantly rouse us, " The wood of Birnam "; and the commemorative spirit, which is one reason for the existence of chronicle-plays, shines through these lines:

* *Defense of Poesy*, ed. A. S. Cook, Boston, etc. [1890], p. 48. Though the Elizabethan public theatres had no formal scenery, properties occasionally indicated locality, a throne, for example, betokening a throne room (*cf*. R. Crompton Rhodes, *The Stagery of Shakespeare*, Birmingham, 1922, pp. 84 ff.). One learns that Henslowe's company even possessed " ij mose [mossy] banckes " (Percy Simpson, " Actors and Acting," *Shakespeare's England*, II, 270, from *Henslowe Papers*, 117).

King Henry. What is this castle call'd that stands hard by?
Montjoy. They call it Agincourt.*

Sometimes the information is contained in the question and merely corroborated in the reply. Plausibly enough, Antigonus asks the Mariner:

> Thou art perfect, then, our ship hath touch'd upon
> The desarts of Bohemia? (*W. T.*, III, 3, 1)

But in the *First Part of Henry VI* (an early, crude play) the Master Gunner appears less interested in his son than in the audience:

	Sirrah, thou know'st how Orleans is besieg'd,
	And how the English have the suburbs won.
Son.	Father, I know. . . .

Master Gunner.	Chief master-gunner am I of this town;
	Something I must do to procure me grace.
	The prince's espials have informed me
	How the English, in the suburbs close
	entrench'd,
	Wont through a secret gate of iron bars
	In yonder tower to overpeer the city.

> (I, 4, 1)

More often, allusions to place are dropped quite casually. There is something of character, something of the speaker's self, in Jack Cade's " Here, sitting upon London-stone, I charge and command " . . . and in Rosalind's " Well, this is the forest of Arden " — to which Touchstone replies,

* 2 *H. IV*, IV, 1, 1; *Macb.*, v, 4, 3; *H. V*, IV, 7, 92.

" Ay, now am I in Arden; the more fool I." Richard the Third's command,

Here pitch our tent, even here in Bosworth field,

has the distinctive note of the chronicle history, and the mention by Octavius of Philippi —

They mean to warn us at Philippi here —

is like the mention of Birnam Forest, immediately arresting. Compare, finally, the naturalness of Menenius's " See you yond coign o' the Capitol," which brings us quite unobtrusively back to Rome, and Joan of Arc's explicit

These are the city gates, the gates of Roan,
Through which our policy must make a breach.*

A much more subtle method of indicating place has sometimes been labelled " pre-localization." This method employs reference in an earlier scene to show the whereabouts of a later one. So at the beginning of *Pericles* we are in Antioch, as Gower the Chorus informs us. Pericles says that he must flee thence. He is, we know, Prince of Tyre, and in the second scene he is issuing orders as if to his subjects — " Let none disturb us." " Here," he says, " pleasures court mine eyes," whereas at Antioch is danger. After a hundred lines or so, Tyre is indeed mentioned, but we are already quite satisfied that we are there. The simpler and more primitive way

* *2 H. VI*, IV, 6, 2; *A. Y. L.*, II, 4, 15; *R. III*, V, 3, 1; *Jul. C.*, V, 1, 5; *Cor.* V, 4, 1; *1 H. VI*, III, 2, 1.

reappears when, at the beginning of the third scene, Thaliard strides on with " So this is Tyre, and this is the court. Here must I kill King Pericles." Or again there is the hovel in *King Lear*. " Here is the place, my lord," Kent says to the King, " good my lord, enter " (III, 4, 1). " The place " is enough, for we remember that Kent and Lear were making toward a hovel when last we saw them, and now they have reached shelter.* Another instance of pre-localization occurs in *All 's Well*. The scene at the beginning of the third act is Florence. For, though the Duke who now appears is a new character, he is accompanied by two of the gentlemen who were on their way to the Italian wars several scenes before. Italy then; but why Florence? Only, I suppose, because still earlier in the play (back in the second scene of Act One, in fact) the King of France had talked with the two gentlemen of sending an answer to " the Florentine," and it is this answer, seemingly, which they are now discussing with the Duke. Shakespeare's confidence in the quickness of his audience must have been limitless! † Pre-localization is dexterously combined with other methods in the Parthian episode (III, 1) in *Antony and Cleopatra*.

---

* *Cf.* III, 2, 61 and 71. Later in III, 4, Gloucester names the hovel, as he orders Edgar in. Probably it was not shown, though a little straw on the inner stage would have served.

† *Cf.* Rhodes, *Stagery of Shakespeare*, 101; W. J. Lawrence, *Shakespeare's Workshop*, Oxford, 1928, p. 17. Both assume that III, 1, is sufficiently pre-localized by II, 1.

Ventidius we have seen already — though hitherto
he has remained mute — and we are expected to
remember these words of Antony's, spoken at the
end of the scene with the Soothsayer more than four
hundred lines earlier:

> Say to Ventidius I would speak with him
>   [*Exit* Soothsayer.
> He shall to Parthia. . . .
>
>   O! come, Ventidius,
> You must to Parthia; your commission's ready;
> Follow me, and receive 't.*

Moreover, when we reach the scene to which Antony's words point forward, we get action, spec-
tacle, to aid us in placing it.[†] " *Enter Ventidius*," the
Folio directs, " *as it were in triumph, the dead body of
Pacorus borne before him.*" " Now, darting Parthia,
art thou struck," Ventidius begins; and Silius,
addressing him by name, says:

>   Noble Ventidius,
> Whilst yet with Parthian blood thy sword is warm,
> The fugitive Parthians follow.   (III, 1, 5)

The effectiveness of the scene if, as is at least argu-
able, it followed without a break the carousal on
Pompey's galley, has been brilliantly demonstrated
by Granville-Barker.[‡]

---

* II, 3, 31, 32, 40–42; *cf.* also II, 2, 15, 16.

† *Cf. Macbeth*, I, 7: " *Ho-boyes. Torches. Enter a Sewer, and divers
Servants with Dishes and Service over the Stage*." . . . Duncan, then, is
dining in an adjacent room as Macbeth enters.

‡ *Prefaces to Shakespeare*, 2nd Series, 120–122.

It must not be forgotten that Elizabethan
" scenes," as divisions in the play, were pretty nebu-
lous things. To an audience at the Globe, scenes, so
far as they existed, were processional, really, a matter of exits and entrances and the grouping and re-
grouping of the characters. Locality, on the other
hand, depended on what the characters said. Thus,
it was permissible not only to represent two places
at the same time (as in the famous tent scene in
Richard III) * but first one place and then another in
the same scene! In *Titus Andronicus*, for instance,
Tamora, Saturninus, and others have gone hunting
early in the morning. Tamora contrives to detach
herself from the rest, and joins her paramour, Aaron.

Tamora. My lovely Aaron, wherefore look'st thou sad,
When every thing doth make a gleeful boast?
The birds chant melody on every bush,
The snake lies rolled in the cheerful sun,
The green leaves quiver with the cooling wind,
And make a chequer'd shadow on the ground.
Under their sweet shade, Aaron, let us sit.

(II, 3, 10)

Bassianus and Lavinia appear, and Tamora quarrels with them. " I pray you, let us hence," Lavinia
says,

And let her joy her raven-colour'd love;
This valley fits the purpose passing well.

And a moment later Tamora, appealing to Chiron
and Demetrius for help, calls the place " a barren
detested vale."

* v, 3. For idealized distance, see pages 44, 45, below.

A barren detested vale, you see, it is;
The trees, though summer, yet forlorn and lean,
O'ercome with moss and baleful mistletoe:
Here never shines the sun; here nothing breeds,
Unless the nightly owl or fatal raven.   (line 93)

More than one Shakespearean editor must have looked anxiously for a break in the action so that he might begin afresh with " *Another Part of the Forest.*" But there is no break. A setting evoked by the spoken word has changed with the changing mood of the scene — that is all. And the passage is remarkable only because of the definiteness with which *both* landscapes are described. A much simpler instance of change of place within the scene is found in the third act of *Measure for Measure.* Claudio in prison is visited successively by the Duke and Isabella. The Duke, lingering, talks with Isabella of laying a trap for Angelo. Isabella now goes out, and the editors begin a new scene with the entrance of Elbow, Pompey, and Officers, on their way to prison, disregarding the fact that the Duke has not left the stage. A Room in the Prison has become the Street before the Prison — but otherwise there is no break in continuity.*

Of the longer descriptions of place there is, curiously enough, much less to say. Some of them —

* Rhodes, *Stagery of Shakespeare*, 90, 91. *Othello*, IV, 2, is another example. Shifts within the scene were sometimes facilitated by manipulation of the inner stage curtain (M. C. Bradbrook, *Elizabethan Stage Conditions*, 32, *Themes and Conventions of Elizabethan Tragedy*, Cambridge [England], 1935, p. 8).

like Iachimo's Renaissance night-piece — justify
themselves on strictly dramatic grounds. Others —
like Romeo's recollections of the needy shop of the
Apothecary — perhaps owe their origin to the fact
that Shakespeare was a poet as well as a playwright.
Stage conditions and the use of the soliloquy fostered such writing; the genius of the age inspired it.
One description, Edgar's of Dover Cliff, stands quite
apart from the rest. After Gloucester has been
blinded he begs Edgar, still disguised as Poor Tom,
to lead him toward Dover:

> There is a cliff, whose high and bending head
> Looks fearfully in the confined deep;
> Bring me but to the very brim of it.
>
> > (*Lear*, IV, 1, 74)

Later they seem to be approaching it.

Gloucester. When shall I come to the top of that same hill?
Edgar. You do climb up it now; look how we labour.
Gloucester. Methinks the ground is even.
Edgar.   Horrible steep:
Hark! do you hear the sea?
Gloucester.   No, truly.
Edgar. Why, then your other senses grow imperfect
By your eyes' anguish.   (IV, 6, 1)

Gloucester fancies that his guide's voice is altered,
but Edgar denies it:

> Y' are much deceiv'd; in nothing am I chang'd
> But in my garments.
Gloucester.   Methinks you 're better spoken.
Edgar. Come on, sir; here 's the place: stand still. . . .

Reading the celebrated description that follows, I have often wondered whether some of Shakespeare's first auditors were not deceived. Here was the method they knew so well: the appeal to their inner vision through charmed words. Were they not to see as actualities what Edgar pictures so vividly? Yet for the practised playgoer there were already, in Gloucester's objections (" Methinks the ground is even . . .") and Edgar's concealment of his identity — perhaps also in the use of the lower instead of the upper stage — grounds for suspicion. And before Gloucester pitches forward on his face and hands, Edgar has in effect pleaded for a suspension of judgment:

> Why I do trifle thus with his despair .
> Is done to cure it.

Shakespeare took few chances, after all.

* * *

" Art," writes Professor Lowes, " deals in *illusion*. Literal accuracy, even when possible, is art's undoing. . . . The tension sensed behind the thirty-one lines, that take less than two minutes to repeat, between ' 'Tis now struck twelve ' and ' the bell then beating one,' in the first scene of 'Hamlet,' *is*, to all intents and purposes, an hour; sixty literal minutes of intervening talk on the stage would drag it to

eternity." And he adds: " These are truisms." *
To smile, therefore, when the writing of a letter is
represented on the stage by four or five quavers
and a flourish, is sophomoric. " Too long! " I
once heard whispered when, in *Camille*, Miss Le
Gallienne approximated plausibility in her writing.
The determination of a norm for these slippery matters was attempted, in 1890, by Dr. Alfred Hennequin in a treatise on playwriting dedicated to Bron-
son Howard and still, I believe, in print.

" Generally," he finds, " the supposed duration of events
upon the stage is about five or six times as long as the actual
period occupied by the representation. That is, at the end of a
dialogue of five minutes, it is allowable to make one of the characters say, ' Here we 've been talking for a whole half-hour.' " †

And of stage letters, he remarks:

Letters or other documents written in the presence of the
audience usually proceed at the rate employed in speaking very
deliberately. The actor does not, of course, do any actual
writing.‡

The amount of supposed time which elapses between scenes is, Hennequin admits, wholly at the
author's pleasure.

Shakespeare's treatment of time is very like his

* *Convention and Revolt in Poetry*, Boston and New York, 1919,
pp. 19, 20.
† *The Art of Playwriting: Being a Practical Treatise on the Elements
of Dramatic Construction* (etc.), Boston and New York, 1890, p. 150.
‡ *Ibid.*, 151.

treatment of place.* Confidence in the imagination of his hearers, an almost characteristic remembering and forgetting — emphasizing and disregarding — are common to both. If the ' wooden O ' of his theatre had, after all, to serve him for a kingdom, so too he ' turns the accomplishment of many years into an hour-glass '; and his startling uses of dramatic condensation of time are accompanied by an equally startling employment of idealized distance. " The one freedom," in Mr. Granville-Barker's phrase, " will imply and enhance the other " — † whether in whole plays or single scenes. Take, for instance, the Coventry episode (v, 1) in the *Third Part of Henry VI*. Warwick, the Mayor of Coventry, and others appear on the walls. Edward, Richard, and their army enter below. " Go, trumpet, to the walls," Edward commands; and the leaders proceed to hold a parley. Then, within less than twenty lines, Oxford leads reinforcements into the city with *Drum and Colors*; Montague leads reinforcements into the city with *Drum and Colors*; Somerset does the same thing with similar pomp; and Clarence, once more with *Drum and Colors*, reinforces Edward! Both armies are now ready for fighting, and, after a few exchanges of defiance, first Edward's battalions, then Warwick's, march across the stage on their

---

* And time is not always indicated felicitously. The Captain's lines in 2 *H. VI*, iv, 1, are as inappropriately highfalutin as those of the Tapster in the epilogue to *The Taming of A Shrew*.

† *Prefaces*, 2nd Series, 70.

way to Barnet. It is almost admittedly a make believe world rather than a world of illusion, but its
proportions, if minute, are symmetrical.

Illusion, amounting almost to hypnosis, justifies
magnificently the swift passing of some of the nights
in Shakespeare's tragedies: the night of Duncan's
murder, and that before Caesar's; the night of Cassio's watch, in *Othello*, which at the beginning of the
scene is " not yet ten o' the clock " and at the end
has become morning.* " By the mass, 'tis morning,"
Iago says (or is it Shakespeare?),

> Pleasure and action make the hours seem short.

Even more daring is the temporal sequence in the
second and third acts of *King Lear*. Night is insisted
on throughout the first scene, and when, called by
Edmund, his father enters, he is accompanied by
" Servants *with torches*." Though the moon is still
shining, the dawn is near when Oswald meets
Kent; and Kent in the stocks waits for sunrise. It is
morning when Lear finds him there. Cornwall and
Regan are not up yet. They come, at length, and
Lear bids them " good morrow " (II, 4, 129), but
before the scene ends " night comes on " once more
— to last through the scene at the farmhouse, late in
the third act. Or if you must have a clock striking

---

* II, 3, 13, 387. See Mable Buland, *The Presentation of Time in
the Elizabethan Drama*, " Yale Studies in English," New York, 1912,
pp. 16, 119.

— as in the great concluding scene in *Faustus* — there is the bedroom scene (ii, 2) in *Cymbeline*. Imogen asks her waiting woman what hour it is, and learns that it is " almost midnight." She will be called " by four." Iachimo presently issues from his chest and, at the end of a long soliloquy, hears the clock: " one, two, three," he counts; " time, time! " *

Frequently, as in this last instance, the lapse of time during a soliloquy — like the lapse of time in Greek tragedy during a choral ode — proceeds apace. At two other points in an Elizabethan play abridgment is more or less to be expected: in the concluding scene and during battles. Shakespeare's most impressionistic battle, the conflict in the fifth act of *King Lear*, is made up of a march across the stage by Lear, Cordelia, and soldiers, four lines of dialogue as Edgar places Gloucester under " the shadow of this tree," an " *Alarum and Retreat within*," and Edgar's return with

> King Lear hath lost, he and his daughter ta'en.
>
> (v, 2, 6)

Shocked by the brevity of this episode, Spedding (in the last century) pleaded for putting the battle between Acts Four and Five — " and let the interval between the Acts be filled with some great battle-

---

* For clocks and bells in the old drama, see W. J. Lawrence, *Those Nut-cracking Elizabethans*, London, 1935, pp. 84 ff.

piece of Handel." On the Shakespearean stage, after all,

such an interval of suspended action, so accompanied with noises of battle in the distance, would have the same effect as a modern inter-Act with an orchestra playing appropriate music; provided only that it were understood to represent a period of indefinite duration.*

As for the anticipations and hurry of the concluding scene — those coincidental sudden marriages, for example — they are traditional, belonging as well to the stories on which the plays are founded. Even Ibsen anticipates. But Tesman and Mrs. Elvsted (in *Hedda Gabler*) were bound to go over Lövborg's notes, sometime, though they sit down to the task with a certain precipitancy.

It is but a step from such slurrings and elisions of time to the curious practice (so frequently discussed since the appearance of Christopher North's celebrated papers in *Blackwood's Edinburgh Magazine*) of employing two clocks, two contradictory sets of time references, in the same play. The explanation seems to lie partly in the character of Shakespeare's plots — full-bodied stories covering, perhaps, a period of months — partly in the very concreteness of his time notes. Starting with plot, and plenty of it,

* " On the Division of the Acts in *Lear, Much Ado*, and *Twelfth Night*," *New Shakspere Society's Transactions*, 1877–79, pp. 19, 20. For a defence of Shakespeare's Actium, see Granville-Barker's *Prefaces*, 2nd Series, 143–145. Attempts have been made to explain away the obviously foreshortened time at the beginning of the *Agamemnon* of Aeschylus.

Shakespeare gathers into vivid sequences episodes which had once been widely separated — which should, in the interests of matter-of-fact plausibility, remain separated. " In spite of an apparently connected and short period in the action," Gervinus writes, Shakespeare " has very often freely scattered indications . . . by which the action, though it passes quickly before the eye, is extended for the ear, for the imagination, to the time which it would naturally require; he has introduced a greater depth of time behind the narrow dramatic fore-ground." * But the process is just the reverse of this. The " greater depth of time " holds over from the original story; it is the " dramatic fore-ground " which has been introduced. At its best, the method combines with the free movement of romantic drama some of the advantages to be got by adherence to the unities. In *Othello*, notably, our sense of propulsion more than offsets the presence of inconsistencies. It may be doubted, moreover, whether in the theatre the inconsistencies would ever be perceived — at least, by persons previously unacquainted with the play.† The spectators' conception of time is " loosely held, and shadowy," a matter, once more, of illusion.

* *Shakespeare Commentaries*, tr. F. E. Bunnett, London, 1863, II, 487.

† But *cf.* E. E. Stoll, *Art and Artifice in Shakespeare: A Study in Dramatic Contrast and Illusion*, Cambridge (England), 1933, pp. 25–27.

Let the Entrances of Othello be four [says Christopher North]
— A, B, C, D. You feel the close connection of A with B, of B
with C, of C with D. You feel the coherence, the nextness; and
all the force of the impetuous Action and Passion resulting. But
the logically-consequent near connection of A with C, and much
more with D, as again of B with D, you *do not feel*. . . . At each
entrance you go back one step — you do not go back two.*

Fast time, in other words, is felt, not computed; and
felt principally in terms of a heightened anxiety and
expectation not incompatible, it may be, with the
sense that time *is* elapsing.

How consciously Shakespeare employed double
time is a hard question. In *Romeo and Juliet*, the interval between the first meeting of the lovers and
their tragic extinction is bounded by a Sunday and
Thursday of the same week. Yet when Angelica
(Juliet's Nurse is, really, so named) tells Romeo that
she angers Juliet " sometimes " by saying that Paris
is " the properer man," or when Juliet speaks of
how the " ancient damnation " had praised Romeo
" so many thousand times," a second, slower clock
seems to be ticking.† And though neither phrase
need be taken at quite its face value, Mr. Granville-
Barker supposes that they have slipped in because
their author had forgotten, or had not yet decided
to use, his fast chronometer.‡ On the other hand,

* " Christopher North " (John Wilson), " Dies Boreales,"
Blackwood's Edinburgh Magazine, May 1850, LXVII, 627.
† II, 4, 218; III, 5, 239.
‡ *Prefaces*, 2nd Series, 3, 4.

early in *Richard II*, when the King is on the point of
visiting John of Gaunt at Ely House, Aumerle brings
word that Bolingbroke (whom the King has
banished) is on his way to take ship from England.
And at the end of the next scene (II, 1), in which the
visit to Gaunt is paid, news comes that Bolingbroke
is returning from France at the head of an army!
With the chronicles before him, Shakespeare must
have been aware that Bolingbroke's weeks were becoming hours.* A familiar variation of double time
occurs when plot and subplot proceed at different
rates of speed. Thus, in the *First Part of King Henry
IV*, when the Gadshill affair is planned (I, 2), there
is mention of a meeting at the tavern in Eastcheap,
the following night. But before this meeting takes
place (II, 4) Hotspur, after defying the King, must
have time to go north and make preparations for
revolt; and, in II, 3, Kate speaks as if he had been
there for two weeks.† Similarly, the forfeiture of
Antonio's bond, in *The Merchant of Venice*, can take
place only after three months, while Bassanio's courtship of Portia, which fills the interval, is a matter
of perhaps two or three days.‡ Conceivably, Shakespeare set each plot going at its own pace, and gave

* Classical precedent for the acceleration of stage journeys is
not wanting — as notably in the *Trachiniae* of Sophocles and the
Captives of Plautus.
† Line 43.
‡ See Mable Buland, *Presentation of Time in the Elizabethan
Drama*, 108–111; Granville-Barker, *Prefaces*, 2nd Series, 69–71.

the matter no further thought; yet in other respects the relations between the stories are worked out with manifest care.

Failure to recognize that in any given instance Shakespeare, consciously or unconsciously, may be departing from the chronology of life, sometimes involves the critic in serious confusion. Thus, Mr. R. Warwick Bond finds that Thurio's serenade ("Who is Silvia?") in the fourth act of *The Two Gentlemen of Verona* need not be the same serenade which Thurio talked of with Proteus two scenes before — *

> And thy advice this night I 'll put in practice.
> Therefore, sweet Proteus, my direction-giver,
> Let us into the city presently
> To sort some gentlemen well skill'd in music.
>
> (III, 2, 89)

The soliloquy of Proteus at the beginning of the serenade scene sounds, indeed, as if much had happened since this talk. But, in the theatre, the connection between the preparations for the serenade and its accomplishment would be made, I am sure, without reference to any vague suggestions of longer time.†

* *The Two Gentlemen of Verona*, Arden Edition, London, 1906, p. 79.

† For an ingenious, though perhaps unnecessary, explanation of *Macb.*, I, 7, 47 ff., in terms of "Double Time," see Lewis Campbell, *Tragic Drama in Aeschylus, Sophocles, and Shakespeare*, London, 1904, p. 220.

The lack in Shakespeare's playhouse of a front curtain, of programmes and artificial lighting, affected his methods of indicating time. In Mr. W. Somerset Maugham's *For Services Rendered*, Eva goes to play chess with Sydney, at the end of Act One, and at the beginning of Act Two they are discovered playing. An Elizabethan audience would have assumed that only a few minutes had elapsed, instead of some twenty hours. But Mr. Maugham — an experienced craftsman — trusts to his programme note and to the lighting to obviate this impression. If, furthermore, some stupid souls did go astray, the lines would set them right. In the modern theatre the readiest way of indicating the passing of time is to drop the curtain — something which Shakespeare could not do. So, though he has a way of killing many birds with one stone, it is possible to discern in his plays speeches, and even whole scenes, which were obviously designed to bridge an interval. When in performance the conversation between Polonius and Reynaldo is cut, Hamlet may seem to have hurried straight from his encounter with the Ghost to Ophelia's closet.* The discourse of Jaques on the Seven Acts and Ages of Man covers the time it takes Orlando to find, and bring on, Adam, whose entrance coincides

---

* II, I. *Cf.* J. Dover Wilson, " The Elizabethan Shakespeare," 1929 (*Aspects of Shakespeare*, Oxford, 1933, p. 215), and G. R. Foss, *What the Author Meant*, London, 1932, p. 21.

effectively with Jaques's " last scene of all." *
" For these two hours, Rosalind, I will leave thee,"
Orlando says; and Rosalind replies, " Alas! dear
love, I cannot lack thee two hours." Then, when
we should lower the curtain, " *Enter* Jaques,
Lords, *and* Foresters," who march across the stage
singing " What shall he have that kill'd the deer? "
and Rosalind can reappear with " How say you
now? Is it not past two o'clock? And here much
Orlando!" †

It is only within very recent years that attention
has been paid to the dramatic propriety of the songs.
We read them, it is true, but read them as inde-
pendent pieces. They were the spoils of the an-
thologist. Detached from their context, they were
even introduced in performances of other plays,
with little or no complaint from persons who should
have known better. Yet on Shakespeare's stage
much was accomplished by means of the songs, and
their value in indicating or implying time and place
was not overlooked. ‡ What, one wonders, would
become of that delectable region, the Forest of
Arden, if the songs were removed? " Blow, blow,

---

* *A. T. L.*, II, 7, 133 ff. For scenes and parts of scenes used to
fill an interval of time, see also Thomas M. Raysor, " The Aes-
thetic Significance of Shakespeare's Handling of Time," *Studies in
Philology*, XXXII (1935), 197–209.

† IV, I, 186; IV, 3, I.

‡ Mr. Richmond Noble's important book, *Shakespeare's Use of
Song*, Oxford, 1923, should be consulted.

thou winter wind," " Under the greenwood tree," and, on the pastoral side, " It was a lover and his lass " do what scenery and lighting can never do and what, in *The Tempest*, " Full fathom five " and " Come unto these yellow sands " do, once more, to perfection. Of another song, " Hark! hark! the lark," in *Cymbeline*, Mr. Noble writes:

> Its use was so subtle that no one but an expert could have been aware that he was witnessing a stage trick. The previous trunk episode [II, 2] had created a heavy stifling atmosphere, which it was necessary to disperse; tragedy was the spirit present, by contrast music acted as relief. Furthermore . . . night was being transformed into dawn; on the modern stage the one episode could be represented almost in total darkness, and by means of artificial lights the gradual approach of dawn could be suggested. Shakespeare . . . made Iachimo announce the time, and Cloten and his companions further to give prominence to the topic, and as a final resource he relied upon the characteristically morning music to give the effect he desired — [*]

the same effect which is gained with so much greater effort before the last act of Puccini's *Tosca*. Of another lyric, the entrance song of Autolycus in *The Winter's Tale*, Mr. Noble finds that it " serves for scene and indicates the season of the year " [†] — spring. But the sheep shearing which follows soon after is, I take it, like the sheep shearing in Thomson's *Seasons*, a summer festival. Perdita, who has no " flowers o' the spring " for her " fair'st friend,"

[*] *Ibid.*, 131, 132.
[†] *Ibid.*, 94.

has for Polixenes and Camillo many flowers " of middle summer." * And Autolycus himself, though he begins vernally enough, introduces a summer note in the third stanza of his song.

" Time and the hour runs through the roughest day." Shakespeare's backgrounds of time accomplish three things, principally. Like the quiet allusions to the weather in Mr. St. John Ervine's *John Ferguson*, they heighten or restore our sense of reality. Then they increase our expectancy. It is usually when some awaited event draws near — Agincourt † or Bosworth Field, Hero's interrupted nuptials or the execution of Claudio — that Shakespeare employs many time notes. The freedom he permitted himself to forget or remember at will is justified, indeed, by the effectiveness of such scenes. Finally, to suspense and reality one must add beauty. And trusting to a feeling for beauty on the part of his audience — or, at least, to their capacity for imagination — Shakespeare again and again set the hands of his clock not at those hours of afternoon which the clocks of Elizabethan London were telling while the play was given but as far away from them as possible. " In *Hamlet*, *Othello*, and *Macbeth*," Bradley notes, " not one scene here and

---

* IV, 3, 103 ff., 113, *cf.* 79–82.
† See pages 200–202, below. Another instance, the scene in Brutus's orchard (*Jul. C.*, II, 1) is described in one of the finest passages in Raleigh's *Shakespeare*, pp. 121, 122.

there but actually the majority of the most impressive scenes take place at night." *

The nocturnal and dawn scenes of *A Midsummer Night's Dream*, though they lack certain characteristic features of Shakespeare's method with time, notably the suggestive or symbolic carrying of torches,† are happily illustrative of what that method often achieves, the quality of beauty. Lysander, in the first scene, will meet Hermia " tomorrow " at " deep midnight " :

> Tomorrow night, when Phoebe doth behold
> Her silver visage in the wat'ry glass,
> Decking with liquid pearl the bladed grass, —
> A time that lovers' flights doth still conceal, —
> Through Athens' gates have we devis'd to steal.
>
> (I, I, 209)

Peter Quince and his actors will rehearse " obscenely and courageously " that same night — " to-morrow night . . . in the palace wood, a mile without the town, by moonlight." ‡ Puck, meeting a Fairy, at the beginning of Act Two, notes that Oberon " doth keep his revels here tonight"; and Oberon's first words are,

---

* *Oxford Lectures on Poetry*, London, 1909, p. 392; Miss Bradbrook, *Elizabethan Stage Conditions*, 45.

† For torches, see W. J. Lawrence, " Light and Darkness in the Elizabethan Theatre," *The Elizabethan Playhouse*, 2nd Series, Stratford-upon-Avon, 1913.

‡ I, 2, 102 ff.

Ill met by moonlight, proud Titania.

(II, 1, 60)

Night is insistently mentioned in the passages which
follow, the nocturnal suggestion reaching a climax
in the song which lulls Titania to sleep. Puck, whom
Oberon has instructed to return " ere the first cock-
crow" — that is, ere midnight * — rejoins his master in Act Three, Scene Two. Venus and the " fiery
oes and eyes of light " are now gaining recognition,
while the moon " looks with a watery eye "; † and
when, after the quarrel of the lovers, Puck is given
fresh commands he says:

> My fairy lord, this must be done with haste,
> For night's swift dragons cut the clouds full fast,
> And yonder shines Aurora's harbinger.
>
> (III, 2, 378)

At the end of the scene, each of the lovers in turn
falls asleep, looking forward to the coming of day.
After Titania has been disenchanted, at the opening of Act Four, Puck again hurries his master —

> Fairy king, attend, and mark:
> I do hear the morning lark —

and next we hear horns blown, and Theseus, entering with Hippolyta, remarks that they have " the

---

* II, 1, 267; S. A. Tannenbaum, " Cock-Crow in Shakespeare,"
The Shakespeare Review, I (1928), 400–406.
† III, 1, 207; III, 2, 61, 107, 188, 356.

vaward of the day." * So persuasive is the atmosphere of the wood that it is with something like consternation that one comes upon old stage directions like " *Enter a Fairie at one doore, and Robin goodfellow at another.*"

* IV, I, 99, III.

Chapter III

SOME CONVENTIONS

Changing Attitude toward Convention — Three Sorts of Soliloquy — Thinking aloud — Talking to Oneself — Talking to Audience — Asides — " To be, or not to be " — Expository Use of Soliloquies — Of Asides — " Drawing-room Asides " — Whispering — Stage Letters — Disguise.

TO EXTOL an intelligent use of convention in the drama requires, nowadays, no great courage. It did, a few years ago, when to say a good word even for the aside was to lay oneself open to the charge of fogyism. " A drama with soliloquies and asides," wrote Archer, " is like a picture with inscribed labels issuing from the mouths of the figures. In that way, any bungler can reveal what is passing in the minds of his personages." *

A wholesome dislike for the abuses of convention in early Victorian drama — abuses manifestly irreconcilable with the ideals of the New Realism — explains this attitude. It led incidentally to fresh inquiry. Are there gradations in evil, it was asked, so that one may prefer, say, the soliloquy to the aside? Are there, even, necessary evils, unescapable defects in the medium itself, like " the un-

* *Play-Making: A Manual of Craftsmanship*, London, 1912, p. 307.

fleshly whiteness of marble statues "? * There are, it was admitted, certain fixed conventions involved in the shaping of a plot, for the influence of the well made play was still very much alive in those days. Selection, at least, is essential, " and with selection begins convention." † There are necessary conventions which have to do with speech. On the stage, even lovers murmuring in a bedroom are required to be audible at considerable distances. Or take characters who might be expected to use an alien tongue. Though Greek was still Greek to Shakespeare's Romans, they speak English without an accent — like the persons of various races whom Mr. O'Neill introduces in *Marco Millions*.

Then there is the celebrated Fourth Wall. I have imagined that missing wall hung, in a performance of *The School for Scandal*, with some of the portraits Charles Surface shows to his amiable uncle. I have watched Falder, in *Justice*, trace with his forefinger the three substantial sides of his cell and then, when he came to the fourth, trace the air. I have even seen the fastidious young hero of a comedy (Mr. Novello's *Truth Game*), after looking over three parts of a tasteless living room, gaze out at the front rows of the orchestra as if they and their occupants, too, were so much bad furniture (That snapped illu-

* Alfred Hennequin, " Writing for the Stage," *The Forum*, February 1890, VIII, 710.
† H. M. Paull, " Dramatic Convention with Special Reference to the Soliloquy," *Fortnightly Review*, May 1899, LXXI, 863.

sion and the audience laughed). The Fourth Wall has become for us something more than a convention: it is an institution, a postulate; it has, we feel, always been. Yet to Shakespeare's audience it was unknown, in the form in which we have it. Their rooms, having no walls, had paradoxically enough four perfectly good ones. The thought is chastening.*

The current attitude toward convention is, as I have suggested, comparatively tolerant. Mr. O'Neill's experiments, his asides and soliloquies and masks, his representation by means of a second actor of the evil traits of a complex character (a device by which soliloquy becomes dialogue!) would have been well-nigh unthinkable a few years ago. Nevertheless, the fact that on our stage these things *are* experimental, distinguishes them at once from the conventions known to Shakespeare. In both cases, a tacit agreement is entered into by the playwright and his audience. But whereas Mr. O'Neill's audience accepts his terms more or less consciously, then waits to see how much it has profited by doing so, Shakespeare's audience, consenting to his terms without giving them a thought, concentrated its attention from the outset on the story. As means to an end, the familiar conventions are least distracting.

* Certain scenes played on the inner stage will be at once recognized as exceptional. For the relations between realism and convention, see a suggestive article, " Dramatic Conventions," in *The Times Literary Supplement*, May 14, 1931.

Of the conventions which Shakespeare employed for expository purposes, the first in importance is the soliloquy.* In his plays, action and gesture, place and hour, find, as we have seen, expression in words. Why not, then, thought as well?

" In all the best dramas," Lamb perceived, " and in Shakspeare above all, how obvious it is, that the form of *speaking*, whether it be in soliloquy or dialogue, is only a medium, and often a highly artificial one, for putting the reader or spectator into possession of that knowledge of the inner structure and workings of mind in a character, which he could otherwise never have arrived at *in that form of composition* by any gift short of intuition." †

Joining with the rhetorical character of Elizabethan drama to make the use of soliloquy natural, was a singular intimacy between the actors and the audience. There on the platform stage, with no scenery behind them and no orchestral gulf before — playing always, as it were, on a runway — the actors were everything. Themselves familiar characters, they looked out, not on a mysterious, darkened auditorium, but on faces as distinctly visible, and some of them as familiar, as their own — the faces, in fact, of the habitués of a stock company.

---

* The shifts of playwrights who, needing a soliloquy, pretend that they are not writing one are often amusing. I have heard, for instance, at least two perfectly good expository soliloquies addressed to cats!

† " On the Tragedies of Shakspeare," in D. Nichol Smith, *Shakespeare Criticism*, 219, 220.

Soliloquy, in such surroundings, is at once explained and conditioned.*

" When a Man in Soliloquy," Congreve writes, " reasons with himself, and *Pro's* and *Con's*, and weighs all his Designs: We ought not to imagine that this man either talks to us, or to himself; he is only thinking, and thinking such Matter as were inexcusable Folly in him to speak." † At its best, the convention is about as Congreve describes it. Unfortunately, there are other sorts of soliloquy as well, and Congreve himself was not always at pains to choose among them. Sometimes the person soliloquizing is conceived of as babbling to himself. So Charlotte, in Porter's *Villain* (1662), concludes a long soliloquy selfconsciously enough with,

> Lord! How I talk? But Womens Hearts oppress'd,
> Will breathe their Secrets to the careless Air,
> Rather than silence keep. ‡

Sometimes, again, the actor — usually, but not always, a low comedian — addresses his monologue straight to the front rows. All three types are represented in Shakespeare's writing, and it is not in every case possible to tell one from another.

Some of the greater soliloquies — " To be, or not

* *Cf.* Matthews, *Shakspere as a Playwright*, 245, and Miss Bradbrook, *Elizabethan Stage Conditions*, 88.
† " Epistle Dedicatory " to *The Double-Dealer* (*Comedies*, ed. Dobrée, p. 115). Scott has a memorable account of the soliloquy in *The Fortunes of Nigel*, chap. xxii.
‡ II, 1 (Ed. 1694, p. 19).

to be "; Brutus's, at the beginning of the orchard
scene; Macbeth's " If it were done when 'tis done "
— are startlingly suggestive of actual thinking.
Shakespeare has ways, too, of setting off, and of
leading into, a soliloquy. He makes use of apos-
trophes and day dreams and prayers. Or, for the
sake of contrast, he flattens out the lines immediately preceding a soliloquy, so that we soar in a
moment from,

> Go bid thy mistress, when my drink is ready
> She strike upon the bell.   Get thee to bed,

to,

> Is this a dagger which I see before me.* . . .

(The actor should, of course, bring out the transition, though I have heard the second line pom-
pously declaimed with insistence on the " she " and
" thee.") On the other hand, in some of the soliloquies which one accepts without question as soliloquies of thought, there are hints that they were
conceived of as speech. Hamlet, for instance, comes
to a full stop with,

> This is most brave
> That I, the son of a dear father murder'd,
> Prompted to my revenge by heaven and hell,
> Must, like a whore, unpack my heart with words,
> And fall a-cursing, like a very drab,
> A scullion!

---

* *Macb.*, II, 1, 31. See, for many of the points made, Arnold,
The Soliloquies of Shakespeare, 20 ff., 141–148. For the day dream,
as in *3 H. VI*, II, 5, 1 ff., see Logan P. Smith, *On Reading Shakespeare*,
London, 1933, pp. 127, 128.

though he adds, the next instant, "About, my brain!" * Another scene from the same play (III, 3) shows strikingly the liberty enjoyed by the Elizabethan dramatist through convention. The agony of spirit which Claudius endures before he prays is given us in words, his prayer is unheard, and he rises from prayer saying:

> My words fly up, my thoughts remain below:
> Words without thoughts never to heaven go.

It would be evidence of insensibility were one to object that the practice of real life has been exactly reversed, Claudius speaking when he would have been silent, and remaining silent when he would have spoken.

So far, we have been at least within sight of actuality. Some of us do on occasion talk to ourselves, and it is understandable that by convention a character on the stage may go a step farther and think aloud. But what are we to make of the third sort of soliloquy, — that in which the character addresses us directly? That strikes at the foundations: for it is surely a necessary convention that the audience are supposed not to exist at all? Shakespeare is never, indeed, a prime offender in this matter. Even Launce does not go so far as, say, Strumbo in *Locrine* (1595), who borrows a knife from the specta-

---

* II, 2, 619 ff.; *cf. Richard II*, v, 5, 55. For overheard soliloquies, see pages 70, 71, 93, below.

tors, asks them what time it is, and, after an absence, greets them cheerfully with, " How do you, maisters, how do you? how have you scaped hanging this long time? " * Yet, leaving out of account all minor, and perhaps apocryphal, indiscretions in the rhymed " tags," one has only to remember Falstaff, as he tells of his ducking (" You may know by my size that I have a kind of alacrity in sinking "), or Autolycus, as he blithely introduces himself, to recognize the fact that Shakespeare did sometimes write soliloquies of the objectionable third sort.† It is noticeable, however, that these soliloquies are beginning to find apologists. There is Miss Doris Fenton, for example. In her lively and instructive thesis, *The Extra-Dramatic Moment in Elizabethan Plays before 1600*, she writes:

> Behind practically all of these speeches . . . lies the desire to make the play more vivid and interesting, to please the public. Because of its personal appeal, the direct address is one of the surest ways of rousing them from boredom or indifference. If not used too frequently, its unexpectedness startles and surprises them into attention. In some instances too, the effect is less of the actor's stepping out of his world, than of drawing the auditors into it, making them feel that they are actually a part of it.

And, making a point which is often overlooked, she adds: " The playwrights as a rule seem to be perfectly aware of what they are doing when they em-

---

* *The Shakespeare Apocrypha*, ed. C. F. Tucker Brooke, Oxford, 1908, pp. 43, 57.
† *Merry Wives*, III, 5, 12; *Winter's Tale*, IV, 2, 13 ff.

ploy this device, and to do so because they wish to, not because they cannot get along without it." * The poet and playwright, Mr. John Drinkwater, who knows from long experience what Shakespeare is like on the stage, goes even farther:

The soliloquy has often in later days been censured as an unnatural device, and so it is when spoken with a ridiculous pretence that the player is talking aloud at length to himself or herself. The player under Shakespeare's direction talked to the audience, and then it was a very different matter. Hamlet murmuring " To be or not to be " in the distance like a minor introspect has but a slack hold on our attention . . . and when Viola in a coy pretence that there is nobody about enquires, " What means this lady? " and goes on for twenty-five lines to consider how will this fadge, she becomes merely a tiresome girl who talks too much.

Whether one agrees with Mr. Drinkwater or not, his candor is refreshing. He continues:

But when Hamlet put all his quick-witted reasoning on suicide bluntly to the people about him, and when Viola asked them point-blank what the devil she was going to do about it, they neither of them said a word too many for their own comfort or anybody's patience.†

The word " aside " has, for our purposes, two distinct meanings. It may refer to something said by one of the dramatic characters to another (or others) not intended to be heard by all of those present. It may also refer to what is very like a soliloquy

* Philadelphia, 1930, pp. 11, 113, 114.
† *Shakespeare*, 86, 87.

(usually short) spoken while other characters are
present — and known to be present by the speaker
— but unheard by them.* An aside in this sense is
not always easy to distinguish from a soliloquy; and
the speaker of asides, like the speaker of soliloquies,
sometimes thinks aloud, sometimes talks to himself,
and sometimes talks to the audience. To the purists,
however, the aside is peculiarly offensive. Thinking
aloud comes more plausibly (they suppose) from an
actor alone on the stage; and, after all, we do not
talk to ourselves when we know that others are
about.

Shakespeare, could, when he chose, externalize
the thought of his characters in a perfect setting.
Witness the third scene in *Macbeth*. The greeting of
the protagonist as Thane of Cawdor is followed in
quick succession by a flash of thought —

> Glamis, and Thane of Cawdor:
> The greatest is behind —

then business — " Thanks for your pains " — then
a single exchange with Banquo, who, turning to
Ross and Angus — " Cousins, a word, I pray you "
— leaves Macbeth momentarily isolated.

Macbeth.   Two truths are told,
> As happy prologues to the swelling act
> Of the imperial theme. . . .

---

* For an aside of this sort, the word " apart " is sometimes
preferred — as by Dr. Arnold.

Business of some kind again interrupts his musing —
" I thank you, gentlemen " — but it is resumed
while Banquo and the messengers first make talk,
then comment on the hero's abstraction. At length,
as Banquo with some surprise addresses him, Macbeth apologizes:

> Give me your favour: my dull brain was wrought
> With things forgotten. *

Some asides are, however, conceived of as actually
spoken, though they may be only partially audible
to other characters present.† So Juliet, after she has
learned of Romeo's identity:

> My only love sprung from my only hate!
> Too early seen unknown, and known too late!
> Prodigious birth of love it is to me,
> That I must love a loathed enemy.
>
> *Nurse.* What 's this, what 's this?
> *Juliet.* A rime I learn'd even now
> Of one I danc'd withal.‡

---

* Lines 116 ff.; *cf.* also *2 H. VI*, v, 1, 23–34, *R. III*, iv, 2, 82–
115. Similar passages are not wanting elsewhere: *e.g. Troublesome
Reign*, ed. Hazlitt, *Shakespeare Library*, Part 2, vol. 1, pp. 231, 232.
In Lodge's *Wounds of Civil War* (1594) is a variation of the formula,
Flaccus asking:
  What maketh Scilla muse and mutter thus?
(ed. J. Dover Wilson, l. 2337).
  † How such asides were habitually spoken may be inferred from
an old stage direction in Dryden's *Secret Love*, II, 5:
Philocles. Hot Irons thank 'em for 't. —
  [*Softly or turning from her.*
Queen. What's that you mutter?
  ‡ 1, 5, 142; *cf. A. & C.*, III, 7, 9; *2 G. Ver.*, II, 1, 151.

In the scene between Suffolk and Margaret, near the end of the *First Part of Henry VI*, these two kinds of aside go hand in hand. After Suffolk's first questioning of himself, Margaret asks: "Why speak'st thou not?" Then as he continues, she says irritably:

> He talks at random; sure, the man is mad.
>
> (v, 3, 85)

And, later still, she picks up and misinterprets a word of his — "he talks of wood." I am afraid that in the following lines from *Richard III*, the second kind gives place to the third, the very reprehensible aside addressed to the audience:

Gloucester [*Aside*]. So wise so young, they say, do never live
         long.
Prince of Wales. What say you, uncle?
Gloucester. I say, without characters, fame lives long.
  [*Aside*.] Thus, like the formal Vice, Iniquity,
        I moralize two meanings in one word.

> (III, 1, 79)

That a sound exegesis of Shakespeare may sometimes depend on understanding of the niceties of convention, is suggested by Professor Stoll's discussion of "To be, or not to be." Polonius and the King are concealed behind the arras throughout this celebrated monologue: and "when eavesdroppers are at hand for the purpose," Mr. Stoll writes, "soliloquies on the Elizabethan stage are overheard." Hamlet may not, therefore, refer to his de-

signs against Claudius, as some critics demand that
he should. Instead, " he plays the King's game "
and " beats him at it. If he is not permitted to know
the King's purposes, he sees a ' cherub that sees
them.' " The spectators would " start up in their
seats " with anxiety, but the hero does not commit
himself, falling instead into " a philosophical discourse and reverie." * Now soliloquies in Shakespeare's plays — the tragedies as well as the comedies — are not infrequently overheard.† But is this
one? Its effect is that of thinking, not speech, and I
believe that Mr. Stoll himself uses the right word
when he calls it a " reverie." The audience, moreover, are carefully prepared for the overhearing by
eavesdroppers of just one thing, the conversation
with Ophelia.‡ There lay the trap which Hamlet
(with what cost to himself!) successfully avoided.
Finally, that it was allowable on the Elizabethan
stage for a character to think aloud without being
overheard, even by persons watching him who
would love to overhear, is shown conclusively by the
scene (III, 2) in *Henry VIII* in which Norfolk, Suffolk,
and Surrey can catch nothing of what Wolsey says

* *Hamlet: An Historical and Comparative Study*, Minneapolis, 1919,
pp. 34, 35; *cf. Shakespeare Studies*, New York, 1927, pp. 135, 136.
† See Arnold, *Soliloquies of Shakespeare*, 90 ff., and " To be, or
not to be, — Again," *Poet Lore*, xxvii (1916), pp. 81–90. Iachimo
and Edmund talk to themselves as if expecting to be overheard —
but are they? (*Cymb.*, I, 6, 32 ff.; *Lear*, I, 2, 152 ff.).
‡ II, 2, 162–167; III, 1, 29–37.

aside. There is, to be sure, this difference, that
Norfolk, Suffolk, and Surrey are not, like Claudius,
concealed.

Soliloquies and asides, whether they stand for
thought or actual speech, form a valuable part of
Shakespeare's technique of exposition. In them,
character and motive are unfolded, plot and coun-
terplot set going, events narrated, and the issues of
the play made clear. There is perhaps exaggeration
in Dr. Arnold's statement that without the soliloquies " Brutus might appear a murderer and Hamlet a madman," but it comes near the truth.* To
the great soliloquies, moreover, one turns confidently not only for an understanding of the plays in
which they occur but for the excitement and the
solace of high poetry.

Sometimes, indeed, the expository intention shows
through, as it was to do so often in the work of less
gifted men, till at last the means itself became suspect. Early in Shakespeare's career, Petruchio
steps forward with these lines:

> Verona, for awhile I take my leave,
> To see my friends in Padua; but, of all
> My best beloved and approved friend,
> Hortensio; and I trow this is his house.
> Here, sirrah Grumio; knock, I say.
>
> (*Tam. Shr.*, 1, 2, 1)

Toward the end of his playwriting, when Shakespeare

---

* *Soliloquies of Shakespeare*, 169.

seems content on occasion to neglect detail, Belarius
is egregiously informative:

> How hard it is to hide the sparks of nature!
> These boys know little they are sons to the king;
> Nor Cymbeline dreams that they are alive.
> They think they are mine; and, though train'd up thus
>   meanly
> I' the cave wherein they bow, their thoughts do hit
> The roofs of palaces.

He dwells on this idea till a noise is heard off stage:

> Hark! the game is rous'd.
> O Cymbeline! heaven and my conscience knows
> Thou didst unjustly banish me; whereon,
> At three and two years old, I stole these babes,
> Thinking to bar thee of succession, as
> Thou refts't me of my lands.   Euriphile,
> Thou wast their nurse; they took thee for their mother,
> And every day do honour to her grave:
> Myself, Belarius, that am Morgan call'd,
> They take for natural father.   The game is up.*

" Myself, Belarius, that am Morgan call'd " — he
could not be more precise.

Sometimes, as we shall see, an expository intention is discovered by critics even in lines which,
coming quite naturally from the character who
utters them, require no apology.† Bradley, on the
contrary, fails to perceive in one of Iago's solilo-

---

* *Cymb.*, III, 3, 79. See Granville-Barker, *Prefaces*, 2nd Series,
239–242.
† Many of the asides in Mr. O'Neill's *Dynamo* are expository,
for that matter.

quies the underlying purpose to inform. Iago says,
of Roderigo:

> I have rubb'd this young quat almost to the sense,
> And he grows angry.   Now, whether he kill Cassio,
> Or Cassio him, or each do kill the other,
> Every way makes my gain: live Roderigo,
> He calls me to a restitution large
> Of gold and jewels that I bobb'd from him,
> As gifts to Desdemona;
> It must not be: if Cassio do remain,
> He hath a daily beauty in his life
> That makes me ugly; and, besides, the Moor
> May unfold me to him; there stand I in much peril.
> No, he must die.   (*Oth.*, v, i, ii)

Bradley is troubled by what he calls " Iago's momentary doubt . . . whether Roderigo and Cassio
must be killed," when " as a mere matter of calcula-
tion it is perfectly obvious that they must." *   In
reality, the speech is a rapid summary of his reasons
for attempting a double murder; and no hesitation
is involved.

Though in this last instance a soliloquy yielded
less, in point of fact, than subtle criticism would
draw from it, the evidence of the soliloquies is sound
evidence, in the main, and to be accepted without
reserve.†   Inattention to what a character says of
himself in his first soliloquy may lead, indeed, to
surprising misconceptions.   Angelo and Jessica will
bear reconsidering from this point of view.   Poor

---

* *Shakespearean Tragedy*, London 1904 (1926), p. 235.
† For Hamlet's self condemnation, see pages 310, 311, below.

little Jessica, in spite of her romantic disguising in boy's clothes and her part in the loveliest of verbal duets, has often been dealt with as harshly as if she were a sort of minor Goneril. She comes on, wistfully, with a tear and a ducat for our friend Launcelot Gobbo. " Farewell, good Launcelot," she says; then in soliloquy:

> Alack, what heinous sin is it in me
> To be asham'd to be my father's child!

(" No sin at all! " the audience would say to themselves.)

> But though I am a daughter to his blood,
> I am not to his manners. O Lorenzo!
> If thou keep promise, I shall end this strife,
> Become a Christian, and thy loving wife.*

She is *not* like her father, and she has decided to elope with a Christian, Bassanio's friend, who has promised to marry her. . . . It is an obvious bid for sympathy. Angelo is a customer of a different kind. We do not like him, certainly, nor is it expected that we should. But he must not be mistaken for a whited sepulchre from the beginning. " I partly think," says Isabella,

> A due sincerity govern'd his deeds,
> Till he did look on me.†

---

* *The Merchant of Venice*, II, 3, 15.

† *Measure for Measure*, v, 1, 446. Even Professor W. W. Lawrence cannot make up his mind on the question (*Shakespeare's Problem Comedies*, New York, 1931, pp. 113, 114). *Cf.* also Stoll, *Shakespeare Studies*, 108, 109.

Her judgment of him is borne out by the terms of his
first soliloquy. Picking up Isabella's grateful " save
your honor," Angelo begins:

> From thee; even from thy virtue!
> What 's this? what 's this?   Is this her fault or mine?
> The tempter or the tempted, who sins most?
> Ha!
> Not she; nor doth she tempt: but it is I. . . .
> What dost thou, or what art thou, Angelo? . . .
>
> O cunning enemy, that, to catch a saint,
> With saints dost bait thy hook!   Most dangerous
> Is that temptation that doth goad us on
> To sin in loving virtue: never could the strumpet,
> With all her double vigour, art and nature,
> Once stir my temper; but this virtuous maid
> Subdues me quite.   Ever till now,
> When men were fond, I smil'd and wonder'd how.
>
> (II, 2, 162)

Angelo is accountable for cupidity — witness his
treatment of Mariana — and for self righteousness,
since he takes pride, as he admits, in his own gravity,* but at the outset he is not a hypocrite and not a
villain.

Iago's motives are expounded in his soliloquies.
Cleopatra's want of soliloquy leaves her enigmatic
and, it may be, all the more fascinating. The
choice of narration, as against representation, for
the murder of the princes in *Richard III*, has found
praise. In his adaptation of the play, Colley Cibber
at first tried the other method, unsuccessfully, and

* II, 4, 9, 10.

smothered them on the stage, whereas Shakespeare really proceeds at two removes, Tyrrell in soliloquy telling us what Dighton and Forrest have told him.*

Some soliloquies, like York's, early in the *Second Part of Henry VI*, and Richard's, near the end of the *Third Part*, look forward with an almost choral sweep. Mr. Masefield writes of the former that

> it gives a terror to what follows. The calm mind makes no mistakes. The judgment of a man without heart seems as infallible as fate, as beautiful, and as ghastly. All happens as he foresees. All the cruelty and bloodiness of the latter half of the play come from that man's beautifully clear, cool brain.†

Other soliloquies, again somewhat choral in effect, look back momentarily, as the action of the play comes to a pause and the speaker sums up the situation which has developed. Viola does so, in the lines which Mr. Drinkwater would have her address to the audience, and the Second Lord, in *Cymbeline*, and Romeo, just before he fights with Tybalt.‡

> *Romeo.* This gentleman, the prince's near ally,
> My very friend, hath got his mortal hurt
> In my behalf; my reputation stain'd
> With Tybalt's slander, Tybalt, that an hour
> Hath been my kinsman. O sweet Juliet!
> Thy beauty hath made me effeminate,
> And in my temper soften'd valour's steel!
>   (III, 1, 115)

---

* IV, 3, 1 ff. *Cf.* A. C. Sprague, " A New Scene in Colley Cibber's *Richard III*," *Modern Language Notes*, XLII (1927), 29–32.

† *William Shakespeare*, London and New York, 1911, p. 57.

‡ *12 N.*, II, 2, 18 ff., *Cymb.*, II, 1, 59 ff.; *cf.* Arnold, p. 65.

As a general caveat against supposing that a good
playwright accomplishes only one thing at a time, it
may be pointed out that Shakespeare, having decided to let Mercutio die off stage, uses this soliloquy as a " link " to cover the interval between
Mercutio's exit and Benvolio's return with

O Romeo, Romeo! brave Mercutio's dead.*

Nor is this all he accomplishes. The hero is to kill
Tybalt and precipitate the tragedy. And this soliloquy, showing Romeo as it does at the limit of his en-
durance, prepares the auditors for what is to come,
and absolves him in their sight from all responsibility for his deed.

Shakespeare's use of asides for purposes of exposition is similar, at certain points, to his use of soliloquies. Thus, Shylock's motives are set forth at large
in his first aside, with a manifest underscoring
of his *personal* malice against Antonio, because of the
latter's refusal to accept interest.† Asides are
more closely fitted into surrounding dialogue than
soliloquies, though occasionally Shakespeare will
ease the transition. The groping asides of Polonius
(" He said I was a fishmonger . . .") are spoken
while Hamlet pores on his book — as if Polonius

* Soliloquies are often so employed — see Arnold, pp. 86, 87, and
R. C. Flickinger, *The Greek Theater and its Drama*, Chicago, 1922,
pp. 309–311.
    † I, 3, 42 ff. For an interesting analysis of the speech, see Louis
Calvert, *Problems of the Actor*, New York, 1918, pp. 69, 70.

were taking advantage of his preoccupation! *
Hamlet's own, " Nay, then, I have an eye of you,"
springs from his perception that Rosencrantz has
spoken aside to Guildenstern; and his aside is covered by theirs.† Stage business, or the show of making talk, is a more usual accompaniment, as when
we see the innocent exchange of courtesies between
Desdemona and Cassio through Iago's eyes:

> He takes her by the palm; ay, well said, whisper; with as
> little a web as this will I ensnare as great a fly as Cassio. Ay,
> smile upon her, do; I will gyve thee in thine own courtship.
> You say true, 't is so, indeed. If such tricks as these strip you out
> of your lieutenantry, it had been better you had not kissed your
> three fingers so oft, which now again you are most apt to play
> the sir in. Very good; well kissed! an excellent courtesy! 't is
> so, indeed. Yet again your fingers to your lips? would they were
> clyster-pipes for your sake!   (*Oth.*, II, I, 168)

Effects of contrast and irony are gained easily in
asides — too easily, it may be, as the familiarities of
the villain in melodrama will testify. There is bite,
though, in Hamlet's

> A little more than kin, and less than kind;

and one would not do without the baleful asides of
Richard at the end of the *Third Part of Henry VI* —

---

* II, 2, 171 ff.; *cf.* Pisanio's asides while Cloten reads the letter
(*Cymb.*, III, 5, 101 ff.).
† II, 2, 308. Effective use is made of this method in *Tit. And.*, V,
2, 137 ff.

So Judas kiss'd his master,
And cried " all hail! " when as he meant all harm.*

The humor scored at Cloten's expense by the Second
Lord, through two whole scenes of *Cymbeline*, employs the same convention.†

Asides have the advantage over soliloquies when
the playwright would mark developing thought.
The famous scene in *The Changeling*, in which De
Flores slowly reaches a comprehension of Beatrice-
Johanna's purpose, and then in a flash perceives
what he himself can make of it, is the supreme example of this use of the aside. The desertion of Antony by Enobarbus — itself a tragedy in little — is
led up to in a series of asides. They show, Mr.
Granville-Barker writes, " what can be done with
thrifty skill in the freedom of the Elizabethan
stage "; and he suggests that earlier in Shakespeare's
career most of them would have been " joined into a
long soliloquy." ‡ As preparation, too, whether for
events still to come or for aspects of character still to
be revealed, the aside is as useful as the soliloquy.
When, overborne at last by his mother's supplica-
tion, Coriolanus consents to give up his vengeance
against Rome, Aufidius is ready with an aside which
implies much of what remains to be accomplished:

* *Hamlet*, 1, 2, 65; *3 H. VI*, v, 7, 33.
† 1, 2; ii, 1; *cf*. Granville-Barker, *Prefaces*, 2nd Series, 298, 299,
and Creizenach, *The English Drama in the Age of Shakespeare*, 275.
‡ *Prefaces*, 2nd Series, 225, note; see also pages 220–223, below.

I am glad thou hast set thy mercy and thy honour
At difference in thee: out of that I 'll work
Myself a former fortune.

(v, 3, 200)

The casual dropping of a platitude by his Lord
Chamberlain is enough to make Claudius feel a
twinge of conscience — and we look forward to the
time, after the acting of *The Mouse-trap*, when he
shall show himself tortured by his sense of guilt.*
Hamlet himself turns from the exhilaration — the
" wild and whirling words " — which succeeded
the departure of the Ghost, to weariness:

The time is out of joint; O cursed spite,
That ever I was born to set it right!   (1, 5, 188)

Finally, brief asides are often inserted to explain
some episode which might seem ambiguous, or
the point of which might be missed. Thus, Mrs.
Quickly, in *The Merry Wives* is at pains to remind the
spectators that she has concealed the good young
man, Simple, in Dr. Caius's closet. Caius sends her
there after " a box, a green-a box." She will fetch
it, she says; then, aside: " I am glad he went not in
himself: if he had found the young man, he would
have been horn-mad." And a moment later —
when the Doctor does go himself — for " some

---

* *Hamlet*, III, 1, 49 ff. *Cf. John*, IV, 1, 25–27, and Lady Macbeth's
brief soliloquy, at the beginning of III, 2, which Mrs. Siddons made
preparatory to the Sleep-walking Scene.

simples " — she exclaims: " Ay me! he 'll find the young man there, and be mad." * Or to turn from farce to tragedy,

> It is the poison'd cup! it is too late,

the terrible exclamation of Claudius as the Queen drinks to Hamlet, calls the attention of an audience preoccupied with the fencing to what is happening up stage.† The part of Edgar in *King Lear* is stocked with these directive or explanatory asides. Of Lear, Edgar says:

> My tears begin to take his part so much,
> They 'll mar my counterfeiting,

and " I cannot daub it further," and later, " O thou side-piercing sight ";

> I would not take this from report; it is,
> And my heart breaks at it,

he cries; and again,

> O! matter and impertinency mix'd;
> Reason in madness!

Besides keeping his own identity and the sympathetic nature of his response clear, the lines echo and enhance the emotion — ' giving sorrow words ' in a way that we shall come to recognize as peculiar-

* I, 4, 47 ff. The second aside is possibly addressed to John Rugby.
† v, 2, 306.

ly Shakespearean.* Edgar, too, takes precautions against any misinterpretation of his treatment of Gloucester in the Dover Cliff episode (" Why I do trifle thus with his despair / Is done to cure it "), just as Imogen, after she has told Lucius that her dead master's name was Richard du Champ, hastens to add in an aside,

> If I do lie and do
> No harm by it, though the gods hear, I hope
> They 'll pardon it.†

Desdemona's lines,

> I am not merry, but I do beguile
> The thing I am by seeming otherwise,

have the same purpose; but they are not, as they are sometimes called, an aside; and, as their context shows, they are perfectly in character.‡ Desdemona on landing has been elaborately saluted by Cassio. As soon as she gets a chance to speak, she thanks him, then immediately asks after Othello:

Desdemona.   I thank you, valiant Cassio.
          What tidings can you tell me of my lord?
Cassio.   He is not yet arriv'd; nor know I aught
          But that he 's well, and will be shortly here.
Desdemona. O! but I fear. . . .

---

  * III, 6, 63; IV, 1, 52; IV, 6, 86, 145, 179; and see pages 160–163, below.

  † *Lear*, IV, 6, 34; *Cymb.*, IV, 2, 377.

  ‡ " A modern dramatist," Schücking writes, " instead of giving this ' aside,' would represent Desdemona as absent-minded and inattentive " (*Character Problems in Shakespeare's Plays*, London, etc. [1922], p. 224).

When " a sail " is cried, off stage, a moment later, the player is trusted to bring out Desdemona's concern. A Gentleman goes to learn what ship has been sighted; and the light talk with Iago begins as they wait.

Desdemona. What wouldst thou write of me, if thou should'st praise me?
Iago.   O gentle lady, do not put me to 't,
            For I am nothing if not critical.
Desdemona. Come on; assay.

Suddenly, she breaks off — " There 's one gone to the harbour? " And when he has satisfied her — " Ay, madam " — it befits her quite frankly and courteously to address him and the others who are present:

I am not merry, but I do beguile
The thing I am by seeming otherwise.
Come, how wouldst thou praise me?   (II, 1, 122)

Nothing has been said, all this while, of the second kind of aside, defined as a remark made by one of the characters to another (or others), not intended to be heard by all of those present. Even the convention-hater, William Archer, thought it " pedantry " to object to asides of this sort, though he saw their weakness too. " It is not the audibility of one group," he wrote, " but the inaudibility of the others, that is apt to strike us as unreal " * (the

* *Play-Making: A Manual of Craftsmanship*, 310, 311. Iago's turning from Montano to speak aside with Roderigo (II, 3, 141)

show of making talk *is* a sorry show at best).
In aside scenes, a great deal depends on grouping.
And when an Elizabethan playwright wished to
introduce some of his persons speaking audibly
and some expressing themselves in pantomime
only, he could, if he saw fit, perch one group
on the upper stage. So, early in Marston's *Antonio
and Mellida*, Rossaline, Flavia, and Mellida *above*
discuss characters *below* who are only assumed to be
talking.* The second scene in *Troilus and Cressida*
might, on an Elizabethan stage, be done effectively
in this way. Pandarus suggests to Cressida that
they " stand up here. . . . Here 's an excellent
place: here we may see most bravely " (line 191).
Cressida consents, and as the Trojan worthies pass
before them in silence, Pandarus gabbles to her
about each in turn.†

The panicky asides of Malcolm and Donalbain
are spoken during the confusion caused by Lady
Macbeth's fainting.‡ And Margaret's swoon, after
the butchering of Prince Edward by the Yorkists,
covers Gloster's asides to Clarence, which point forward to yet another royal murder:

---

is sufficiently implausible. *Cf.* the extreme conventionality of Mol-
ière's *Le festin de Pierre*, II, 4.

  * *Cf.* Massinger's *Virgin Martyr*, II, 3. The great soliloquy scene
with which *The Revenger's Tragedy* opens is similarly staged.

  † *Cf. R. II*, III, 3 — a scene in which distance is startlingly con-
ventionalized.

  ‡ II, 3, 126 ff.

King Edward. What! doth she swoon? use means for her re-
          covery.
Gloucester.   Clarence, excuse me to the king, my brother;
          I 'll hence to London on a serious matter:
          Ere ye come there, be sure to hear some news.
Clarence.   What? what?
Gloucester.   The Tower! the Tower!   (*3 H. VI*, v, 5, 45).

It is notable that in neither instance were these
asides necessary. Malcolm and Donalbain have
their chance to confer when the stage is cleared, a
few lines below. And after Margaret has been led
out, Edward turns to Clarence:

King Edward. Where 's Richard gone?
Clarence.   To London, all in post; and, as I guess,
          To make a bloody supper in the Tower.
King Edward. He 's sudden if a thing comes in his head.

Evidently Shakespeare felt that the asides con-
tributed in themselves to the effects of contrast and
confusion, or of cruelty general and particular,
which he wished to produce. At times, indeed, his
asides are far less plausible. In the midst of a formal
speech to Saturninus, Tamora, suddenly dropping
her voice, urges him to dissemble with the hated
faction of Andronicus.

> I'll find a day to massacre them all,

she promises. Then, speaking once more for all to
hear, she pleads for the " good old man " (1, 1, 442).
Not least among the " awkward snags " for a producer
of *The Winter's Tale*, Mr. Foss writes, is " the en-

trance of Leontes in Act II, Scene 1, with its twenty-four important lines before the group of ladies listening to Mamillius' sad tale become aware of the presence of their King." * Perhaps, the ladies should notice Leontes a good deal earlier than Mr. Foss thinks — and even if they did the awkwardness might remain.

Asides of this sort — " drawing-room asides," I should like to call them — are useful for exposition. *King John* opens on the note of patriotism as Chatillon, the French Ambassador, gets England's defiance for an answer. But England is divided, is *not* true to itself.

> Our strong possession and our right for us,

cries John. But Elinor caps him:

> Your strong possession much more than your right,
> Or else it must go wrong with you and me:
> So much my conscience whispers in your ear,
> Which none but heaven and you and I shall hear.
>
> (I, 1, 39)

Sebastian and Antonio do not carry much terror with them, but their asides, just before the magical banquet in *The Tempest*, remind us that there is still some thunder in the air. And at a very different feast, in *The Taming of the Shrew*, when Kate has at last thanked Petruchio and some concession on his

* *What the Author Meant*, 136.

part seems inevitable, he turns quickly to Hortensio:

> Eat it up all, Hortensio, if thou lov'st me,

and Hortensio falls to. A much more striking example occurs in the scene of Julius Cæsar's return from the games. Standing apart with Cassius — the grouping has its significance — Brutus calls attention to the faces, then waits for a chance to signal Casca; while Cæsar, with one glance at Cassius, sums him up in the thrice-familiar lines to Antony.[*]

Asides are nowhere set to work more efficiently, however, than in the scene on Pompey's galley in *Antony and Cleopatra.* Pompey at first puts off Menas as he whispers to him — " Forbear me till anon." Then, as Antony explains to poor Lepidus the nature of that " strange serpent," the crocodile, Menas returns.

Menas. If for the sake of merit thou wilt hear me,
    Rise from thy stool.
Pompey.   I think thou'rt mad.   The matter?
                                   (II, 7, 62)

and, with a " Be jolly, lords," flung back at the revellers, Pompey leaves the table. The offer of Menas — " Wilt thou be lord of the whole world? " — is made, and rejected. Pompey rejoins the others;

---

[*] *Temp.,* III, 3, 11 ff.; *Tam. Shr.,* IV, 3, 50; *Jul. C.,* I, 2, 181–213.

and the scene to which a few brief exchanges have given suspense and contrast ends in irony:

Enobarbus.   Hoo! says a'.   There's my cap.
Menas.   Hoo! noble captain! come.

Even the great scene in which Melantius outfaces Calianax (in *The Maid's Tragedy*) seems by comparison mere claptrap.*

Asides of both kinds are occasionally delivered in a stage whisper, but this is a clumsy compromise. The inaudible whispering, which is called for, or implied, by Shakespeare's text, is a different thing, and serves a variety of purposes. It may stand for dialogue which is omitted in the interest of economy. Or it may warn the audience that something is brewing — what, they must wait to see. Thus Richard, giving Tyrrel his final directions for the murder of the little princes, "*whispers.*" † And shortly before the death of Brutus, when Clitus has brought word that Statilius must have been taken prisoner or slain, Brutus says:

> Sit thee down, Clitus; slaying is the word;
> It is a deed in fashion.   Hark thee, Clitus.
> *[Whispers.*

---

* " Drawing-room Asides " are now and then overheard (as in *Merry Wives*, II, 1, 173–176, and Wycherley's *Love in a Wood*, v, 5, Mermaid Ed., pp. 118, 119), and may even be feigned (as in *The Braggard Captain* of Plautus, IV, 6, tr. Thornton, I, 227 ff., and Jonson's *Alchemist*, I, 1, Mermaid Ed., III, 297).

† IV, 2, 78; see also pages 129, 130, and 153, 154, below.

Clitus.	What, I, my lord? No, not for all the world.
Brutus.	Peace, then! no words.
Clitus.	I 'll rather kill myself.
Brutus.	Hark thee, Dardanius. [*Whispers.*
Dardanius.	Shall I do such a deed?
Clitus.	O, Dardanius!
Dardanius.	O, Clitus!
Clitus.	What ill request did Brutus make to thee?
Dardanius.	To kill him, Clitus. (*Jul. C.*, v, 5, 4)

Brutus now turns to Volumnius and, asking for the third time, speaks aloud:

> Hold thou my sword-hilts, whilst I run on it.

The impressiveness of the scene gains greatly from the dramatist's privilege of employing suggestion.

* * *

" I never could make out his writing," Paula Tanqueray remarks, handing her letter to Aubrey, who reads it aloud. Pinero wished us to hear the letter in question, and he contrives it beautifully. There is Paula's carelessness of consequences, her concern, as well, to avoid the imputation of desiring to conceal anything. There is the touch of realism. And there is the subtle reminder, which Aubrey does not miss, of his wife's former intimacy with Ardale.* Pinero is, as ever, a master of economy.

* *The Second Mrs. Tanqueray*, Act IV.

Through convention, Shakespeare's persons enjoy certain liberties, akin to the soliloquy and the aside, in connection with the reading of their correspondence.* These liberties, nevertheless, they seldom abuse, for they read their letters or have their letters read to them much as they would in real life. Thus, when the frenzy of Malvolio is under discussion near the end of *Twelfth Night* and a communication from him is brought by Feste, Olivia bids the latter " Open it, and read it." Feste does not get far. " ' *By the Lord, Madam . . .* ' " he recites, and Olivia turns quickly to the more reliable Fabian: " Read it you, sirrah." Bardolph, again, is the bearer of a flamboyant missive headed: " *Sir John Falstaff, knight, to the son of the king nearest his father, Harry Prince of Wales, greeting.*" The Prince has time to look at it while Poins asks Bardolph about Falstaff's health. Then Hal gives the letter to Poins, who reads it aloud critically, finding before he is done references to himself of an unfortunate nature. " My lord," he cries, " I 'll steep this letter in sack and make him eat it " (*2 H. IV*, II, 2, 149). In *The Merchant of Venice*, Bassanio at the request of Portia reads aloud his letter from Antonio telling of the forfeiture of the bond, and at Shylock's trial the Duke has his clerk read to the court the letter which serves as Portia's credentials; but Lorenzo, with equal

---

* The letters are conveniently collected in R. L. Mégroz, *Shakespeare as a Letter-Writer and Artist in Prose*, London, 1927.

naturalness, does not read to the other young men his letter from Jessica.*

The practice of reading letters aloud is so familiarly associated with the soliloquy that it is a trifle disconcerting to find Archer judging between them, or rather, maintaining that the letter soliloquy is the only kind of soliloquy that is quite reputable.

"A letter," he urges, "has an actual objective existence. The words are formulated in the character's mind and are supposed to be externalized. . . . Thus the letter has, so to speak, the same right to come to the knowledge of the audience as any other utterance. It is, in fact, part of the dialogue of the play, only that it happens to be inaudible. A soliloquy, on the other hand, has no real existence. It is a purely artificial unravelling of motive or emotion." †

Shakespeare, it may be supposed, felt no such distinctions. At any rate, the reading of letters by Brutus and Malvolio, by Kent, Lady Macbeth, and Mrs. Page, is made to appear a natural accompaniment of their soliloquies — or *vice versa*.‡ No letter need, of course, be quoted entire. Nor is Lady Macbeth to be thought of as reading part of Macbeth's letter to herself and part aloud. As a matter of fact, she enters in the act of reading and we hear only

* II, 4, 29 ff.; III, 2, 315 ff.; IV, 1, 149 ff. Claudius makes a point of reading to Laertes the letter from Hamlet (IV, 7, 41 ff.).

† *Play-Making*, 310. For letter soliloquies, see Arnold, pp. 67, 68.

‡ *Jul. C.*, II, 1, 36 ff.; *12 N.*, II, 5, 92 ff.; *Lear*, II, 2, 167 ff.; *Macb.*, I, 5, 1 ff.; *Merry Wives*, II, 1, 1 ff.

that part of the letter which we need to hear. Malvolio is overheard as he reads, and we get from the eavesdroppers a sort of apology for what is coming:

Malvolio [*Seeing the letter.*] What employment have we here?
Fabian. Now is the woodcock near the gin.
Sir Toby. O, peace! and the spirit of humours intimate reading
    aloud to him!

There is no abruptness. Malvolio comments first on the writing, then on the inscription, then on the seal. Once accept the convention which permits him to soliloquize and to be overheard, and (Sir Toby to the contrary) the reading of the letter aloud follows logically.

The reading of letters is combined, on occasion, with the speaking of asides. There is no particular reason why this should not be done, though a purist may feel that for the most part it comes off somewhat uneasily. The Countess in *All 's Well* is, in fact, momentarily relieved of the Clown's company while she reads her letter from Bertram. Horatio, on the other hand, makes no bones of reading Hamlet's letter in the presence of the sailors who brought it. Early in *Lear*, Gloucester probably reads the forged letter from Edgar aside, and not to Edmund, turning to him afterwards with, " When came this to you? Who brought it? " And in the fourth act, when Edgar reads in Gloucester's presence the incriminating letter carried by Oswald, a soliloquy spoken by Gloucester, immediately after, shows that he has not heard it — one convention serving to help out another.*

Some of the letters already mentioned — Kent's, foreshadowing Cordelia's intervention; Bassanio's, about the bond; Horatio's, from Hamlet — contain information of real consequence. And to these might be added the letter, summarized by Hotspur, which tells that Northumberland will not be with the rebels at Shrewsbury, and the letter, quoted from by Pisanio in soliloquy and later read by Imogen, setting forth the vengeful purpose of Imogen's husband.† Many letters however, contain what is to us stale news. The chief importance of these letters, which are seldom given in full, lies in the effect they produce on the characters who receive them. Thus, we have heard the witches' prophecies, but Lady Macbeth has not, and what she makes of the letter recounting them is of the utmost interest. Or there is the letter which invites Falstaff to the disastrous assignation at Herne's Oak. In this scene, the Falstaff of Mr. Otis Skinner showed in his face the recollection of all his former ill-usage — the beating and the buckbasket — and shrinking from the thought of further harm, he would at first have nothing to do with the messenger. Then, as she persisted and dangled the letter temptingly before his eyes, a

---

* *All's Well*, III, 2, 11 ff.; *Hamlet*, IV, 6, 13 ff.; *Lear*, I, 2, 50 ff.; IV, 6, 262 ff.
† *1 H. IV*, IV, 1, 13 ff.; *Cymb.*, III, 2 and iii, 4.

different look came into them, and he resisted no longer.* This use of letters is, as it were, a short cut to character.

As far as exposition is concerned, disguise in drama is an occasion rather than a means. It is regularly prepared for, notably by soliloquies, so that we may not miss whatever special values, as of humor or irony or pathos, the artifice affords.† Edgar in *Lear* not only tells the audience what he will look like as a Bedlam beggar, but familiarizes them with the professional whine which he will employ — " poor Turlygood! poor Tom! " ‡ The likelihood of a successful disguise was increased, as far as the Elizabethans were concerned, by four things: the elaborate distinctions of contemporary costume; the fashionableness of beards; the practice on the stage of doubling minor parts; and the performance of women's parts by boys. On the other hand, disguise does not always conceal the identity of the character who adopts it — as Tamora, for instance, finds to her cost.§ And what makes as much for probability as against it, the face or voice

* *Merry Wives*, IV, 5, 129 ff. See also page 11, above, for the varying responses of Warwick, Margaret, and others to the news of Edward the Fourth's marriage.

† Yet, on the Bartley principle, I suppose, Mr. Randle Ayrton, as the Duke in *Measure for Measure*, threw back his monk's cowl, at the beginning of II, 3, and showed us his face.

‡ II, 3. For these soliloquies, see Arnold, pp. 56, 57.

§ *Tit. And.*, V, 2; *cf. Timon*, III, 4, 42. Disguises are repeatedly seen through in *The Downfall of Robert Earl of Huntington* (1598).

of the person disguised may seem to some beholder vaguely familiar. Cymbeline says of " Fidele " :

> I have surely seen him;
> His favour is familiar to me.   Boy,
> Thou hast look'd thyself into my grace,
> And art mine own;

and Gloucester remembers that ' his son / Came then into his mind ' when he saw Poor Tom in the storm.*

---

* *Cymb.*, v, 5, 92; *Lear*, iv, 1, 32. For disguise, see also P. V. Kreider, " The Mechanics of Disguise in Shakespeare's Plays," *Shakespeare Association Bulletin*, ix (1934), 167–180.

Chapter IV

THE BEGINNING AND THE END

Rise of Curtain — Programmes — Identification of Characters — Comparison with Greek Tragedy — Keynote Scenes — *Hamlet* — *Otello* and *Othello* — Butlers and Parlor Maids — Openings of Comedies — Of Histories — Ending a Play — Recapitulation of Events — Friar Laurence — Stratagems to avoid Recapitulation — Closing Speeches.

EVEN for one who goes often and critically to the theatre, there remains something of excitement, something of credulous anticipation, in the moment when at last the lights begin to go down and he watches for the rise of the curtain. What happens immediately afterwards is frequently a disappointment: and one of the tasks of a playwright is that it should not be so. " He has to impart to the audience," Bradley writes, " a quantity of information about matters of which they generally know nothing and never know all that is necessary for his purpose. But the process of merely acquiring information is unpleasant, and the direct imparting of it is undramatic." * For a playwright, moreover, the task is complicated — as the novelist's somewhat similar task is not — by conditions over which he has little or no control. There are the noises

* *Shakespearean Tragedy*, 42. See also *Hamlet*, ed. J. Q. Adams, Boston, etc. [1929], pp. 173–175.

made by an audience settling down to listen and the even more harassing noises made by late-comers. There is the apparent incapacity of many actors to understand that, while we are getting used to their voices, they must speak more slowly, and more distinctly, than usual. No wonder that the first place on a vaudeville programme is an unenviable one, or that the leading actor in a play is seldom on the stage when the curtain goes up.*

Elizabethan practice included, it is true, the possibility of opening with a lively or informative prologue.† But against this advantage enjoyed by Shakespeare and his contemporaries must be set off many serious difficulties occasioned by the nature of their stage. The scene of Lord Dunsany's play, *The Glittering Gate*, is " a Lonely Place ":

The Lonely Place is strewn with large black rocks and uncorked beer-bottles, the latter in great profusion. At back is a wall of granite built of great slabs, and in it the Gate of Heaven. The door is of gold.

Below the Lonely Place is an abyss hung with stars.

The rising curtain reveals Jim wearily uncorking a beer-bottle. Then he tilts it slowly and with infinite care. It proves to be empty. Faint and unpleasant laughter is heard off.

Scenery and lighting have told us a great deal. So has pantomime — which is common property. There remains the programme, listing as the *dramatis personae*: " Jim, *lately a burglar* "; " Bill, *ditto* ";

---

* Shakespeare usually postpones the entrance of his tragic heroes, showing a like consideration for Henry V, Falstaff (in all three plays,) Shylock, and Petruchio.

† See pages 194 ff., below.

" *Both dead.*" Before a word has been uttered, we have come into possession of enough information to carry us far. The Globe was without scenery and artificial lighting, and its frequenters were not provided with programmes.

How much we actually learn from our programmes — rather less, I believe, than is commonly assumed — is matter for inquiry. Many persons besides the late-comers certainly do not consult their programmes before the play begins. Those who do will be edified, it may be, by discovering that there are such-and-such Joneses, variously related, and that they are to be acted by players with familiar names and players with unfamiliar ones. During the intermissions, some in the audience who are curious, or who have nothing else to do, looking at their programmes again, may find them really useful as a means of checking impressions. And people in the theatre do seem concerned about the amount of time which is supposed to elapse between scenes, though unfortunately this concern is sometimes expressed only after the lights have been lowered. The modern playwright, in a word, shows wisdom if he makes his piece self-explanatory.

Without programmes, the identification of the characters depended almost wholly on the lines.*

* Mr. W. J. Lawrence suggests that the frequent doubling of rôles in Elizabethan performances would make careful identification particularly necessary (*Shakespeare's Workshop*, 15).

Shakespeare now and again finds room in a soliloquy for the speaker's name (" Myself, Belarius, that
am Morgan call'd " falls in a class by itself) and for
the name of the person who is entering as the soliloquy closes.* Shakespeare, too, takes advantage of
the brief interval between the appearance of a new
character at one of the regular entrance doors and
his joining other characters down stage to give us the
newcomer's name, so that " See where he comes "
passes into something like a formula. " Who comes
here? " Duncan asks, early in *Macbeth*. " The
worthy Thane of Ross," Malcolm replies. And
Lennox comments:

> What a haste looks through his eyes!   So should he look
> That seems to speak things strange.

Then, and then only, Ross speaks: " God save the
king! "† On our stage, Duncan, Malcolm, and
Lennox would, I suppose, gaze into the wings. The
catalogue method is utilized, as well, notably during
the muster of Falstaff's recruits, in the *Second Part of
Henry IV* (III, 2), and when Peter Quince and his
fellow amateurs are preparing for their rehearsal, in
A Midsummer Night's Dream (I, 2). In both scenes,
there is fun in the names themselves. Falstaff en-

---

* See page 73, above, and Arnold, *Soliloquies of Shakespeare*,
53 ff.

† I, 2, 46; see Raleigh, *Shakespeare*, 124. Some of Shakespeare's
methods are as old as the Greeks (*cf.* Flickinger, *Greek Theater and
its Drama*, 208).

joys it as much as we do. " Yea, marry," he says,
" let 's see *Bullcalf*." Finally, the greater distinctiveness of Elizabethan costume and Elizabethan forms
of address is always to be reckoned with. Costume,
Raleigh remarks, was " a note of rank, profession,
or trade, and so helped to tell the story." * Shakespeare, at any rate, trusts chiefly to ecclesiastical
robes and a sprinkling of ' my lords ' to identify the
Archbishop of York, on his first appearance in
Henry IV.†

If, for a comparison, one turns from the luxuries
of the moderns to the austerities of the Greeks,
Shakespeare's problems at the beginning of a play
appear to shrink perceptibly. Thus, Professor
Chandler R. Post maintains that by choosing to give
us only the last phase of a tragic story Aeschylus
found himself

in a dilemma of exposition exactly twice as difficult as falls to
the lot of the modern playwright. The modern has only to make
clear to his audience the relationship of his characters, and the
qualities of the characters themselves, while he can fall back
upon the action of the play itself to explain the intricacies in
which he proposes to involve them.

Aeschylus had to explain " those very intricacies the
results of which, and only the results of which," his

---

* *Shakespeare*, 120. Revivals in modern dress can recover only a
little of this distinctiveness of costume.

† *I H. IV*, IV, 4. The speeches make it clear which side he is on,
and we know that the Archbishop is on that side. Note also " My
cousin Scroop " (line 3).

tragedy was to exhibit. At the beginning of *Lear*, Mr. Post continues, the characters " have as yet done nothing which will affect the catastrophe." * *Hamlet* and *The Tempest* are the clearest exceptions. The Ghost's narration, led up to as it is and broken from time to time by Hamlet's passionate interjections, has the full momentum of tragic drama; Prospero's almost stands still. But though the Greek dramatist had more to tell by way of preliminary exposition, he could take for granted the familiarity of his auditors with the legends on which he built his plot, and he possessed in his chorus a readier means of imparting information than any at Shakespeare's disposal. Again there are exceptions. For before the Elizabethans went to see *Henry V*, they had heard of Agincourt. " Julius Caesar " meant something, emotionally; " Pandarus " and " Cressida " were proverbial names. Acquaintance with the subject-matter of certain of Shakespeare's plays may be assumed, furthermore, on the part of some in the audience who had seen the older pieces on which these plays were founded. But *King Lear* must have startled persons who remembered *The True Chronicle History of King Leir*, and recollections of the old *Hamlet* were possibly more confusing than helpful to those who saw the new. Finally, it must not be overlooked that the Elizabethans usually had

* " The Dramatic Art of Aeschylus," *Harvard Studies in Classical Philology*, XVI (1905), 20, 21.

double-deckers to launch. In *Lear*, the Gloucester plot requires an introduction of its own. There are four distinct groups of characters in *A Midsummer Night's Dream*, and each gets its due. Theseus and Hippolyta, at the beginning, talk of what is uppermost in their minds, not forgetting, however, to drop a hint of those later " merriments" in which the " hard-handed men " are to figure. The abrupt entrance of Egeus leads swiftly to a knowledge of the affairs of the lovers. We see the Thespians getting their parts from Peter Quince. Robin and a Fairy meet, dreading a collision between the opposing factions to which they belong.

What has to be told of transactions antecedent to the first words of a play may be given us as a lump sum at the outset, or doled out gradually as such knowledge becomes indispensable. The first method is characteristic of Euripides and Seneca; the second, of Sophocles and Ibsen. Shakespeare in many of his best plays finds still a third way, which is neither lavish nor parsimonious.

There are manifest advantages in acquainting an audience early with what has gone before. As we shall see, Shakespeare prefers preparation to surprise. Cajoling us with a sense of our omniscience, he exploits to the full the knowledge he imparts. On the other hand, even a popular audience is willing within reason to wait. " Fie upon 'em, little infidels," cries the Citizen in *The Knight of the Burning*

Pestle, " what a matter 's here now! Well, I 'll be
hanged for a half-penny, if there be not some abomination knavery in this play." * He is not insistent
on knowing everything at once — nor are we,
through the long first scene in Mr. Rice's *Counsellor-
at-Law.* Moreover, after our attention has once
been caught by things, exciting in themselves, about
which we should like to hear more, the process of
being informed becomes painless.† And Parthian
shots into the past, momentary reminiscences or
scraps of narration, may be extraordinarily effective
when they concern characters whom we know.
Helena is afraid of Hermia:

> I pray you, though you mock me, gentlemen,
> Let her not hurt me. . . .

> O! when she 's angry, she is keen and shrewd.
> She was a vixen when she went to school
> (*M. N. D.*, III, 2, 299, 323).

And Othello, at the end of the tragedy:

> And say besides, that in Aleppo once,
> Where a malignant and a turban'd Turk
> Beat a Venetian and traduc'd the state,
> I took by the throat the circumcised dog,
> And smote him. . . .‡

---

* I, I (Beaumont and Fletcher, *Works*, ed. Dyce, II, 139).

† The familiar sequence at the beginning of a novel — " an
opening scene, a retrospect, and a summary "— is significant in
this connection (*cf.* Lubbock, *Craft of Fiction*, 66).

‡ Mr. Dobrée's discussion of the " panoramic " and " relation "
methods should be consulted (*Restoration Tragedy*, Oxford, 1929,
pp. 73, 74).

" His usual plan in tragedy," Bradley writes of Shakespeare, " is to begin with a short scene, or part of a scene, either full of life and stir, or in some other way arresting. Then, having secured a hearing, he proceeds to conversations at a lower pitch, accompanied by little action but conveying much information." * These initial excitements were not designed merely to thrill the groundlings. The swordplay of the Capulets and Montagues and the clamor of the Roman mob, had, like the tryst-keeping of the witches and the " solemn march " of the Ghost in armor, a tragic import for those who could perceive it. Romeo is a Montague, Juliet a Capulet, and the " fearful passage " of their love is " death-mark'd " by the hate of the Houses. Against the inconstancy of the populace, the honorable man, Brutus, and the brave man, Coriolanus, are alike helpless. Similarly, the infatuation of Antony is stated in the opening lines, so that Cleopatra, entering with

> If it be love indeed, tell me how much,

has already been answered:

> Nay, but this dotage of our general's
> O'erflows the measure.

And Iago is at work before we see Othello. " At the very outset," Bradley resumes, we are given " a

† *Shakespearean Tragedy*, 43.

strong impression of the force which is to prove fatal to the hero's happiness . . . when we see the hero himself, the shadow of fate already rests upon him.''*

When all is said, no play opens better than *Hamlet*. The first lines, scrutinized as they have been by critic after critic, seem capable, still, of revealing subtleties hitherto unperceived. On the stage comes a sentry, armed with a partizan, walking his round. A sentry — to guard against what? Then there is a challenge, but not from the expected person, and with a flutter of anxiety in it. The sentry, challenging in his turn, gets the countersign. In clipped speeches, we hear of the time — past midnight — and of the cold. The sentry is " sick at heart." Then, with a certain pointedness the newcomer asks: " Have you had *quiet* guard? " And Francisco's reply — " Not a mouse stirring " — gives us the silence. Horatio and Marcellus enter, and again there is the challenge, and again, the staccato phrasing — groups of four words each, predominating. Marcellus asks:

> What! has this thing appear'd again tonight?

And " this thing " becomes, only a little less vaguely, " this dreaded sight," and at length, " this apparition." Bernardo begins to repeat what had

---

* *Ibid.*, 44, 45. For these " key-note scenes," *cf.* Freytag, *Technique of the Drama*, tr. E. J. MacEwan, Chicago, 1895, pp. 118, 119.

happened, the night before, when " yond same
star " (he points to it) was just " where now it
burns." The time, that is, was the same — " The
bell then beating one " — and as it strikes — " *Enter* Ghost." Critics have grumbled over the later
speeches devoted to Fortinbras. Horatio is charged
with keeping " an eye on the audience "; Marcellus is scolded for his unwarrantable ignorance
of recent Danish history.* Undoubtedly, the pace
relaxes. But should it not? For by changing speeds
Shakespeare makes the reappearance of the Ghost
far more dramatic. As for Scenes Two and Three,
so much is accomplished in them that when we
are once more waiting in the " dead vast and
middle of the night," we need to hear only what the
Ghost, and the Ghost alone, can impart. And that
in time will be told again, twice over, in the play
within the play.

In Boito's libretto for the *Otello* of Verdi, we start
with the landing of the Moor in Cyprus. The obvious rightness of this beginning, in Verdi's opera,
must often have suggested that the merits of Shakespeare's first act have perhaps been taken too much
for granted. It *is* prologue-like. Bradley speaks of
it as filled with " a kind of preliminary conflict between the hero and Brabantio."

* Quiller-Couch, *Shakespeare's Workmanship*, Cambridge (England), 1931, p. 137; Archer, *Play-Making*, 72–77; *cf.* also Miss Bradbrook, *Themes and Conventions of Elizabethan Tragedy*, 116, 117.

It is devoted [Moulton finds] to bringing out the situation of the various parties at the opening of the story. This is just what a classical dramatist, tied by the unities, would merely assume, and bring it out by incidental reference.*

On the other hand, setting aside its numerous felicities of detail, which no lover of Shakespeare would willingly part with, the first act represents with the utmost vividness things which it is essential for us to remember: the strangeness and beauty of the circumstances of Othello's marriage; and the completeness of his trust in Iago. " Tush! never tell me," Roderigo begins. He and the Ancient are already in the midst of conversation, and we hear them as we might hear two characters in real life when a door is quietly opened.† If for once we deliberately set aside all our associations with the play, and read it as if it were wholly new, a certain daring will be discovered in these first speeches. For Iago poses as that most sympathetic of stage characters, the veteran soldier deprived of his just dues. And by whom? An unknown Moor, one who had witnessed the proofs of Iago's soldiership,

---

* *Shakespearean Tragedy*, 65; *Shakespeare as a Dramatic Artist*, 3rd ed., Oxford, 1893, p. 240.

† The same method may be used in a soliloquy or aside. Thus Bassanio's " So," which has been mistaken for a reference to the supposed implications of the song, " Tell me where is fancy bred," is in reality a picking up of his hitherto unspoken train of thought. He has been doing silently what Morocco and Arragon did aloud. *Cf.* the Folio direction: Song " *whilst* Bassanio *comments on the Caskets to himselfe* " (*Mer. Ven.*, III, 2, 73).

> At Rhodes, at Cyprus, and on other grounds
> Christian and heathen,

but, " loving his own pride and purposes," had chosen instead, contrary to seniority, Michael Cassio, the mere theorist. And the same Moor (still before we see him) is abused by Roderigo in the vilest terms. Very quietly our sympathies are re-adjusted. Iago's cynicism and self-seeking, his dis-ingenuousness and actual malice, begin to show through. His companion, and Iago himself, lose our respect rapidly in the scene with Brabantio. But almost a hundred and fifty lines have passed before we get the first hints of Othello's reputation and high place; and in the theatre it is perhaps even later before the slower-witted among the spectators have quite caught up.* Meanwhile, through the famous address to the Venetian signiors, our interest has never flagged; and when at the close of the act we know all the things that we have wanted most to know, we are still anxious to go on.

To the other " key-note scenes " may be given only a word or two more. It is notable that in *Romeo and Juliet* (as in *Julius Caesar*), there is a little coarse humor at the outset, humor which quickly turns sour on the tongue and then is forgotten in the clashing of swords. Indeed, it is only when Romeo

---

* Allowance must be made for the casting of the parts. Cibber makes it plain, for instance, that on the Restoration stage a character acted by Sandford became, *ipso facto*, a villain.

is inquired for that we begin to hear strains of the play's characteristic lyricism. Although a sense of the " ancient grudge " pervades it, this first scene looks forward rather than back, foreshadowing the later flareup of the quarrel, but with no mention of the quarrel's origins. Again, as becomes a youthful tragedy still a little formal in tone, the grouping of the characters is as symmetrical as that of a ballet.

Two Capulet men-servants are first introduced, next two Montague men-servants; then Benvolio on the Montague side, then Tybalt on the Capulet side; then on each side citizens; then old Capulet and Lady Capulet, then Montague and Lady Montague; finally, as keystone to bind all together, the Prince.*

The opening of *Macbeth* is distinguished by its swiftness. The Weird Sisters have come and gone in just sixty-one words! The battle of the second scene is not, like that in which Hamlet's father " smote the sledded Polacks on the ice," an old conflict but contemporaneous with the account of it. In terms of lines, Duncan has reached Macbeth's castle while Hamlet is just beginning to hear the story of Horatio's watch, and before Juliet has spoken more than a dozen words. In *Antony and Cleopatra*, it is the arrangement of the opening speeches to which I would direct attention. Demetrius and Philo, two " ordinary honest fellows " of the sort we shall be concerned with later, frame with their strictures the

* Dowden, *Shakspere: A Critical Study of his Mind and Art*, New York and London [1918], p. 53.

gorgeous eroticism of Antony's " soft hour ": his infatuation is acted out before us, then designated
anew almost on the principle stated by Bartley.*
And Demetrius concludes:

> I am full sorry
> That he approves the common liar, who
> Thus speaks of him at Rome.

Yet one of the most brilliant critics of the present day
writes that in the light of the first three acts of *Antony and Cleopatra*, " it would not be at all incon-
gruous for the play to end as a comedy " — " a
result," he adds, " unthinkable " in *All for Love*! †

The technique of beginning a modern play has as
its poles the pistol shot and the age-old confidences
(which have not yet quite ceased) between the butler and the parlor maid.   Shakespeare, though his
characteristic opening is the " key-note scene," was
not above giving us the Elizabethan counterparts of
the talkative couple just mentioned.   *His* butler and
parlor maid belong, indeed, to a different station in
life, and one of them is likely to have had the advantages of foreign travel.   Now and then they are
given names.   Essentially, however, they remain the
First and Second Gentlemen, as we get them at the
beginning of *Cymbeline*.   " But what 's the matter,"
the Second asks?   And through some seventy lines

---

* See pages 172–177, below.
† Dobrée, *Restoration Tragedy*, 72.

Shakespeare allows the First to tell him, with only such relief as the Second's feeble " And why so," or " How long is this ago," will afford. Camillo, in *The Winter's Tale*, does amount to something later, but he talks at the beginning with an " Archidamus," who is never addressed by name, and who disappears as soon as the conversation is over. It may even be suggested that, in *Henry V*, the Archbishop of Canterbury and the Bishop of Ely are not without resemblances to a First and Second Gentleman. Canterbury, as we shall see, becomes momentarily important when the Salique Law falls under discussion.* But aside from their interest in the question of taxing church property — a question which slows up still further a first scene in no sense lively — the pair are virtually uncharacterized, and Ely gets only one little speech thereafter.

It is easy to hold a brief against butlers and First Gentlemen, and I do not wish to be too hard on them. Mr. Granville-Barker would have it that Shakespeare, in the beginning of *Cymbeline*, aimed at suggesting the conscious " artlessness " of the play. John Bailey commends the quiet opening of *The Winter's Tale*, which he likens to the quiet openings of Scott's novels. Louis Calvert is against " putting in ' punch' at the start." For, he argues, " naturally at the beginning of any play the audience are cold. . . . To appeal to them successfully the

* Page 290, below.

author and the actors must go gently." * One thing
is sure. A character ought not to describe at length
matters with which his hearer on the stage would already be acquainted; and minor characters in quiet
opening scenes have a way of doing just that.† In
The Critic, Sneer protests: " But I think you manage
ill: for there certainly appears no reason why Sir
Walter should be so communicative." And Puff,
with his sublime merging of art and reality, answers:
" For, egad now, that is one of the most ungrateful
observations I ever heard — for the less inducement
he has to tell all this, the more I think, you ought to
be oblig'd to him." If Puff is right, we must acknowledge a considerable obligation to Lucentio for
his first speech in *The Taming of the Shrew*, which is
exactly of the sort described.‡ Somewhat different
is the case of Charles, in *As You Like It*:

Oliver. Good Monsieur Charles, what 's the new news at the
new court?
Charles. There 's no news at the court, sir, but the old news:
that is, the old duke is banished by his younger brother
the new duke. . . .

And he continues in the same vein, not without encouragement from Oliver. On the stage, neverthe-

* *Prefaces to Shakespeare*, 2nd Series, 245, 246; *Shakespeare*,
" English Heritage Series," 1929, pp. 203, 204; *Problems of the
Actor*, 142.
† Hennequin seems to accept the practice as inevitable, refer-
ring to it as one of the " conventions of the dialogue " arising from
" the necessities of exposition " (*The Art of Playwriting*, 154).
‡ I, I, 1–24; cited also by Stoll, *Poets and Playwrights*, 58.

less, the implausibilities involved amount to nothing. We have seen Orlando take his brother by the throat; and Oliver's fragments of soliloquy, just before the scene with Charles, were sinister enough to create tension. The bad brother is only waiting for his chance to speak. And when Charles is done with his " old news," Oliver asks quietly, " What, you wrestle to-morrow before the new duke? " (I, I, 128).

Two of the comedies, *Twelfth Night* and *The Tempest*, open with something like " key-note scenes ": with music and an amorous discourse in the one case, and in the other with a storm.

'A tempestuous noise of thunder and lightning' is heard, foul and technical words draw the audience's attention and the play is on its way. If that be unavailing, ' Enter Mariners wet,' and ever-powerful realism completes the conquest.*

Beyond the fact that during a storm a ship is in danger of going aground, we are not expected to learn much from this first scene in *The Tempest*. But we make out that a king and a prince are aboard; we get a glimpse of Gonzalo, and laugh at his joke about the boatswain's being born to be hanged — Shakespeare even counts on our remembering it.† The first words in Scene Two are

* J. Isaacs, " Shakespeare as Man of the Theatre," *A Series of Papers on Shakespeare and the Theatre . . . by Members of the Shakespeare Association*, London, 1927, p. 111.

† I, I, 32; V, I, 217. If you " are setting out to tell the incredible," writes Sir Arthur Quiller-Couch, " nothing will serve you so well as to open with absolute realism " (*Shakespeare's Workmanship*, 84).

richly suggestive, poetry having all the advantage when it comes to insinuating facts rather than stating them:

> If by your art, my dearest father, you have
> Put the wild waters in this roar, allay them.

Then, almost immediately, we settle down to Prospero's narrative, which, for all Miranda's sympathetic little comments and his own injunctions to listen, proves tedious enough. Sensitive critics agree that in *Twelfth Night* the first speech, and even the first line, have a singular appropriateness — are in keeping with the spirit of " a play compact of harmony." *   And it is notable that, just as in some of the tragedies, we pass in Scene Two to more or less ordinary expository writing, with Viola, a stranger, asking a captain who was " bred and born " in Illyria simple questions—"What country, friends, is this?" "Who governs here?" "What is his name?" —and getting in reply plenty of solid information.

As for the other comedies, though *The Two Gentlemen of Verona* moves slowly through two whole acts, another early play, *The Comedy of Errors*, opens admirably.   It is indispensable, Brander Matthews observes, that the spectators

should be told plainly, at the very beginning, all about the two sets of twins, and that they should have explained to them the

* See especially Raleigh, 123; John Bailey, *Shakespeare*, 144, 145.

strange combination of circumstances which has resulted in
bringing both pairs of brothers together unexpectedly in the
same city, the one master and his servant having every reason
to believe that the other master and the other servant have
been lost at sea.[*]

And Shakespeare so contrives it that the story told
by Aegeon, which accomplishes all this, is natural
for him to tell and interesting for us to hear. The
beginning of *The Merry Wives* derives a certain ani-
mation from Shallow's wrath against Sir John
Falstaff. And this episode is not inconsequential.
Sir John makes it an occasion for turning away his
followers, beginning with Bardolph; and in revenge
Pistol and Nym betray to the threatened husbands
Falstaff's designs on Mrs. Ford and Mrs. Page.
All's Well, on the other hand, gets under way
quietly and without fuss. In the course of a little
over a hundred lines, we learn everything that it is
essential for us to know, become acquainted with
three of the major characters, and, in the soliloquy
spoken by Helena, grow intimate with her and are
made ready for the coming of Parolles.

That Shakespeare, even in the days of his appren-
ticeship as a playwright, was capable of writing good
first scenes, is shown not only by *The Comedy of
Errors* but by several of the early histories. If there
is not too much else to praise in the *First Part of*

[*] *A Study of the Drama*, Boston [1910], pp. 188, 189. For *The
Two Gentlemen*, see Baker, *The Development of Shakespeare as a Dramatist*, 118.

Henry VI, the beginning, at least in design, is above reproach. Our attention is caught instantly by expressive action, the passing of a funeral procession — not this time at the end of a play, as was customary, but before a word has been spoken. Then, voice after voice taking it up to produce an effect essentially musical in character, there begins the lamentation for a dead king, England's warrior-king, Henry the Fifth. For thirty lines it continues; but with an abrupt turn disharmony sets in:

Winchester. The battles of the Lord of hosts he fought:
   The church's prayers made him so prosperous.
Gloucester. The church! where is it? Had not churchmen pray'd
   His thread of life had not so soon decay'd:
   None do you like but an effeminate prince,
   Whom like a school-boy you may over-awe.

Henry VI has succeeded Henry V. Messengers crowd in with tidings of English losses and of the disputes of English factions. The good days are over. And with the machinations of a prelate who would " sit at chiefest stern of common weal," the scene ends. It is almost two acts later before, in a passage emotionalized by the circumstances of the speaker, we hear from the dying Mortimer of old quarrels and old claims, the tangled rights and wrongs of the Houses of York and Lancaster.* Although the

---

* II, 5. Mr. Masefield writes of it memorably (*William Shakespeare*, 53). For the opening scene, *cf.* Wendell, *William Shakspere: A Study in Elizabethan Literature*, New York, 1894, 78, 79.

opening of the *Second Part of Henry VI* is less poeti
cally conceived, it is technically even more interest
ing. A steadily diminishing group is employed, so
that we proceed from a crowded stage, at the beginning of the scene, to the single figure of York, at the
end. Henry receives Margaret as Queen of England. After the reading of the distasteful marriage
treaty he goes out, with Margaret and Suffolk; and
Humphrey, Duke of Gloucester, begins at once to
speak against Suffolk and the treaty. After the
departure of Gloucester — the exits throughout
are structural — the Cardinal rails at him, then
goes out in his turn. Somerset talks aside with
Buckingham:

> Cousin of Buckingham, though Humphrey's pride
> And greatness of his place be grief to us,
> Yet let us watch the haughty cardinal:
> His insolence is more intolerable
> Than all the princes in the land beside. . . .

Exeunt Buckingham and Somerset. Salisbury and
Warwick remain with York; and Salisbury proposes
that they do what they can

> to bridle and suppress
> The pride of Suffolk and the cardinal,
> With Somerset's and Buckingham's ambition;
> And, as we may, cherish Duke Humphrey's deeds. . . .

Salisbury and Warwick now go, leaving the stage
to the archplotter, York, who in soliloquy discloses
his ambition " to raise aloft the milk-white rose."

Take for contrast *Richard III*, which is boldly launched by Richard himself:

> Now is the winter of our discontent
> Made glorious summer by this sun of York.

Wrong as it is from the point of view of yesterday's manuals of dramatic technique — for the principal character is on at the start and may scarcely be excused from the charge of directly addressing the audience — the speech prevails, nevertheless. Richard, who is to dominate the play, begins it swiftly and surely. Poetry shines through his rhetoric: and poetry, as Shakespeare wrote it for the Elizabethan stage, could itself be drama.

Finally, *King Lear* and the *First Part of Henry IV* have, in each case, a special interest.* In both parts of *Henry IV*, but especially in the first, the amount of retrospection is striking. The immediate occasion of the revolt against Bolingbroke — the matter of Hotspur's prisoners — is brought out promptly. For the casual author of a chronicle play who thought in terms of the company's money-chest and, giving the public what it wanted, was not concerned to please himself — for Shakespeare, in short, as he is sometimes depicted today — the immediate occasion would have been enough. For the author of

---

* I am passing over many plays. The opening of *Titus Andronicus* — a very competent one — is excellently treated by Baker, *The Development of Shakespeare as a Dramatist*, 125 ff.

Henry IV, it plainly was not. The past, " Richard's time," is lived over again in passage after passage. Northumberland, Worcester, and Hotspur talk of it in the first act; Bolingbroke draws lessons from it for Prince Hal; Hotspur makes Blunt listen to stories about it; and, just before Shrewsbury, Worcester brings it up once more in his final expostulation with the King.* The landing of Bolingbroke at Ravenspurgh, his usurpation of the crown, the contrast between Richard and Henry — Shakespeare, I take it, was still so fascinated by these things that he had to recur to them, whether the people in the theatre were interested or not. Those who remembered his *Richard II* might have been. As for *King Lear*, it opens with a few lines of unexciting prose. The two strands of the plot are brought together neatly, as Kent and Gloucester talk of the proposed division of the kingdom and of the birth and upbringing of Edmund. Then, with Lear's entrance, we begin as it were at the beginning, yet with a scene which is dramatic, having both conflict and suspense. It is made practically self-explanatory. Cordelia's asides are needed, perhaps; but the palpable honesty of Kent's opposition, and the equally palpable generosity of France, could not well be missed by any audience. The reason for Lear's wrath is brought out unmistakably by France. " Is it but this? " he asks,

* I, 3, 145 ff.; III, 2, 39 ff.; IV, 3, 54 ff.; V, I, 32 ff.

> a tardiness in nature
> Which often leaves the history unspoke
> That it intends to do?

Cordelia looks forward, almost prophetically, as she bids farewell to her sisters. " I know you, what you are," she says:

> Time shall unfold what plighted cunning hides;
> Who covers faults, at last shame them derides.
>
> (lines 272, 283)

And we are left with Regan and Goneril and the vague menace of their concluding speeches.*

* * *

In studies of Shakespeare's dramatic technique, his methods of beginning a play are likely to receive plenty of attention, his methods of ending one, very little. Beginnings are difficult. But so are endings. In particular, though near the close of a play the author may still have many things to explain, he will need tact in explaining them. The analogy with life holds, but only momentarily. At the conclusion of a sequence of exciting events, we do of course talk them over, questioning each other about this detail or that, and commenting with great sagacity on how what has happened came about. But when the same events have been shaped into a

---

* See pages 306, 307, below.

play, it is different. Having shared the confidence
of the author (who knows everything) the audience
know more about what has happened than many,
if not all, of the dramatic characters, so that perfectly natural questions and comments become tiresome and must be put over into the silent void which
lies beyond epilogues and last curtains. In the
theatre, furthermore, one Aristotelian precept is
rigorously if unconsciously applied. The story may
or may not have a beginning and a middle. It certainly must have an end. And once the audience
feel, with a relaxing of the tension, that the end has
come, they will put up with no nonsense. Then it
happens that the reader, untroubled by such scru-
ples, may delight in the last pages of a play, only
to discover, when he sees the play acted, that just
there it perceptibly drags.*

"A repetition in narrative of matters already
seen in action is the grossest of technical blunders,"
Archer writes.† If so, Shakespeare blundered often.
Puck's long recapitulation at the beginning of Act
Three, Scene Two, of *A Midsummer Night's Dream*, is
an example. At Oberon's bidding, Puck tells exactly
what has occurred: the planting of the "ass's nowl"
on Bully Bottom's head; the panic of the "rude
mechanicals"; Titania's waking and her infatua-

* Mr. Drinkwater's pleasant comedy, *Bird-in-Hand*, I offer as an
example — though allowance must always be made for variations
in performance.
† *Play-Making*, 75.

tion. Yet the speech is not tedious. When the
" translated " Pyramus was spied by his associates,
Puck says:

> As wild geese that the creeping fowler eye,
> Or russet-pated choughs, many in sort,
> Rising and cawing at the gun's report,
> Sever themselves, and madly sweep the sky;
> So, at his sight, away his fellows fly,
> And, at our stamp, here o'er and o'er one falls;
> He murder cries, and help from Athens calls.
> Their sense thus weak, lost with their fears thus strong,
> Made senseless things begin to do them wrong;
> For briars and thorns at their apparel snatch;
> Some sleeves, some hats, from yielders all things catch.

Fresh details have been added. The whole account
is suffused with the colors of poetry.

> I led them on in this distracted fear,
> And left sweet Pyramus translated there;
> When in that moment, so it came to pass,
> Titania wak'd and straightway lov'd an ass.

The repetition is as delightful as the thing repeated.
In a footnote, Archer somewhat dilutes the
strength of his statement. What he had in mind, he
makes it clear, was repetition merely for the sake of
conveying information. And he cites *Romeo and
Juliet*, in which Shakespeare allowed Friar Laurence to " re-tell the whole story of the tragedy."
" Even in so early a play," Archer comments, " such
a manifest redundancy seems unaccountable."
Now if the purpose of Friar Laurence's recapitulation was to supply information, the passage would

certainly be redundant, for the Elizabethans, unless I am much mistaken, were quite as capable of following an intricate plot as we are. Moreover, unlike Puck's speech — which came, we should remember, in the middle and not at the end of the play — Friar Laurence's narrative adds no details of interest and is without any great poetical distinction. What, then, was its purpose? Romeo, Paris, and Juliet have been discovered dead. Some of the Watch, called by the County's page, have arrested Balthasar, Romeo's man; and others bring on the Friar, whom they have found lingering near the tomb. A general alarm has been given, and the people come hurrying in " with open outcry." At last, the Prince quiets the tumult.

> *Prince.*   Seal up the mouth of outrage for a while,
> Till we can clear these ambiguities,
> And know their spring, their head, their true
>   descent. . . .
>
> Bring forth the parties of suspicion.
> *Friar Laurence.* I am the greatest, able to do least,
> Yet most suspected, as the time and place
> Doth make against me, of this direful murder.
>   (v, 3, 216)

And he tells his story. Balthasar and the page add a few details, and Balthasar gives the Prince a letter left by Romeo for his father. The Prince reads it.

> *Prince.*   This letter doth make good the friar's words. . . .
>
> Where be these enemies? — Capulet! Montague!
> See what a scourge is laid upon your hate.

And we pass to the beauty and tranquillity of the concluding speeches. Now it is obvious that Friar Laurence's speech makes for verisimilitude. For if the play was to go on at all, after Juliet's death — and Elizabethan custom demanded that it should — some such ' clearing of ambiguities ' must take place. Again, though the good Friar is in no great danger, perhaps, it does behoove him to establish his innocence — and thus, in some degree, suspense is revived. Above all, his narrative forms a necessary transition from the tragic outcome to its interpretation. Romeo and Juliet are sacrifices to the enmity of the Houses; but not vain sacrifices, since hate passes in the " glooming peace " which their love has won.* If in performance the play is to answer Shakespeare's intention, we must put up with Friar Laurence.

Toward the end of *Titus Andronicus* the crimes against the protagonist are recounted time after time: in Aaron's forced confession; by Titus himself as he gloats over Chiron and Demetrius; and finally, on a grand scale, by Lucius and Marcus as they excuse themselves for killing Saturninus.† Such exhaustive recapitulation is designed, I take it, rather to evoke sympathy for the avengers than to explain, or merely recall, the labyrinthine horrors

---

* The theme announced in the prologue is, thus, recalled in the last lines (see page 198, below; and G. S. B., *A Study of the Prologue and Epilogue in English Literature*, London, 1884, p. 35 n.).

† v, 1, 87 ff.; v, 2, 169 ff.; v, 3, 67 ff.

of the story. Iachimo's disclosures in the last act of *Cymbeline* have to do, once more, with things already familiar. In the study, we are likely to resent his departures from fact, the running together, as it would seem, of two distinct episodes, one in France and one in Italy. On the stage, such variations in detail would doubtless pass unnoticed. Why they are there is another question. Shakespeare may have been preoccupied with achieving a brilliant, perhaps a too brilliant, dénouement.* A last example comes from *The Comedy of Errors*. Pooling their knowledge, the bewildered characters go over everything that has occurred, and the " repetition in narrative of matters already seen in action " is one of the most amusing passages in the whole play. Until the appearance of the Abbess with Antipholus of Syracuse and Dromio of Syracuse — the two masters and the two servants now at last fairly confronted — no headway can possibly be made. Even afterwards, confusion is not quite over. " Master," asks Dromio of Syracuse, " shall I fetch your stuff from shipboard? " And the *wrong* Antipholus answers:

> Dromio, what stuff of mine hast thou embark'd?
>
> *Dromio of Syracuse.*   Your goods that lay at host, sir, in the Centaur.

---

* See also page 253, below. The intricacies of the last scene are analyzed by Wendell, *William Shakspere*, 358–361.

Antipholus of Syracuse. He speaks to me. I am your master,
                 Dromio.*

As a rule, however, Shakespeare avoids recapitu-
ation at the close of a play. Rupert Brooke found
n *The Devil's Law-Case* a " device that is so auda-
ious in its simplicity as to demand admiration.
Leonora . . . interrupts the growing flood of explanations with

> Cease here all further scrutiny. This paper
> Shall give unto the court each circumstance
> Of all these passages!

One is too relieved to object," is Brooke's comment.† But the paper trick did not originate with
John Webster. Northumberland, entering at the
beginning of the last scene in *Richard II*, tells Bolingbroke that he has sent to London

> The heads of Salisbury, Spencer, Blunt, and Kent.
> The manner of their taking may appear
> At large discoursed in this paper here.

And Portia, in *The Merchant of Venice*, has at last
good news for Antonio:

> Unseal this letter soon;
> There you shall find three of your argosies
> Are richly come to harbour suddenly.
> You shall not know by what strange accident
> I chanced on this letter —

---

* v, 1, 411. I like to associate with these lines the subtle empha-
is, at the end of Goldoni's *Il Ventaglio*, on the fan itself, which has
aused so much trouble.

† *John Webster and the Elizabethan Drama*, 117, 118.

it is enough for all purposes that she has it.* Shake
speare's usual way of paying his respects to verisi
militude is to introduce a simple statement, by one o
his personages, postponing the detailed discussion o
what has happened.   Even after Friar Laurence'
diffuseness, the Prince in *Romeo and Juliet* bids the
assembled company

> Go hence, to have more talk of these sad things;

and similarly, at the end of *The Comedy of Errors*, the
Abbess invites the other characters

> To go with us into the abbey here,
> And hear at large discoursed all our fortunes.†

The formula — for it amounts to that — is a usefu
one. It is realistic in a small way, and it is unobtru
sive. In the shape of an invitation, it serves to ge
the characters off the stage at the end of a comedy
just as the funeral procession gets them off at the
end of a tragedy. Though such invitations ofter
come from persons of high rank (including severa
dukes), the most pleasant is Mrs. Page's:

> Good husband, let us every one go home,
> And laugh this sport o'er by a country fire;
> Sir John and all.   (*M. W. W.*, v, 5, 267)

At other points in a play besides the end, Shake
speare sometimes employs stratagems to avoid a
recapitulation. In the last scene but one in *Th*

---

* v, 1, 275.
† *R. & J.*, v, 3, 307; *Com. Er.*, v, 1, 397.

Taming of the Shrew, Lucentio tells briefly how he has contrived to marry Bianca. Vincentio hurries off to take vengeance on Tranio; and Baptista, who needs further enlightenment, follows Vincentio " to sound the depth of this knavery " (line 142). Everything has been cleared up when the last scene begins, and we pass without further ado to what to-day might be called an epilogue. Or again, in *The Merry Wives of Windsor*, Mrs. Ford and Mrs. Page decide to acquaint their husbands with the deceit they have practised on poor Falstaff. Leaving the stage, they are replaced momentarily by the Host and Bardolph. Then the Fords and Pages enter with Sir Hugh Evans. And Evans begins:

'T is one of the pest discretions of a ' oman as ever I did look
    upon.
Page. And did he send you both these letters at an instant?
Mrs. Page. Within a quarter of an hour.
Ford. Pardon me, wife.* . . .

As an alternative to consigning recapitulations to a supposed parley off-stage, Shakespeare could set his characters whispering. This is done effectively in the second act of *As You Like It*. Orlando brings in Adam,

    Oppress'd with two weak evils, age and hunger.
                       (II, 7, 132)

---

* IV, 4, I. *Cf.* Thaler, *Shakspere's Silences*, Cambridge (Massachusetts), 1929, p. 51; and Creizenach, *The English Drama in the Age of Shakespeare*, 272.

The Duke bids him " fall to." While he does so, and under cover of the song, " Blow, blow, thou winter wind," the Duke and Orlando talk apart; and at the conclusion of the song the Duke says:

> If that you were the good Sir Rowland's son,
> As you have whisper'd faithfully you were, . . .
>
> Be truly welcome hither.*

In novels and plays, the natural place for distinguishing issues and summing up ideas is the end. In Shakespearean tragedy, " after the hero's death-scene the survivors, face to face with the majesty of death, cast a last comprehensive glance at the personality and life-work of the departed." † His body must be borne out, for there is no front curtain. The closing speeches have a quiet dignity not unlike that of classical tragedy. They are, with one or two exceptions, " full of the spirit of atonement and forgiveness " — even *Titus Andronicus* looks forward, at the end, " to a better time about to dawn." ‡ By convention, the last speech of all is entrusted to the character highest in rank. Thus, Fortinbras closes *Hamlet*; Albany, *Lear*; and Lodovico, *Othello*. Octavius, not Antony, has the last word in *Julius Caesar*.

* *Cf.* Noble, *Shakespeare's Use of Song*, 73; and for whispering, see pages 89, 90, above.
† Creizenach, *The English Drama in the Age of Shakespeare*, 270.
‡ *Ibid.*, 271. See also Lewis Campbell, *Tragic Drama in Aeschylus, Sophocles, and Shakespeare*, 76, 90, 91.

" The closing funeral orations," Professor Stoll maintains, " are always spoken by the dramatist himself " — that is, " so far as authority is concerned." * This is sound enough, as a generalization, but it must not be made inflexible. Malcolm, at the termination of *Macbeth*, says:

> What 's more to do,
> Which would be planted newly with the time,
> As calling home our exil'd friends abroad
> That fled the snares of watchful tyranny;
> Producing forth the cruel ministers
> Of this dead butcher and his fiend-like queen . . .
>
> We will perform in measure, time, and place.

Coming from the speaker, " this dead butcher " is quite proper. As Shakespeare's final designation of Macbeth, it will not do.† Octavius, who concludes two tragedies, retains something of his accustomed frigidity on both occasions. The contrast in tone between Antony's fervent eulogy of Brutus —

> His life was gentle, and the elements
> So mix'd in him that Nature might stand up
> And say to all the world, " This was a man! " —

and the formality of Octavius's

> According to his virtue let us use him,
> With all respect and rites of burial,

---

* *Hamlet*, 22, 23 and note; *cf. Othello: An Historical and Comparative Study*, Minneapolis, 1915, pp. 14, 15.

† *Cf.* George Saintsbury, *Shakespeare*, Cambridge (England), 1934, p. 99.

is of the sort Shakespeare excelled in. At the end of
the later tragedy, Octavius seems awed, a little, by
Cleopatra's beauty in death —

> She looks like sleep,
> As she would catch another Antony
> In her strong toil of grace —

though he appreciates, as well, the skill with which
she has outwitted him. Assenting to the explanation
given of her death, he notes with the least possible
touch of contempt:

> Her physician tells me
> She hath pursu'd conclusions infinite
> Of easy ways to die.

Then he becomes gracious:

> She shall be buried by her Antony:
> No grave upon the earth shall clip in it
> A pair so famous.

But note what follows:

> High events as these
> Strike those that make them; and their story is
> No less in pity than his glory which
> Brought them to be lamented.

He has contrived, at the last, to praise himself.*

---

* The final point is MacCallum's (*Shakespeare's Roman Plays and
their Background*, 389).

Chapter V

PREPARATION AND SURPRISE

Kinds of Surprise — Preparation for Scenes to come —
Lady Macbeth's Sleep-walking — Shylock — Preparation for Unusual Characters — Malvolio's Letter — Surprise of *Dramatis Personae* — Irony — Sometimes Imperceptible to First Audience — Instances of Surprise in
Shakespeare — Whispering again — Hermione lives.

M R. SAMUEL PEPYS, who as a theatre-goer is
for ever anticipating our experiences, admits,
on one occasion, that his " having a book " spoiled
his pleasure, " a little," in the play. The question of
whether or not one should read such-and-such a
piece before seeing it, is still asked; the answer de-
pending, of course, on the tastes of the person who
asks it and the nature of the play he is to see. Closely
related to this question — so closely, indeed, that
the two are sometimes confused — is another,
which has been much debated by critics: whether
or not preparation is better than surprise.

Surprise is commonly associated with the lower
dramatic *genres*, with melodrama and farce. * The

---

* Coleridge writes that " as the feeling with which we startle at
a shooting star, compared with that of watching the sunrise at the
pre-established moment, such and so low is surprize compared
with expectation " (*Shakespearean Criticism*, ed. T. M. Raysor,
Cambridge, Massachusetts, 1930, 1, 225).

authority of the Greek tragic writers tells against it. Even today it is likely to be frowned on, in theory. In practice, however, since Ibsen, surprise has taken on new forms. We have grown accustomed to a technique which, as in *The Wild Duck*, by withholding information at the outset, effects a reversal of our sympathies. The sustained attack on " the middle-class fetish," whether seriously or out of mere fondness for prank and paradox, has been conducted, in plays innumerable, by giving to a conventional situation some startling, or at least unexpected, turn. As early as the eighteen-nineties — at *Arms and the Man* or *The Gay Lord Quex* — audiences were being taught to distrust first impressions. The lesson, time has shown, needed to be learned. But surprise may appear on a still higher level. From greater knowledge of the characters, a dramatist may, in Lord Dunsany's phrase, " surprise by truth." * The double ending of *The Cherry Orchard* is an unforgettable instance. And in Shakespeare — for this sort of surprise is not new — there is Beatrice, and her " Kill Claudio," and Juliet's Nurse, with her recollection of how lovely a gentleman Paris is —" Romeo's a dishclout to him." †

Yet by means of preparation, by imparting knowledge to the spectators and building on that

* " The Carving of the Ivory," *The Art of Playwriting: Lectures Delivered at The University of Pennsylvania on the Mask and Wig Foundation*, Philadelphia, 1928, p. 60.
† *Much Ado*, IV, 1, 294; *R. & J.*, III, 5, 221.

knowledge, advantage may be gained both tactically and strategically. Tactically, the playwright
who takes us into his confidence beforehand is
able to make the most of ingeniously complicated
situations,

the ironies of disguise or mistaken identity, of deception or
slander, of playing a part or overhearing, or of prophecies or
oracles coming true upon the stage. The audience ought to
know (as it does) that the youth whom Orlando is wooing is
Rosalind, and that Lady Teazle is behind the screen.*

Strategically, a dramatist may by the same means
persuade us of the inevitability of the action as a
whole. His methods inspire confidence. And if, as
the play closes, we feel that the end has in some sort
been kept before us from the beginning, we are unlikely to ask awkward questions.†

Further implications of the two methods, preparation and surprise, belong to the realm of aes-
thetics, into which I have no intention of pursuing
them. Shakespeare inclines definitely toward preparation. In his plays, first impressions are not
strikingly reversed, the adjustment of our sympathies is effected early and maintained afterwards.
Iago may be allowed to deceive us, but only momentarily.‡ The fact that Claudius was the murderer of

* Stoll, *Poets and Playwrights*, 61 (Mr. Stoll is, nevertheless, inclined to defend surprise).

† " The aim of the great artist is not to surprise the spectator
with an unforeseen, but to gratify him with an ' inevitable, ' action "
(A. B. Walkley, *Drama and Life*, London, 1907, p. 116).

‡ See pages 108, 109, above.

Hamlet's father is withheld, but not for long. In particular, the manner in which Shakespeare makes us ready for a full enjoyment of scenes to come is well worth study.

Preparation in this sense occurs before Lady Macbeth's sleep-walking. Through the long scene at the English court — an episode which seems to be even longer than it is — we have been out of touch with things in Scotland, though we have heard of the tyrannies practised by " devilish Macbeth," who is now, Malcolm remarks grimly, " ripe for shaking." * Lady Macbeth has been absent even longer than her lord (we last saw her talking wearily with him, after the banquet). Now " *enter a* Doctor of Physic *and a* Waiting-Gentlewoman," who speak as follows:

> *Doctor.*   I have two nights watched with you, but can perceive no truth in your report. When was it she last walked?

The confident naturalness of the " she " is noteworthy. The person whom they are discussing goes unnamed.

> *Gentlewoman.*   Since his majesty went into the field, I have seen her rise from her bed, throw her night-gown upon her, unlock her closet, take forth paper, fold it, write upon 't, read it, afterwards seal it, and again return to bed; yet all this while in a most fast sleep.

The Doctor comments on the strangeness of this. Then he asks:

* IV, 3, 237.

> In this slumbery agitation, besides her walking and other actual performances, what, at any time, have you heard her say?
>
> *Gentlewoman.* That, sir, which I will not report after her.

Lady Macbeth enters an instant later. It should be observed, in the first place, that we have been told enough to appreciate, without distraction, the import of what follows. " Economy of attention " has been assured.* We have learned that Lady Macbeth is asleep, that we are to hear her, doubtless with a certain horror, when she is off her guard. Furthermore, the words of the Doctor and the Gentlewoman pique our curiosity. After all, we know Lady Macbeth so much better than they can possibly know her! Notice, also, how much is left us to discover for ourselves. More is promised, that is, than the representation before our eyes of what has already been described in full. Lady Macbeth *says things* — which the Gentlewoman " will not report after her." †

The importance of preparatory evidence and, perhaps, the dangers attendant upon rigidity in interpreting it, are brought out by examination of a celebrated passage in *The Merchant of Venice.* The two " Sallies " (Salarino and Salanio) enter, to-

---

* Clayton Hamilton, *The Theory of the Theatre*, New York, 1910, 98, 99. So, he adds, Cyrano's nose is described before it is seen.

† With this scene, compare the episode of Cardinal Beauford's death — a gruesome miniature — and the preparation for it (*2 H. VI*, III, 2, 368 ff.).

ward the end of the second act, to describe the outcome of Jessica's bid for freedom. Shylock, we learn,
was too late to overtake the lovers; and Salanio says:

> I never heard a passion so confus'd,
> So strange, outrageous, and so variable,
> As the dog Jew did utter in the streets.

It is, he explains, a mingled lamentation — for the
loss of the Jew's daughter, " two rich and precious
stones," and much money. Salarino suggests how
Shylock's passion is to be taken:

> Why, all the boys in Venice follow him,
> Crying, his stones, his daughter, and his ducats.

And Salanio's comment shows the bearing of all
this on Antonio:

> Let good Antonio look he keep his day,
> Or he shall pay for this.   (II, 8, 12)

Salarino is reminded of a story, told him by a
Frenchman the day before, to the effect that a
Venetian vessel, possibly one of Antonio's, had mis-
carried at sea. We pass at this point to Belmont and
Portia; but the " Sallies " reappear at the beginning
of Act Three. The loss of Antonio's ship is now a
certainty, Salarino notes, adding: " I would it
might prove the end of his losses." Shylock enters.
While Salanio and Salarino are present, he keeps
some control over his passion. As soon as they have
gone, he gives it full vent. In reply to his interrogation, Tubal says that he has been unable to find

Jessica. Shylock falls at once into the confused outcry we have been waiting for. One of the two missing jewels, a diamond, comes first, then his daughter
and his ducats. His passion is bizarre. To an
Elizabethan audience, it must have been ludicrous
as well. " I would my daughter were dead at my
foot," he exclaims, " and the jewels in her ear!
would she were hearsed at my foot, and the ducats
in her coffin!" Tubal cheers him with tidings of
Antonio's " ill luck," the loss of another ship. Shylock's note changes to one of exultant hate: " I
thank God! I thank God! Is it true?" The same
sequence is repeated, as Tubal tells him of Jessica's
lavish spending: again the jingle of daughter and
ducats; again the recurrent menacing of Antonio.
Then at last we come to the crucial lines. Shylock's
second stone was a turquoise.

Tubal. One of them showed me a ring that he had of your
daughter for a monkey.
Shylock. Out upon her! Thou torturest me, Tubal: it was my
turquoise; I had it of Leah when I was a bachelor: I
would not have given it for a wilderness of monkeys.

(III, 1, 126)

The pathos of this — for it is, I contend, pathetic —
would be lost, a little earlier, in the midst of incon-
gruous elements. The speech comes, however,
virtually at the end of the scene. " But Antonio is
certainly undone," Tubal says; and we close, at
once, with Shylock's preparations for the arrest of

his enemy. Thus, the emotions of an audience are
not, as I see it, the impossibly combined emotions of
hate, humor, and pathos, but hate and humor
mingled — and then suddenly, for an instant only,
pathos.* That this interpretation of the scene may,
on the stage, be made brilliantly effective was demonstrated, a few years ago, by Mr. Maurice Mos-
covitch. To sum up. The usefulness of Salanio and
Salarino in enabling us to catch, at the outset, the
general drift of the episode is fully admitted. What
is denied is that they anticipate, or were intended
to anticipate, its whole import.†

We might expect that the first appearance of an
unusual character would be preceded, with some
regularity, by an account of his eccentricities, but
preparation of this sort is rare.‡ On the contrary,
Shakespeare sometimes postpones the description
until we have had a look at the person described,
or, when it suits his convenience, falls back upon
soliloquy. Parolles, indeed, is pretty well analyzed
by Helena before the rascal comes on; and, in the

* For a very strong statement on the other side, see Stoll,
Shakespeare Studies, 311 ff. (*cf.* also Creizenach, *The English Drama
in the Age of Shakespeare*, 245).

† For the " Sallies " themselves, see Granville-Barker's *Prefaces*,
2nd Series, 81–83. Many instances of preparation are passed over:
e.g. King Lear, III, 1, in which Lear's identification with the storm is
made clear, as also the part played by the Fool — " who labours
to outjest " his master's injuries.

‡ Tragic heroes are, however, likely to be talked about before
we see them.

story told by the First Lord, the characteristic
moralizing of the melancholy Jaques is anticipated.*
Otherwise, Parolles might deceive a goodly portion
of the audience and Jaques might puzzle them. A
more interesting example comes from the *Second
Part of Henry VI*, where, in York's long soliloquy,
we are told all about the " headstrong Kentish-
man," Jack Cade, who is to be imposed upon the
people as " that John Mortimer, which now is
dead." † Thus, when, much later, Cade appears,
proclaiming himself to be what we know he is not,
we are in a position to enjoy the racy comments of
Dick the Butcher and Smith the Weaver:

Cade. My father was a Mortimer. —
Dick [Aside]. He was an honest man, and a good bricklayer.
Cade. My mother a Plantagenet, —
Dick [Aside]. I knew her well; she was a midwife.
Cade. My wife descended of the Lacies, —
Dick [Aside.] She was, indeed, a pedlar's daughter, and sold
many laces.
Smith [Aside.] But now of late, not able to travel with her
furred pack, she washes bucks here at home.‡ . . .

Preparation for scenes which might, without it,
be difficult to follow comes frequently from characters engaged in conspiracy. Iago guides us before
the drinking scene. Sicinius and Brutus are as
lucid as possible about Coriolanus's final ' stooping

* *All's Well*, I, I, III ff.; *A. Y. L.*, II, I, 25 ff.
† III, I, 356, 372.
‡ IV, 2, 42.

to the herd.' After making it clear that she intends
to be perverse with Antony, Cleopatra whispers, as
he enters: " I am sick and sullen." Likewise, in
comedy, Petruchio explains to the spectators the
first moves in his campaign against Katharina; the
two French Lords tell exactly what they propose to
do to Parolles and how he will behave; and Hero
outlines to her women the method they are to follow
in deceiving Beatrice.* The preposterous conduct
of Malvolio is enjoyed, more than once, in anticipation. Malvolio himself signifies what is coming;
then Maria, the archconspirator, interprets for him:

> If you will, then see the fruits of the sport, mark his first
> approach before my lady; he will come to her in yellow stock-
> ings, and 't is a colour she abhors; and cross-gartered, a fashion
> she detests; and he will smile upon her, which will now be so un-
> suitable to her disposition, being addicted to a melancholy as
> she is, that it cannot but turn him into a notable contempt. If
> you will see it, follow me.   (II, 5, 218)

Two scenes later, " the fruits of the sport " are near
picking:

Maria. ·If you desire the spleen, and will laugh yourselves into
stitches, follow me. Yond gull Malvolio is turned heathen.
. . . He 's in yellow stockings.
Sir Toby. And cross-gartered?
Maria. Most villanously; like a pedant that keeps a school i' the
church. . . . He does obey every point of the letter that

---

* *Oth.*, II, 1, 273 ff. and II, 3, 51 ff.; *Cor.*, III, 3, 1 ff.; *A. & C.*, I, 3,
13; *Tam. Shr.*, II, 1, 171 ff.; *All's Well*, III, 6, 22 ff. and IV, 1, 1 ff.;
Much Ado, III, 1, 1 ff. — the plot against Benedick is kept clear by
asides spoken during its execution (but *cf.* II, 1, 381 ff.).

I dropped to betray him: he does smile his face into more
lines than are in the new map with the augmentation of
the Indies. You have not seen such a thing as 't is.

(III, 2, 75)

We must wait still, through fifty lines of Sebastian
and Antonio; but then Olivia, entering with Maria,
asks:

> Where is Malvolio? he is sad, and civil,
> And suits well for a servant with my fortunes:
> Where is Malvolio?   (III, 4, 5)

In the delectable passages which follow a great deal
depends on Olivia, whose consternation is a measure
of the completeness of Malvolio's undoing.

Our pleasure in the surprise experienced by the
characters when some particular event which we
have been waiting for takes place, is a notable asset
of preparation. It is to comedy something like what
irony is to tragedy, inspiring, not awe, not realiza-
tion of the insecurity of life, but a joyous sense of our
own superiority. The last scene in *The Taming of
the Shrew* might be studied to advantage from this
point of view. Or, to cite a modern instance, who
can forget the tableau, in Mr. Lennox Robinson's
Far-Off Hills, just before Marian's climactic entrance
in the new dress: Susie, down front, mumbling
prayers; the men and girls, huddled at the back,
listening in dismay to the thundering blows on
Marian's door? " It is not nearly so amusing to be

fooled," Mr. Clayton Hamilton observes, " as it is to watch other people being fooled. . . . Against this fundamental fact, the success of a dozen or a hundred surprise-plays can scarcely be regarded as weighing down the balance." *

Irony, as it is usually defined, presupposes knowledge on the part of the audience. A thing is said or done, a situation is conceived, ironically, when appearance and reality are contrasted. More definitely, irony depends, we are told, on our perception of a hidden significance, in words or actions, pointedly at variance with their outer meaning. The character who speaks or behaves ironically may be conscious of this hidden significance. " He that's coming/Must be provided for," says Lady Macbeth of Duncan, not without appreciation of the disquieting ambiguity of her words.† But quite as often, the ironist is too confident, or too preoccupied with the immediate, to be aware of any element of incongruity, and the inner significance of what he does or says altogether escapes him. Thus Caesar, setting out to go to the Capitol, addresses Trebonius, one of the conspirators,

> Remember that you call on me today:
> Be near me, that I may remember you.

---

* *Problems of the Playwright*, New York, 1917, p. 35.

† *Macb.*, 1, 5, 67. For a brief but excellent description of irony, see A. E. Haigh, *The Tragic Drama of the Greeks*, Oxford, 1896, pp. 174 ff.

" Caesar, I will," Trebonius replies. Then, as if to make sure that the irony should not go unmarked, he adds aside:

> And *so near* will I be,
> That your best friends shall wish I had been further.
>
> (II, 2, 122)

Caesar's invitation will be accepted — but in a different sense from Caesar's own. Like many another unconscious ironist, he has unwittingly stumbled upon the truth.

A situation, a whole play even, may be conceived ironically. Duncan, about to enter the castle of his enemy, pauses to remark on its peacefulness. The porter at the same castle fancies himself, not without reason, porter of hell gate. The irony in *Troilus and Cressida* extends beyond the scene in which Cressida bids her name become a byword if she prove false.* In this last scene, the method is practically that of the Greek tragic writer, who by dramatizing a familiar story could count on a swift apprehension of its ironic values. On the other hand, by the time Duncan reaches Macbeth's castle we regard him as already doomed; and the Porter's vaporings follow hard upon the terrible whispers of the murderers. Shakespeare is building, once more, on the knowledge he has himself imparted.

So in disguise scenes, the conscious ironist may ring the changes on appearance and reality, and

* III, 2; *Macb.*, I, 6; II, 3.

whatever his mood is, whether merry or wistful or sardonic, we miss nothing of the effect desired. We know that Henry V may well call himself " Harry *le Roy* "; that the Doctor will certainly be Portia's bedfellow; and that Viola is far from talking at random when she tells Orsino about the love of women for men.* Knowing, likewise, that Titus is not deceived by Tamora, when she comes to him in the " strange and sad habiliment " of Revenge, we can feel the full force of these lines, in which irony is capped with irony:

Tamora.   Farewell, Andronicus: Revenge now goes
            To lay a complot to betray thy foes.
Titus.   I know thou dost; and, sweet Revenge, farewell.

(v, 2, 146)

We are even allowed to follow the ironies indulged in by villains and deceivers.

> I pray you, uncle, give me this dagger,

the little Duke of York begs; and Richard who has made it clear, in his asides, that he is continually ' moralizing two meanings in one word,' answers:

> My dagger, little cousin? with all my heart.

(III, 1, 110)

And, in the same play, Clarence is promised " wine enough . . . anon " — after we have been told of the malmsey butt. As for comedy, there is Mrs. Ford's

---

* *H. V*, IV, 1, 49; *Mer. Ven.*, v, 1, 233; *12 N.*, II, 4, 105 ff.

asseveration to Falstaff: " Well, heaven knows how I love you; and you shall one day find it." *

Thus, by means of preparation — by keeping us, as it were, well abreast of the march of events — Shakespeare regularly facilitates our perception of conscious irony. Sometimes, but much less frequently, the presence of unconscious (or " dramatic ") irony is made clear in the same way. When, in *Cymbeline*, Imogen misses her bracelet she says:

> Confident I am
> Last night 't was on mine arm, I kiss'd it;
> I hope it be not gone to tell my lord
> That I kiss aught but he.   (II, 3, 150)

Pisanio, as he reads the letter commanding him to murder Imogen, exclaims that some " false Italian " must have deceived Posthumus. Imogen, immediately after, is all eagerness to reach " this same blessed Milford "; and later still, when she is with Arviragus and Guiderius, and Arviragus promises to love her as a brother, she says aside: " Would it had been so, that they/Had been my father's sons," † In every one of these cases, the irony would be apparent even to a first audience. At times, indeed,

---

* *R. III*, 1, 4, 170; *M. W. W.*, III, 3, 87; *cf.* also *W. T.*, I, 2, 177–181.

† III, 2, 4 and 49 ff.; III, 6, 75. The certainty of Desdemona that Othello is " made of no such baseness/As jealous creatures are " is perhaps Shakespeare's most subtle instance of irony — for she is not wrong, really, but triumphantly right (III, 4, 28).

Shakespeare seems desirous of driving in his point.
Trebonius, as we saw, labels, and almost spoils, the
unconscious irony of Caesar's command —

> Be near me, that I may remember you.

Far more cunning is the contrivance by which Duncan's sad reflection on the Thane of Cawdor's
treachery —

> There 's no art
> To find the mind's construction in the face:
> He was a gentleman on whom I built
> An absolute trust —

is followed, the next instant, by the appearance of
Macbeth. It might even be urged that Henry the
Sixth's confidence in the loyalty of his subjects —

> No, Exeter, these graces challenge grace:
> And, when the lion fawns upon the lamb,
> The lamb will never cease to follow him —

becomes ironic only when his words are drowned
out by the shouts of the victorious Yorkists.[*]

Yet, time after time, the irony in Shakespeare's
plays would be imperceptible to a first audience.
The fact is an important one. Moulton, with
Greek tragedy in mind, defines irony as " ignorance
of the sequel on the part of the personages represented clashing with knowledge of it on the part of
the audience." [†] Baker holds that

---

[*] *Macb.*, I, 4, 11; *3 H. VI*, IV, 8, 48.
[†] *The Ancient Classical Drama: A Study in Literary Evolution*, 2nd
ed., Oxford, 1898, p. 128.

dramatic irony depends on a preceding planting in the minds of the auditors of information which makes what is true contrast sharply with what the characters of the particular scene suppose to be true.*

But in Shakespearean drama, a first audience would often be quite ignorant of the sequel; and irony sometimes occurs without any previous planting of information. On the other hand, Sir Arthur Quiller-Couch finds that Shakespeare's irony is not always of the traditional kind. It is often "retrospective rather than prophetic. It does not prepare the spectator for what is to come; but rather, when it comes, reminds him as by an echo that it has been coming all the while." And he cites Lady Macbeth's confident words, just after the murder,

> A little water clears us of this deed,

which find their answer in the sleep-walking scene.† Now it is possible that some keenly observant spectator at the first performance of *Macbeth*, when he saw with horror Lady Macbeth's vain efforts to remove the blood, cast his mind back, and recalled the irony which lay in a single line three acts before.‡ But take another example. In the play scene

---

* *Dramatic Technique*, Boston and New York, 1919, pp. 202, 203.
† *Shakespeare's Workmanship*, 50, 51; *cf.* G. G. Sedgewick, "Dramatic Irony," Harvard dissertation (unpublished), 1913, pp. 340 ff.
‡ Few persons could have missed the general connection between the two scenes, and few would have forgotten the *sight* of the murderers' bloody hands.

in the *First Part of Henry IV*, Falstaff (as the Prince) comes to his peroration:

> No, my good lord; banish Peto, banish Bardolph, banish Poins; but for sweet Jack Falstaff, kind Jack Falstaff, true Jack Falstaff, valiant Jack Falstaff, and therefore more valiant, being, as he is, old Jack Falstaff, banish not him thy Harry's company: banish not him thy Harry's company: banish plump Jack, and banish all the world.   (ii, 4, 528)

To which Hal says simply, " I do, I will." There is plenty of irony in that! But to appreciate it, the Elizabethans who first saw Falstaff stride the boards were required to wait until the *Second Part of Henry IV* had been composed and produced. Then, in the last scene of the last act of that play, their patience may have been rewarded.

No, in many cases, Shakespeare could not have been thinking in terms of the first time of acting and the immediate success. On the contrary, he introduced the ironic for no other reason, I suppose, than that it pleased him as an artist to do so. If there were those who desired to see his plays a second time, so much the better.* But their pleasure — *our* pleasure — comes swiftly. For, like the pleasure taken by a Greek audience in the irony of Sophocles, it is founded on a knowledge of the outcome. So when Othello, greeting Desdemona with ecstatic joy after his landing in Cyprus, cries:

---

* See also pages 119, 120, above. Professor J. D. Wilson's portrait, *The Essential Shakespeare*, will come as a refreshment of spirit to those who are weary of Sir Sidney Lee's commercial playwright.

> If it were now to die,
>   'T were now to be most happy,

we, who know the sequel, find a deeper significance
in his words than any which the first audience could
have perceived in them.* " Fail not our feast,"
Macbeth says to Banquo. " My lord, I will not,"
he replies; and we know how he came. Or there is
Juliet, expostulating with her mother,

> Delay this marriage for a month, a week;
> Or, if you do not, make the bridal bed
> In that dim monument where Tybalt lies;

or Angelo, in his false security, saying of Claudio,

> You may not so extenuate his offence
> For I have had such faults; but rather tell me,
> When I, that censure him, do so offend,
> Let mine own judgment pattern out my death,
> And nothing come in partial;

or Timon, confessing he had often wished himself
poorer, so that he might come nearer his friends.† . . .
Out of our acquaintance, with the event, it is even
possible to imagine ironies which may not have
been a part of the author's intention. I remember
the sinister emphasis which Mr. George Arliss

---

* II, I, 192. I am willing to grant that some sensitive persons
shivered, even then — as perhaps they did, in R. & J., at II, 6, 3–8.
Foreshadowings of the tragic event are not without their immediate
value.

† Macb., III, I, 28; R. & J., III, 5, 201, M. M., II, I, 27; Timon,
I, 2, 105. See also Miss Bradbrook, Themes and Conventions of
Elizabethan Tragedy, 33, 34, 86.

placed upon the word " man " in one of Shylock's
first speeches —" the *man* is, notwithstanding, sufficient." It was effective, without doubt — so effective that perhaps it was right.

* * *

Although the general frankness of Shakespeare's
methods is beyond question — frankness, in this
connection, implying a preference for taking the
audience into his confidence rather than fooling
them — his plays are not without instances of surprise. Some of these are mild enough. Thus, the
skill with which, in *The Comedy of Errors*, Aegeon's
wife is kept out of sight until she is needed at the
very end, has found praise.* But, granted that it is
satisfactory for the Lady Abbess to turn out to be
the person she is, still the discovery does not really
startle us. We feel, I take it, very much as we feel
about the safety of Antonio's ships at the end of *The
Merchant*, that the rules of romance are being observed — that is all. In *Love's Labor's Lost*, where
for some unknown reason they are broken, Berowne
for Shakespeare, or Shakespeare in the person of
Berowne, duly apologizes:

> Our wooing doth not end like an old play;
> Jack hath not Jill.   (v, 2, 882)

---

* Thaler, *Shakspere's Silences*, 54.

On occasion, characters whisper among themselves; and such whispering may serve as a vague
warning that some surprise is being hatched. The
proper attitude for us to take is suggested by Mr.
Bayes in *The Rehearsal*. His Gentleman-Usher and
Physician have gone out " *whispering*," and Smith
asks:

> But pray why all this whispering?
> *Bayes.* Why, Sir, . . . because they are suppos'd to be Politi-
> cians; and matters of State ought not to be divulg'd.
> *Smith.* But then, Sir, why —
> *Bayes.* Sir, if you 'l but respite your curiosity till the end of
> the fifth Act, you 'l find it a piece of patience not ill re-
> compenc'd.*

One or two examples of premonitory whispering
have already been adduced.† A notable instance is
the Countess of Auvergne episode in the *First Part
of Henry VI*. Talbot receives from the Countess a
graciously phrased invitation " to visit her poor
castle." Bedford teases him a little:

> Is it even so?   Nay, then, I see our wars
> Will turn into a peaceful comic sport,
> When ladies crave to be encounter'd with.
>
> (II, 2, 44)

He declines to accompany Talbot, and the last
lines in the scene are these:

> *Talbot.*   Well then, alone, — since there 's no remedy, —
> I mean to prove this lady's courtesy.

---

* II, 1, ed. Montague Summers, pp. 16, 17.
† Pages 89, 90, above.

Come hither, captain. [*Whispers.*] You perceive my
mind.
Captain. I do, my lord, and mean accordingly.
[*Exeunt.*

The Countess herself now enters with the porter of
her castle; but there is still mystery. She bids him
remember her orders and, when he has carried
them out, " bring the keys to me." The soliloquy
which follows is threatening but enigmatical:

Countess. The plot is laid: if all things fall out right,
I shall as famous be by this exploit
As Scythian Tomyris by Cyrus' death.
Great is the rumour of this dreadful knight,
And his achievements of no less account:
Fain would mine eyes be witness with mine ears,
To give their censure of these rare reports.

(II, 3, 4)

Talbot has scarcely begun to speak with the Countess when he learns that he is a prisoner. Then, in a
moment, the tables are turned. He winds a horn,
and his soldiers who, unknown to the Countess,
have been waiting outside, force in the gates.
There are possibilities in the scene, though the
young Shakespeare, or whoever wrote it, has not
fully realized them.*
Antonio is delivered from Shylock's clutches by a
trick which has evoked much nonsensical grumbling
from persons who refuse to enter into the spirit of

---

* *Cf.* Baker, *Dramatic Technique*, 97, 213; and Creizenach, *The
English Drama in the Age of Shakespeare*, 265, 266.

the play. It is a good trick, nevertheless, and in romance one of unquestionable legality. As for its theatrical effectiveness, that is still demonstrated by the spontaneous laughter, and even applause, of simple people seeing the comedy for the first time. Preparation is replaced, in this instance, not by inaudible whispering but by an equally inaudible conversation off stage.* Or, rather, we *are* prepared, quite satisfactorily, for the sight of Portia and Nerissa " accoutred like young men "; and we are informed, besides, that Portia is secretly in communication with her Paduan cousin, Doctor Bellario. What we do not know is how Portia hopes to save Bassanio's friend. " I'll tell thee all my whole device," she says to Nerissa,

> When I am in my coach, which stays for us
> At the park gate.   (III, 4, 81)

During the trial, moreover, Portia seems unable to help. Her plea for mercy is eloquent, but it is refused. She examines the bond, only to find that its terms are clear. Shylock praises her repeatedly. She appears to sum up in his favor:

> A pound of that same merchant's flesh is thine:
> The court awards it, and the law doth give it.

Then, and only then, she springs the trap.†

* *Cf.* Creizenach, p. 266.
† Yet the readiness of Portia and Nerissa to fall into what Shylock calls trifling, just before sentence is demanded (IV, 1, 289–295) suggests the possibility that the scene is usually played too tragically.

Very different is the shock which we experience at the end of *King Lear*. Full preparation is replaced, on this occasion, by reference to a paper which Edmund gives the Captain. But Edmund's words are scarcely ambiguous —" to be tender-minded," he observes, is unbecoming in a soldier. We know, without being told, what is in the paper. " I'll do't my lord," says the Captain (v, 3, 35). Yet even after Edmund, dying, has said plainly that his writ

Is on the life of Lear and on Cordelia,

the entrance of Lear carrying Cordelia's body takes us unawares. To the first audience, with their recollections of the happy ending of the old *King Leir*, it must have been as terrifying as it was unforeseen. Things seem, indeed, to be shaping themselves toward such an ending. Albany has asserted himself, on our side. Edgar is victorious against Edmund. The evil characters are dead, or dying. We hope still, as Albany invokes the gods to protect Cordelia: " The gods defend her! " It is like Edgar's " Pray that the right may thrive," before the beginning of the battle, and it brings a similar answer: " *Enter* Lear, *with* Cordelia *dead in his arms*." *

Shakespeare's most artistic use of surprise is in

* See page 46, above. Bradley's discussion of the present passage should be consulted (*Shakespearean Tragedy*, 63, 326). Othello's suicide is, of course, startling; and Lodovico's speech just before (v, 2, 329 ff.) throws us off our guard even more completely than Albany's (v, 3, 297 ff.) just before the death of Lear.

Lear; his most brilliant, in *The Merchant of Venice*. A few other instances remain to be mentioned. The scene between Macduff and Malcolm, in the fourth act of *Macbeth*, depends for its effectiveness (which is not great) on the withholding of a secret from the audience. Malcolm is suspicious, at the beginning, but there is no hint that he is testing Macduff. Indeed, if the scene had been composed a little later in the author's career we should, doubtless, be assured by historians of the drama that Shakespeare was here trying his hand at the sort of *coup de théatre* in which Beaumont and Fletcher excelled. Another surprise — which may not be a surprise at all — occurs near the close of the *First Part of Henry IV*. Falstaff has been watching the single combat between Hotspur and Prince Hal when, in the words of the old stage direction, " *Enter Dowglas, he fights with Falstaffe, who fals down as if he were dead*." There he remains while Hotspur, who has been mortally wounded, expires. The Prince speaks well of his enemy. Then he spies Falstaff:

> What! old acquaintance! could not all this flesh
> Keep in a little life?   Poor Jack, farewell!

And he concludes:

> Embowell'd will I see thee by and by:
> Till then in blood by noble Percy lie.   (v, 4, 102)

Exit. Whereupon, Falstaff arises and addresses the audience. Now Morgann has painted a most distressing picture of the behavior of eighteenth-century actors at this point.* Certainly, as they managed it, there could have been no surprise for the spectators when Falstaff arose; and, as certainly, low comedians are a law unto themselves. Falstaff should, I believe, seem actually to breathe his last. How great, then, will be our joy and relief when, after a long pause to be sure that there is no one about, the mountain stirs! " Embowell'd," indeed! †

Finally, in *The Winter's Tale*, Shakespeare went a step farther. Quite deliberately, and no doubt enjoying what he was doing, he played a hoax on his audience, keeping it up for two whole acts. Hermione, after she hears the news of her son's death, is borne out, swooning, by her ladies. Paulina returns, some twenty lines later, and announces, with mingled outcries and denunciations, that her mistress is dead.

> I say she 's dead; I 'll swear't: if word nor oath
> Prevail not, go and see: if you can bring
> Tincture or lustre in her lip, her eye,
> Heat outwardly, or breath within, I 'll serve you
> As I would do the gods.   (III, 2, 204)

And she falls, again, into full-mouthed reviling of Leontes.‡ But this is as nothing to what we get in

---

* *Dramatic Character of Sir John Falstaff*, London, 1777, p. 25.
† That excellent actor Mr. Roy Byford, did the scene in this way some years ago.
‡ See pages 250, 251, below. Sir Arthur Quiller-Couch suggests

the next scene. Antigonus, left alone with the in-
fant Perdita on the sea-coast of Bohemia, addresses
his charge:

> Come, poor babe:
> I have heard, but not believ'd, the spirits o' the dead
> May walk again: if such thing be, thy mother
> Appear'd to me last night, for ne'er was dream
> So like a waking.

The apparition, coming to him " in pure white
robes, / Like very sanctity," had bidden him leave
the child in some remote part of that country.

> " And, for the babe
> Is counted lost for ever, Perdita,
> I prithee, call't: for this ungentle business,
> Put on thee by my lord, thou ne'er shalt see
> Thy wife Paulina more."

Antigonus is obeying, he says, at all points.

> I do believe
> Hermione hath suffer'd death; and that
> Apollo would, this being indeed the issue
> Of King Polixenes, it should here be laid.

His own death follows swiftly — even as the dream
intimated. For Hermione to come to life again
after all this is, I protest, cozenage and swindling.*

---

that " if, as members of the Globe audience, we know our Shakespeare of old," we ought to guess, " in Paulina's protestations, a
something held up his sleeve " (*Shakespeare's Workmanship*, 232).
Familiarity with Shakespeare's methods would, as I see it, work
exactly the other way.

* See further pages 183 ff., below. The effectiveness of the
statue scene itself is not for an instant denied — but that is another
matter.

Chapter VI

TESTIMONY

Responsiveness of Surrounding Characters — Ophelia's
Mad Scene — Characters Compared to Witnesses — Effect
of Repeated Praise or Blame — Malvolio as his Fellows
see him — Coriolanus — First and Second Gentlemen —
Messengers — Antony and the Soothsayer — Supernatural Testimony — Margaret — Ghost in *Hamlet*.

"HALF of our work," writes Louis Calvert, in
his fine book on acting, " is to make our
own speeches effective, half of it is to make effective
the speeches of our associates in the piece." * So,
quite recently, the letter scene in *Twelfth Night*
(II, 5) has been given fresh enchantment by the
listening of a notable Maria — though, from the
mere text, one might suppose that Maria, so far
from listening, was not present at all! The actors of
small parts in Shakespeare's plays have a heavy
obligation to fulfil. For, as Professor Stoll has
shown, they are asked, like a Greek chorus, to reflect and vivify the emotions of others. " Without
the awestruck comments of the Doctor and the
Waiting-woman," Mr. Stoll suggests, " Lady Macbeth's tragic mutterings and murmurings would
fall a little dully and feebly upon our ear" — they

* *Problems of the Actor*, 97.

would be less thrilling, certainly. And so with
comedy: the " laughter crackles on the stage before it resounds in gallery and pit." *

Thus, the passionate lamentations uttered by
York, when, set upon a molehill and crowned with
a paper crown, he is given the napkin steeped in
his son's blood, are made even more pitiful by the
comments of Northumberland, one of his enemies:

> Beshrew me, but his passion moves me so
> That hardly can I check my eyes from tears.

And again,

> Had he been slaughter-man to all my kin,
> I should not for my life but weep with him,
> To see how inly sorrow gripes his soul.†

Or there is the glorification of Falstaff's figure. No
one seems able to resist holding forth on that subject. Even the Sheriff and the Carrier enjoy it.
Prince Hal asks them what men they are pursuing.

Sheriff. One of them is well known, my gracious lord,
  A gross fat man.
Carrier.   As fat as butter.   (*1 H. IV*, II, 4, 567)

The poignancy of Ophelia's mad scene is expressed and defined by the lookers-on. First, a
Gentleman prepares us for what is to come. Ophelia "is importunate, indeed distract: / Her mood will

---

* *Poets and Playwrights*, 75–77.
† *3 H. VI*, I, 4, 150, 169; *cf. R. III*, I, 4, 64, 65.

needs be pitied." " Her speech," he continues, "is nothing,"

> Yet the unshaped use of it doth move
> The hearers to collection; they aim at it,
> And botch the words up fit to their own thoughts;
> Which, as her winks, and nods, and gestures yield them,
> Indeed would make one think there might be thought,
> Though nothing sure, yet much unhappily.   (IV, 5, 2)

He has noticed, also, that "she speaks much of her father." The pauses in Ophelia's prattle are filled by Claudius and Gertrude with sympathetic comments and interjections — " Alas! sweet lady, what imports this song? " " Alas! look here, my lord," " How do you, pretty lady? " " Pretty Ophelia." And Claudius, who has called part of what she said " conceit upon her father," explains, after her departure:

> O! this is the poison of deep grief; it springs
> All from her father's death.

When Ophelia returns, Laertes is present, and he alone interprets for her:

> Is't possible a young maid's wits
> Should be as mortal as an old man's life?
> Nature is fine in love, and where 't is fine
> It sends some precious instance of itself
> After the thing it loves.   (IV, 5, 158)

This is " a document in madness," he cries, " thoughts and remembrance fitted." Then, as the scene becomes unendurable to him:

Thought and affliction, passion, hell itself,
She turns to favour and to prettiness.

The responsiveness of the surrounding characters is, in Shakespeare's plays, a means of emotional intensification. But, as a good dramatist is continually accomplishing more than one thing at a time, the comments spoken during Ophelia's mad scene will be found to possess further values. Thus, the Gentleman's speech is an excellent instance of the sort of preparation we have come to expect of Shakespeare before scenes which might otherwise be difficult to follow. Moreover, the remarks of the King and Laertes contribute not a little toward our knowledge of the speakers. Claudius pities Ophelia. The fury of Laertes is stilled. When, after Ophelia's exit, the King begins to ply him once more, it is, indeed, a different, almost a subdued, Laertes whom he faces — one who descends to explanation, if not to apology. Nevertheless, his desire for vengeance, far from disappearing, has taken deeper root. From now on, Claudius will have no difficulty with him. Laertes is doomed.

In the same scene, a cause is assigned for Ophelia's madness — her grief over the death of Polonius — and anyone familiar with Elizabethan technical methods will accept this as the true cause. Alone, the King's word might not be enough. Ophelia has had to bear the knowledge of Hamlet's supposed malady, a malady which she must have attributed to her own enforced unkindness. The reality of her distress is brought out in her soliloquy at the end of the nunnery scene. Fortunately, we have other witnesses besides Claudius. Their testimony is quite conclusive.

The author of a play may not, it will be remembered, directly address us. For enlightenment on many matters, we look to the characters. What, we ask, do they tell us about themselves? What do they say of one another? What are *their* explanations of motives and events? The analogy between such statements and the testimony of witnesses is, within limits, a useful one. For, in a play as in a court-room, not everything that is affirmed is, of course, to be admitted as evidence, and some characters are more worthy of credit than others. On the other hand, it would be manifestly absurd to carry the analogy too far. So, in the absence of evidence to the contrary, we are ready to bring in a verdict of " guilty " against one of Shakespeare's personages, even on the strength of hearsay, or of his own uncorroborated testimony. Yet so remarkable is the credibility of the witnesses in Elizabethan drama that unless they are contradicted, or are known to have a reason for departing from the truth, we are usually justified in believing whatever they say.*

* This is, of course, a very broad generalization. See, especially, pages 298 ff., below.

The mere repetition of praise or blame is a means of determining where we should bestow our sympathies. Coleridge wrote of Helena, in *All's Well*, that " it required all Shakespeare's consummate skill to interest us for her; and he does this chiefly by the operation of the other characters,— the Countess, Lafeu, &c. We get to like Helena from their praising and commending her so much."* In *Henry VIII*, a difficult, paradoxical play, *both* Katharine and Anne Bullen are consistently lauded, while Wolsey is almost as consistently denounced. Anne pays tribute to Katharine's virtues; and Wolsey admits that Anne is "virtuous / And well deserving." † For all that, one has only to recall the scolding of Juliet by Old Capulet, and Iago's reputation for honesty, to perceive that there is nothing mechanical about the Shakespearean distribution of censure and applause.

Everything that is said of a character by his fellows will be carefully heeded by those critics who desire a means of checking the accuracy of their own impressions. What, for instance, was Malvolio really like? We know, of course, what he does and says. We recognize, it may be, a certain individuality — difficult to define but present, nevertheless — in his tones, or manner of speech.

---

* *Shakespearean Criticism*, ed. Raysor, II, 357.

† II, 3, 1 ff.; III, 2, 98 ff. Cromwell has a good word for his master, but only after Wolsey's fall. It is left for Katharine and Griffith to sum up his merits and defects (IV, 2).

We are even permitted, once or twice, to enter into his thoughts as they are externalized for us in soliloquy. There remains the testimony of the other characters. Feste calls Malvolio a fool, and refers to Sir Toby Belch as of the same opinion. Olivia, speaking very much to the point, says: " O! you are sick of self-love, Malvolio, and taste with a distempered appetite. To be generous, guiltless, and of free disposition, is to take those things for bird-bolts that you deem cannon-bullets." * There, at the outset, is a directive comment the force of which would not be missed by an experienced audience. To Viola, Malvolio is merely " this churlish messenger." Sir Toby Belch, with a tremendous flourish, calls him " a Peg-a-Ramsey "— which is not very helpful. Later, however, when Malvolio has descended upon his revels, Sir Toby has a glimpse of the eternal verities: " Dost thou think," he demands, " because thou art virtuous, there shall be no more cakes and ale? " † Maria, who has already given an instance of her shrewdness by the manner in which she has hit off Sir Andrew, now asserts that she can " gull " the steward " into a nayword."

Sir Toby. Possess us, possess us; tell us something of him.
Maria. Marry, sir, sometimes he is a kind of puritan.
Sir Andrew. O! if I thought that, I 'd beat him like a dog. . . .

---

* *12 N.*, I, 5, 96.
† II, 2, 24; II, 3, 84, and 124.

Maria. The devil a puritan that he is, or anything constantly
but a time-pleaser; an affectioned ass, that cons state
without book, and utters it by great swarths: the best
persuaded of himself; so crammed, as he thinks, with
excellences, that it is his ground of faith that all that
look on him love him; *and on that vice in him will my
revenge find notable cause to work.*　　　　　(II, 3, 151)

In other words, the veracity of the portrait will be
demonstrated by the success of her stratagem. Sir
Toby's wrath at Malvolio's presumption, in the
letter scene, yields only such epithets as " rogue,"
" scab," and " brock "; while Sir Andrew keeps up
bravely with, " Fie on him, Jezebel! " Just before
the transformation, however, we are reminded of
the dignified Malvolio of the beginning. Olivia
asks:

Where is Malvolio? he is sad, and civil,
And suits well for a servant with my fortunes.
　　　　　　　　　　　　　　(III, 4, 5)

" Poor gentleman," she says of him when, near the
close of the comedy, she remembers that he is
" distract." And " gentleman " should be noted,
though, shortly after, it is replaced by another
word:

Alas, poor *fool*, how have they baffled thee!*

Feste was right, after all.

In *Coriolanus*, as befits a tragedy of character, the
testimony concerning the hero is voluminous.† Of

---

* v, 1, 290 and 381.
† *Cf.* Stoll, *Art and Artifice in Shakespeare*, 148.

the witnesses, some, like the Citizens and Aufidius, are the hero's enemies; some, like Menenius, his friends. And two particularly impressive witnesses seem to be neutral. At the beginning, mutinous citizens discuss the protagonist. He is, one of them declares, "chief enemy to the people . . . a very dog to the commonalty."

> Second Citizen. Consider you what services he has done for his country?
> First Citizen. Very well; and could be content to give him good report for 't, but that he pays himself with being proud.
> Second Citizen. Nay, but speak not maliciously.
> First Citizen. I say unto you, what he hath done famously, he did it to that end: though soft-conscienced men can be content to say it was for his country, he did it to please his mother, and to be partly proud; which he is, even to the altitude of his virtue.
> Second Citizen. What he cannot help in his nature, you account a vice in him. You must in no way say he is covetous.
> First Citizen. If I must not, I need not be barren of accusations: he hath faults, with surplus, to tire in repetition.

Barring this last vague imputation, which is sufficiently explained by the hostility of the speaker, every item in the description is accurate.* Marcius is proud. He hates the plebeians. His courage, which is magnificent, is actuated by personal honor — scarcely by patriotism. As for Volumnia's influence over him, the full force of it appears only

---

* The earlier speeches strike " the keynote of the entire play " (Miss H. E. Fansler, *The Evolution of Technic in Elizabethan Drama* Chicago and New York [1914], p. 238).

when he consents to forgo his vengeance.   Shakespeare, that is to say, had already begun to motivate a scene which occurs almost at the end of the play.

Sicinius and Brutus, the next witnesses, again mention the pride of the hero.   They discover another defect in him, a want of self-control. Marcius did not conceal his anger at their being " chosen tribunes for the people."

Brutus.   Being mov'd, he will not spare to gird the gods.
Sicinius. Bemock the modest moon.
Brutus.   The present wars devour him; he is grown
     Too proud to be so valiant.   (I, 1, 262)

It is upon these qualities that they build, throughout.   Sicinius is not discouraged when Coriolanus seems likely to be made consul:

    He cannot temperately transport his honours
    From where he should begin and end, but will
    Lose those he hath won.
Brutus.   In that there 's comfort.*

And when Volumnia has persuaded her son to lay aside his austerity and attempt to placate the multitude with soft words, Brutus knows what course to pursue:

    Put him to choler straight.   He hath been us'd
    Ever to conquer, and to have his worth
    Of contradiction: being once chaf'd, he cannot
    Be rein'd again to temperance; *then he speaks*
    What 's in his heart; and that is there which looks
    With us to break his neck.   (III, 3, 25)

---

* II, 1, 243; *cf.* II, 3, 266.

We may not, however, attach the same degree of credit to everything that the Tribunes say. Why, Sicinius wonders, is Coriolanus willing to serve under another? Brutus's reply, which he accepts and enlarges upon, seems quite wide of the mark.* Unlike themselves, Coriolanus is no Machiavellian. " He's the devil," cries one of the Volscian soldiers. " Bolder," Aufidius corrects, " though not so subtle." † When, late in the play, Sicinius and Brutus are discussing the hero with Menenius, they again go too far:

> *Brutus.*   Caius Marcius was
>   A worthy officer i' the war; but insolent,
>   O'ercome with pride, ambitious past all thinking,
>   Self-loving, —
> *Sicinius.*   And affecting one sole throne,
>   Without assistance.
> *Menenius.*   I think not so.   (IV, 6, 29)

Menenius, himself, might be held unacceptable as a witness because of his manifest bias in favor of the hero. " I have been," he admits,

> The book of his good acts, whence men have read
> His fame unparallel'd, haply amplified.   (V, 2, 14)

Yet what he says of Coriolanus is substantially true. Thus, in the following lines we have, once more, the quality which the Tribunes exploited — only, this time, it is not looked upon with contempt:

* I, 1, 269 ff. *Cf.* II, 1, 12–15.
† I, 10, 16.

First Patrician. This man has marr'd his fortune.
Menenius.   His nature is too noble for the world:
                    He would not flatter Neptune for his trident,
                    Or Jove for 's power to thunder. His heart's
                       his mouth:
                    What his breast forges, that his tongue must vent;
                    And, being angry, does forget that ever
                    He heard the name of death.   (III, I, 253)

Aufidius belongs with the chorus characters in
the next chapter.* Of the remaining witnesses —
there are several — I call attention to the two unnamed Officers whom we see laying cushions in the
Capitol, just before the return of Coriolanus from
the Volscian war. There are, say the Officers,
three candidates for consulships, but " 'tis thought
of every one Coriolanus will carry it." " That's a
brave fellow," the First Officer remarks, " but he's
vengeance proud, and loves not the common
people." At least he does not flatter them, the
Second replies: Marcius does not care whether they
love him or hate him, " and out of his noble carelessness lets them plainly see it."

First Officer. If he did not care whether he had their love or
        no, he waved indifferently 'twixt doing them neither
        good nor harm; but he seeks their hate with greater de-
        votion than they can render it him; and leaves nothing
        undone that may fully discover him their opposite. Now,
        to seem to affect the malice and displeasure of the people
        is as bad as that which he dislikes, to flatter them for their
        love.

---

* Pages 228, 229.

Second Officer. He hath deserved worthily of his country.

(II, 2, 18)

And on that note the Officers close. Sir E. K. Chambers suggests that they " are in sympathy by birth with the plebeians, and by office with the patricians. They are not, therefore, extreme on either side." * The rank and file of Elizabethan playgoers would certainly have accepted their testimony, as no doubt they were intended to do.†

Though Shakespeare's characters — villains and all — make, on the whole, surprisingly trustworthy witnesses, some of them inspire greater confidence than others. Thus, we should listen with particular attention to the ordinary honest fellows, and the mere Lords and Gentlemen, who abound in the plays. We have already had a glimpse of them, as Elizabethan counterparts of the butler and parlor maid, doing their duty in Act One, Scene One.‡ Fortunately, they do not confine their helpfulness

---

* Furness, *Variorum Shakespeare*, 220.

† *A. & C.* is like *Cor.* in the frequency with which the hero's character is commented upon (see Logan Pearsall Smith, *On Reading Shakespeare*, 122–124; and Gervinus, *Shakespeare Commentaries*, II, 379, 380). Soliloquies, it should be noted, are not much used in either play.

‡ See pages 111, 112, above. " Every audience knows that such a faithful expositor is not misleading them," writes Professor Lawrence of the First Gentleman in *Cymb.*, I, I (*Shakespeare's Problem Comedies*, New York, 1931, p. 203); yet Arthur Symons advises us to take his praises of Posthumus " at the valuation of common rumour " (*Studies in the Elizabethan Drama*, New York [1919], p. 135).

to the beginning. And when Fielding burlesqued them, in *The Tragedy of Tragedies*, Doodle (or is it Noodle?) is slain, as a bearer of ill tidings, during the holocaust at the very end of the play. Their character as witnesses is unimpeachable. Or, to speak by the card, the fact that they have no characters, that they are only Salanio and Salarino, in *The Merchant of Venice*, or the First and Second Officers, in *Coriolanus*, makes it likely that their speeches will be purely informative.

In *Henry VIII*, expository " Gentlemen " are very active indeed. Two of them are employed, at the beginning of the second act, to tell us about the trial and conviction of Buckingham, with whom they sympathize. Wolsey bears the blame. " Certainly," says the Second Gentleman, " the cardinal is the end of this." " 'Tis likely," his companion replies — and proceeds to give reasons for thinking so. " All the commons," the Second Gentleman concludes,

> Hate him perniciously, and o' my conscience,
> Wish him ten fathom deep: this duke as much
> They love and dote on.   (II, 1, 39)

Buckingham himself is brought in, guarded. He addresses the bystanders, then goes off to be executed. " O this is full of pity! " cries the First Gentleman, gathering up the emotion of the scene. The Second Gentleman has a weighty secret to impart:

> Did you not of late days hear
> A buzzing of a separation
> Between the king and Katharine?   (II, 1, 147)

His friend has heard, but is incredulous. The
Second Gentleman assures him that it is

> Held for certain
> The king will venture at it.   Either the cardinal,
> Or some about him near, have, out of malice
> To the good queen, possess'd him with a scruple
> That will undo her.

" 'Tis the cardinal," is the First Gentleman's ready
comment; and he goes on to name Wolsey's motive.
We have turned an important corner in the play.
At the beginning of the fourth act, the Gentlemen
appear once more, taking pains to remind us of
their identity —" at our last meeting," the Second
remarks,

> The Duke of Buckingham came from his trial.

Now, however, they are waiting to see Anne " pass
from her coronation "; nor do they wait in vain.
With all possible splendor the procession moves
across the stage while the two Gentlemen point out
one august personage after another. At the conclusion of the show, a third Gentleman appears,
who gives the others a lively account of what went
on in the Abbey. And toward the end of the scene,
we again turn a corner. The Second Gentleman

asks who the two bishops were " that went on each side of the queen."

Third Gentleman.	Stokesly and Gardiner; the one of Winchester, —
	Newly preferr'd from the king's secretary, —
	The other, London.
Second Gentleman.	He of Winchester
	Is held no great good lover of the archbishop's,
	The virtuous Cranmer.
Third Gentleman.	All the land knows that:
	However, yet there 's no great breach; when it comes,
	Cranmer will find a friend will not shrink from him. (IV, 1, 100)

Wolsey, by this time, is dead; Katharine is dying. And just as the Gentlemen eased the earlier transition, from the fall of Buckingham to the matter of the King's divorce, so now they lead us gently forward into the new concerns, centering about Cranmer, with which the last part of the play has to do.

When Timon finds himself in need of money, he sends confidently to three of his friends, Lucius, Lucullus, and Sempronius. Lucullus, in the first of three parallel scenes, puts off Timon's servant, Flaminius, whom he attempts to bribe. Flaminius refuses his money and passionately denounces him.* In the next scene, Lucius enters with " three Strangers." They tell him that Timon is ruined; and when Timon's servant comes for money,

* III, 1. See page 248, below.

Lucius makes excuses and will not send any. The three Strangers are left to discuss what they have heard.

First Stranger. Why this is the world's soul; and just of the same
                          piece
                    Is every flatterer's spirit.   Who can call him
                    His friend that dips in the same dish? for, in
                    My knowing, Timon has been this lord's father.

And he concludes the scene with:

> Men must learn now with pity to dispense;
> For policy sits above conscience.

Though to us the insincerity of Lucius seems transparent, the author took nothing for granted.   He found, moreover, in the dispassionate moralizing of the chorus-like Strangers, contrast where contrast was needed.   Each refusal is unlike the others.   And it is notable that after the third, which immediately follows the departure of the Strangers, Timon's servant strikes a new note — one of bitter scorn.

> Excellent! Your lordship's a goodly villain.   The devil knew not what he did when he made man politic; he crossed himself by 't: and I cannot think but in the end the villanies of man will set him clear.* . . .

When Shakespeare's " Citizens " are members of a mob, they assume a certain collective character and cease to be mere honest fellows who comment and explain.   The three Citizens who have a scene

* III, 3, 27.

to themselves in *Richard III* are just that.* They tell us, it is true, nothing that we did not know before. The action of the play stands still. Yet, through them, we become conscious of a broader significance in what we are witnessing. Edward IV is dead, they say. The passing of a king is no mean matter. It touches the lives of countless simple men, like these.

> Woe to that land that 's govern'd by a child! —

one of them exclaims. Henry VI was a child, too; but he had " virtuous uncles " to protect him:

> O! full of danger is the Duke of Gloucester!

The First Citizen makes light of their fears. " All will be well," he says. But the Third Citizen knows better:

> When clouds are seen, wise men put on their cloaks;
> When great leaves fall, then winter is at hand. . . .
>
> All may be well; but, if God sort it so,
> 'T is more than we deserve, or I expect.
>
> (II, 3, 32)

After the shrill outcries of the scene before, this moment of quiet is more than welcome.

Bearers of news, in Shakespeare's plays, are undistinguished persons, as a rule, and some of them are mere " Messengers." Perhaps, like their expository cousins, the First and Second Gentlemen,

---

* The weaknesses of masters are sometimes shrewdly noted below stairs — see especially *A. & C.*, II, 7, 1–19.

they are the more trustworthy for being without
character. Sometimes they say what is not so.
But the audience, on these occasions, have already
been acquainted with the facts, and are not deceived, with Antony, into believing that Cleopatra
is dead, or, with Romeo, that Juliet is dead, or,
with Northumberland, that the rebels have won at
Shrewsbury.* On the other hand, what is news to
us may be already known to the person who receives it. Blunt breaks in upon the interview between Henry Bolingbroke and Prince Hal, in the
First Part of Henry IV, with word that Douglas and
the English rebels have joined forces at Shrewsbury.

> *King Henry.* The Earl of Westmoreland set forth today,
> With him my son, Lord John of Lancaster;
> For this advertisement is five days old.
>
> (III, 2, 170)

It is like Henry, we feel, to have known, and
acted, so promptly. The scene, too, has been given
fresh movement — it ends with a rush. No wonder,
Shakespeare tried the device again. In the *Second
Part of Henry IV*, Northumberland gives way to
grief when he hears of the real outcome at Shrewsbury. " This strained passion doth you wrong," he
is told. All is not lost. And Morton describes at
length the revolt of the Archbishop of York.

* *A. & C.*, IV, 12; *R. & J.*, V, 1; *2 H. IV*, I, 1. See also page 307,
below.

Northumberland. I knew of this before; but, to speak truth,
          This present grief had wip'd it from my mind.
                                        (I, 1, 210)

The author's intention — to forward his exposition
without losing touch with the principal character
concerned — is plain enough.

Messengers' speeches in Greek tragedy, writes
Moulton, " give the impression that for a time
dramatic effect is suspended, and, as a substitute,
the recognized features of Epic Poetry supply a
new interest."* In Shakespearean drama, the pre-
rogatives of the formal Messenger are distributed.
But bearers of news are still allowed to employ a
heightened style, on occasion; and with the departure from realism which the use of this style involves, is discernible, at times, a certain broadening
of the scope of their speeches. So, at the beginning
of the *First Part of Henry VI*, a Messenger brings
" sad tidings " out of France:

          Guienne, Champaigne, Rheims, Orleans,
          Paris, Guysors, Poictiers, are all quite lost.

" How were they lost? " he is asked, " what treachery was us'd? "

Messenger. No treachery; but want of men and money.
          Among the soldiers this is muttered,
          That here you maintain several factions;
          And, whilst a field should be despatch'd and fought,
          You are disputing of your generals. . . .

---

* *The Ancient Classical Drama*, 145.

> Awake, awake, English nobility!
> Let not sloth dim your honours new-begot:
> Cropp'd are the flower-de-luces in your arms;
> Of England's coat one half is cut away.
>
> (I, 1, 68)

It is like a page from some Elizabethan versified history.*

* * *

A critic, who on Shakespearean matters is usually very right indeed, goes astray, I believe, in his interpretation of the scene between Antony and the Soothsayer. Antony's " spirit all afraid to govern him near Caesar! Is it, indeed!? " expostulates Mr. Granville-Barker:

> Caesar has all the luck at dicing and cock-fighting. No doubt! But the naked truth is that the sensual man in him must find excuse for the
> " I will to Egypt. . . .
> I' the East my pleasure lies."
> and any is better than none.†

Now, in Plutarch, the Soothsayer says what he does to Antony, " either to please Cleopatra, or else for that he found it so by his art." ‡ We may judge which explanation Shakespeare preferred by

---

* The high style lasts on in the narratives of Ross and the Sergeant, in *Macb.*, 1, 2. See also Miss Bradbrook, *Themes and Conventions of Elizabethan Tragedy*, 114.

† *Prefaces*, 2nd Series, 195; *A. & C.*, II, 3, 38.

‡ Hazlitt, *Shakespeare's Library*, Part 1, vol. III, p. 352.

urning back, a few pages, for we have already had
. taste of the Soothsayer's art.

> You shall outlive the lady whom you serve,

ie told Charmion. And his words come true. She
loes outlive her lady, by ever so little. The fortunes
f Charmion and Iras are, as he described them,
 alike.'"* But a broad principle is involved, as
vell. In Elizabethan tragedy, anything like *super-
atural testimony* (which is what the Soothsayer's
varning to Antony purports to be) must be taken
vith the utmost seriousness. If, in other words,
>hakespeare had expected us to doubt the state-
nent that Antony's genius was " rebuk'd " under
Caesar, it would have been necessary for him to
how us clearly why we should do so. Fraud would
ave had to be established, and there is no evidence
•f fraud.†

Fortunately, it is no longer necessary to labor the
>oint that Shakespeare's ghosts are real ghosts, or
hat the Weird Sisters are something far more
angible than an externalization of Macbeth's own
vil nature — imagine allowing Macbeth's own
vil nature to herald the coming of James to the

---

* 1, 2, 33 ff. Charmion's reply,
> O excellent! I love long life *better than figs*,
hows where the dramatist's thoughts were.
   † Notice, too, that the Soothsayer is justified by the event when
ie tells Antony that Caesar's fortunes will " rise higher " than his.
Iow Shakespeare regarded the Soothsayer is shown clearly by
Macb., III, 1, 56, 57.

English throne! The reality of supernatural manifestations in the plays is, or should be, taken for
granted. Where, as in the last act of *The Merry
Wives*, a spook is not a spook, the fact is made
abundantly clear. But even in matters which
fringe the debatable region of coincidence, we are
not permitted to rationalize. Brander Matthews
states, with some exaggeration, that in Shakespeare

prophecies are always accomplished, curses always work out
and presentiments are always justified; to him prophecies,
curses, and presentiments are dramaturgic devices for arousing
attention and exciting expectancy.*

Just before the rebel lords are arrested as traitors,
in the *Second Part of Henry IV*, we see them drinking
with Lancaster and Westmoreland.

Westmoreland. Health to my lord and gentle cousin, Mowbray.
Mowbray.   You wish me health in very happy season;
           For I am, on the sudden, something ill.
Archbishop. Against ill chances men are ever merry,
           But heaviness foreruns the good event. . . .

           Believe me, I am passing light in spirit.
                                        (IV, 2, 78)

Yet in the miserable sequel, Mowbray and the
Archbishop share alike. The presentiments of
doomed men are not, then, all of one sort. Romeo's
" cheerful thoughts " are but " a lightning before
death "† — as ironic as the riddling oracles that

* *Shakspere as a Playwright*, 322.
† *R. & J.*, v, 1, 1 ff.; v, 3, 88–90.

' lie like truth.' Along with portents and omens, presentiments are introduced to create an atmosphere appropriate to tragedy, or the threat of tragedy. Antonio's sadness, at the beginning of *The Merchant of Venice*, is justified by subsequent events. Hero, as she dresses on the morning of her wedding, has reason to discover that her " heart is exceeding heavy." * And, on the other hand, a happy outcome is not always unheralded. Bassanio feels that he could win Portia if only he had means to compete for her:

> I have a mind presages me such thrift,
> That I should questionless be fortunate.†

Our sense of tragic mystery is heightened by the fulfilment of dreams, of prophecies, and even, sometimes, of curses. In *Richard III*, Margaret's curse strikes down victim after victim. It is recalled by them, and by her. The whole play echoes with it — yet it is only a beginning of marvels. In the confidence of hate, Anne curses Richard's wife, and so, ironically, herself.‡ Buckingham, in a " feigned prayer," calls down God's punishment on himself, and what he " begg'd in jest " is " given in

---

* *Much Ado*, III, 4, 25. For portents and omens, see Stoll, *Shakespeare Studies*, 229 and note.

† *Mer. Ven.*, I, 1, 176; *cf. 3 H. VI*, v, 1, 71. But note that Gloucester's foreboding of evil (*3 H. VI*, IV, 7, 10) proves groundless.

‡ I, 2, 26 ff.; IV, 1, 71 ff.

earnest." * Clarence dreams of his own death, and his account of his dream falls between the instructing of his murderers and their performance of the deed. Richard, too, has dreams.

> Ill rest betide the chamber where thou liest,

cries Anne, early in the play.† The apparitions which troop past the tents of Richard and Richmond, on the night before Bosworth Field, are definitely looked forward to, in the Duchess of York's imprecations:

> Therefore take with thee my most grievous curse . . .
>
> My prayers on the adverse party fight;
> And there the little souls of Edward's children
> Whisper the spirits of thine enemies
> And promise them success and victory.
>
> (IV, 4, 188)

In the comprehensiveness of this later scene (V, 3) the distinctions between past and future are obliterated. The dreams of the rival captains are controlled by the ghosts of those whom Richard has murdered. They bid him dream of his " cousins smother'd in the Tower " and of how he stabbed Prince Edward at Tewksbury. To Richmond and Richard alike, they send visions of the morrow.‡ Richmond is to

> Dream of success and happy victory.

---

* II, 1, 32 ff.; v, 1, 13 ff.

† I, 2, 113; cf. IV, 1, 84.

‡ For the reality of these ghosts, see Stoll, *Shakespeare Studies,* 217 ff.

But Richard must dream " of bloody deeds and
death "; and he starts out of his sleep with,

> Give me another horse! bind up my wounds!

There are, finally, the prophecies and curses of
earlier days — Henry's prophecy " that Richmond
should be king "; the curse laid upon Margaret by
Richard, Duke of York — and these, too, are remembered and fulfilled.*

As a matter of fact, it is hard to find dreams and
prophecies in Shakespeare which are *not* fulfilled.†
In *Richard III*, Hastings receives a warning from
Stanley. " This night," says the messenger,

> He dreamt the boar had razed off his helm.
> (III, 2, 10)

Hastings does not hearken; and he pays for his
incredulity with his life. Stanley escapes. The
emphasis is all on Hastings — and in drama it is
emphasis which counts. In the *Second Part of
Henry VI*, Gloucester describes to his Duchess the
" troublous dream " which has saddened him.
She makes light of it, and tells him of the dream
she has had:

> Methought I sat in seat of majesty
> In the cathedral church of Westminster,
> And in that chair where kings and queens are crown'd;
> Where Henry and Dame Margaret kneel'd to me,
> And on my head did set the diadem.   (I, 2, 36)

---

* IV, 2, 94 ff., I, 3, 174 ff.; *cf. 3 H. VI*, IV, 6, 68 ff., I, 4, 164.
† But see pages 158, 159, above.

This dream, of course, does not come true: nor is there any need that it should, if, as seems likely, the Duchess made up the whole thing. She has an obvious motive for doing so. Again, when Henry IV is expostulating with his son he tells him:

> The hope and expectation of thy time
> Is ruin'd, and the soul of every man
> Prophetically do forethink thy fall.

But we already know Prince Hal well enough to have our own opinions about his future. Hotspur's dying words —" O! I could prophesy "— are more to the point.* As for the sinister croak of Brabantio, at the end of the senate scene in *Othello* —

> Look to her, Moor, if thou hast eyes to see:
> She has deceiv'd her father, and may thee —

wrong as the sequel shows him to be, still he speaks a kind of truth. " My life upon her faith! " is Othello's answer. The passage is not ironic, precisely, yet it shades off into irony. A literal fulfilment of prophecy would be far less terrible.

Curses, on the other hand, frequently miss their mark. The fatalism of Shakespeare is not that of Greek tragedy. He was, it is clear, far more interested in the emotions of the imprecator than in the working out of the imprecation. *Richard III* is exceptional. For in *Richard III* a special problem, the dramatic representation of factional hate,

* *1 H. IV*, iii, 2, 36; v, 4, 83.

carried forward from the past and renewed under
a tyranical king, found, in Margaret's malediction
and its fulfilment, an artistic solution. When, however, in *Richard II*, the Duchess of Gloucester curses
Mowbray —

> O! sit my husband's wrongs on Hereford's spear,
> That it may enter butcher Mowbray's breast.
> Or if misfortune miss the first career,
> Be Mowbray's sins so heavy in his bosom
> That they may break his foaming courser's back,
> And throw the rider headlong in the lists! —

her words have no effect. The duel is stopped; and
Mowbray, after his long wars against the pagans,
dies peacefully.[*] Similarly, the impassioned curse
levelled by Coriolanus against the Roman people
does them no harm; and, in *Lear*, Goneril's death is
not accompanied by any reference to

> Th' untented woundings of a father's curse.[†]

Sometimes, as we shall see, the essential import
of a play finds expression in the prophetical utterance of a chorus character like Antony, in *Julius
Caesar*, or Exeter, in the *First Part of Henry VI*,
" The sense of a recurrent pattern " in Shakespeare's histories is derived, in great part, from
his use of prophecies.[‡] Richard's admonitions

---

[*] I, 2, 47; IV, i, 91 ff.
[†] *Cor.*, III, 3, 118 ff. *Lear*, I, 4, 324.
[‡] See Miss Bradbrook, *Elizabethan Stage Conditions*, 72, 73.

to Northumberland, in *Richard II*, are repeated, musingly, by Henry, far on in the *Second Part of Henry IV.** Henry VI hails the advent of Richmond to the English throne — and his saying is remembered when the time for its accomplishment draws near. The evil witches in *Macbeth* " have more in them than mortal knowledge "; and even the trumpery Spirit which is conjured up for Duchess Eleanor foretells the future with disconcerting accuracy. [†]

Finally, in two plays — *The Winter's Tale* and *Hamlet* — there are supernatural pronouncements which require careful attention. The " seal'd-up oracle " brought from Delphos by Cleomenes and Dion presents, it is true, only a momentary difficulty. The bearers are reported, at the end of the second act, to have reached Sicilia. They are " hasting to the court "; and, at the beginning of the third act, we see them waiting for fresh horses. [‡] Cleomenes and Dion are honest fellows who sympathize with Hermione. The low-pitched scene in which they talk of Delphos lends dignity to the oracle, and we become more and more eager to know what it contains. On the stage, indeed, the reading is definitely a climax:

* *R. II*, v, 1, 55 ff.; *2 H. IV*, III, 1, 65 ff.

† *Macb.*, I, 5, 3; *2 H. VI*, I, 4.

‡ The whereabouts of III, 1, is given by the New Cambridge editors as " Before an inn upon a high road in Sicilia," which does very well.

Hermione is chaste; Polixenes blameless; Camillo a true subject;
Leontes a jealous tyrant; his innocent babe truly begotten; and the king
shall live without an heir if that which is lost be not found!

(III, 2, 133)

Now Leontes, quite clearly, is not habitually either
jealous or tyrannical. An amiable king at the beginning of the play, he becomes the victim of an
obsession. He is " in rebellion with himself."*
To a definite question, however, the oracle gives a
peremptory answer. Leontes has been " a jealous
tyrant " in his recent conduct. To that, and that
alone, the oracle refers.

But how is the Ghost to be understood when he
speaks of Hamlet's " almost blunted purpose "?

After the performance of *The Mouse-trap*, Hamlet
is sent for by his mother. On his way to her
closet he has an opportunity to kill Claudius, but
does not take it — for reasons to be considered
later.† The scene with Gertrude opens violently.‡
She calls for help; and Hamlet kills Polonius, behind the arras, mistaking him for the King. Then,
in the lines which follow, an important point is established as unobtrusively as possible:

Queen.   O! what a rash and bloody deed is this!
Hamlet.   A bloody deed! almost as bad, good mother,
          As kill a king, and marry with his brother.   (III, 4, 27)

---

* I, 2, 355.   † Pages 295 ff., below.
‡ In the First Quarto Gertrude tells Claudius:
          I first bespake him faire,
    But then he throwes and tosses me about. . . .
Hamlet, nowadays, is inclined to be too gentle with his mother.

But the Queen does not understand what he means.
" As kill a king! " she says wonderingly. " Ay,
lady, 'twas my word." She was not, as Hamlet now
perceives, an accomplice in the murder; and he
turns at once to other matters.* His passion rises as
he talks of Claudius. Gertrude has yielded, but he
is not satisfied. In spite of her intreaties, he continues to denounce his uncle, falling at last into
mere railing:

> A cut-purse of the empire and the rule,
> That from a shelf the precious diadem stole,
> And put it in his pocket!
> Queen.   No more!
> Hamlet. A king of shreds and patches.

It is at this moment that the Ghost enters — not, as
before, in armor, but "in his habit as he liv'd."

> Hamlet. Save me, and hover o'er me with your wings,
>   You heavenly guards! What would your gracious
>   figure?
> Queen. Alas! he 's mad!
> Hamlet. Do you not come your tardy son to chide,
>   That, laps'd in time and passion, lets go by
>   The important acting of your dread command?
>   O! say.
> Ghost.   Do not forget: this visitation
>   Is but to whet thy almost blunted purpose.
>   But, look! amazement on thy mother sits;

---

* In the First Quarto Gertrude swears that she " neuer knew
of this most horride murder " (A. J. A. Waldock, *Hamlet: A Study
in Critical Method*, Cambridge [England], 1931, p. 64; see also, for
the Ghost, pp. 89–91).

O! step between her and her fighting soul;
Conceit in weakest bodies strongest works:
Speak to her, Hamlet.

No detailed consideration of the general problem
of Hamlet's delay is possible within the limits of the
present inquiry. Of late, indeed, the margins of
difference have been perceptibly narrowed. To some
critics the delay is wholly explained by difficulties
over which Hamlet has no control, particularly, the
necessity he is under of verifying what has been
told him by an apparition. When Hamlet says, in
soliloquy, "The spirit that I have seen / May be the
devil," it is plain that the Elizabethan audience
would have heard him with sympathy and understanding. By other critics, these difficulties are
sometimes granted, but they are not regarded as
essential. Rather, it is contended that what really
stands in the hero's way is a weakness in his own
character resulting from melancholy, as melancholy was understood by the Elizabethans. But
as some of these critics grant that Hamlet has, also,
obstacles to overcome which are not of his own
making, so some of those who absolve Hamlet from
responsibility for the delay admit that he is melancholy.*

The testimony of the Ghost is not neglected by
either side. Those who find Hamlet not at fault
show that it is the Ghost's function to urge ven-

---

* The foregoing statement is, of course, a drastic simplification.

geance. His reproaches are not reproaches at all, in Mr. Stoll's opinion, but exhortations.* Nor should the Ghost be expected to have much sympathy for Hamlet's previous doubts, knowing as he does that they are unfounded — that he is not a devil! † He is naturally impatient to have his commands obeyed. In any case, it is urged, he does not continue to chide his son, but immediately calls his attention to the distress and alarm of the Queen. If, on the other hand, the Ghost's statements are accepted at their face value, as reproaches, importance is attached to the fact that Hamlet himself anticipates the accusation —

Do you not come your tardy son to chide? . . .

Ghosts, too, were more or less traditionally informative in Elizabethan drama — as this one has already been.‡ His ' honesty,' questioned by Hamlet, has been triumphantly established. He comes from beyond the grave and has 'more in him than mortal knowledge.'§ If, he says, he were permitted

* *Hamlet*, 16; *Art and Artifice in Shakespeare*, 94 ff.

† This point is Professor Kittredge's. The ghost passionately, and quite humanly, reviles Claudius.

‡ Senecan Ghosts are very expository (*cf.* C. E. Whitmore, *The Supernatural in Tragedy*, Cambridge [Massachusetts], 1915, pp. 97 ff.).

§ " What the Ghost says is true . . . since, as every Elizabethan who believed in the ' honesty ' of ghosts would acknowledge, the Ghost sees Hamlet *sub specie eternitatis* and follows the secret motions of his heart " (J. Dover Wilson, ed., *Hamlet*, Cambridge [England], 1934, p. lxi).

to tell us the 'secrets of his prison-house,' they would
' harrow up our souls.'

This visitation
Is but to whet thy almost blunted purpose. . . .

Doubtless, the audience at the Globe knew how
the words were to be taken. At this distance it is
hard to be sure.

Chapter VII

THE CHORUS CHARACTER AND OTHERS

Prologue and Epilogue — Induction — Sly — Chorus
in *Henry V* — Gower — Chorus Character — Definition
and Relationships — Patmore's Point of Rest — Tags and
Sentences — Enobarbus — Other Chorus Characters —
Friar Laurence — Spokesman for Audience — Three
Varieties Distinguished — Gratiano — Kent — Paulina.

"ENTER PROLOGUE . . ." He appeared at
the third sounding of a trumpet, a dignified
personage in a " grave, long old cloak " of velvet,
standing on a traditional spot and making a traditional bow. Ours is " an old form of petition," *
says one of Beaumont and Fletcher's Prologues:

> The cloaks we wear, the legs we make, the place
> We stand in, must be one, and one the face, —
> Nor alter'd, nor exceeded.†

By way of novelty, Jonson begins *Cynthia's Revels*
with a group of child actors squabbling over possession of the Prologue's cloak; and Tom Heywood
brings on " three in black cloaks " (like the ravens

---

* The Prologue's pedigree is a long and complicated one. Sir
E. K. Chambers traces the mediaeval line to " the priest who
read the pseudo-Augustinian Christmas *lectio* from which the
Prophetae sprang " (*Mediaeval Stage*, II, 148). On the classical side,
there are the Chorus, and the very informative prologues of Latin
comedy.

† *The Humorous Lieutenant* (*Works*, ed. Dyce, VI, 419).

of the Ballad) to introduce his *Four Prentices of London*. *Troilus and Cressida* has an armed Prologue, suitable to its martial theme. The Prologue to the *Second Part of King Henry IV* is Rumor " painted full of tongues."

Sometimes a chorus speaks the prologue; sometimes the speaker of the prologue returns at intervals as an informal chorus. The important prologue to *Romeo and Juliet* is consigned to a chorus, which returns, however, only once — at the end of the first act — and then not too effectively.* Gower, on the other hand, does his duty by *Pericles*, acting as Prologue to the play and reappearing on seven occasions in the course of it. Another way of beginning was to dramatize one's preliminaries as a separate scene (the " Induction "), afterwards, if one chose, seating the characters on the upper stage to comment on the action and serve, themselves, as a framework for it. Epilogues, finally, were not yet the highly finished compositions which Dryden and his fellows turned out almost at will.† Shakespeare's tragedies are without epilogues. In his comedies they consist merely of an actor's falling out of his part to solicit the applause of the spectators. Rosa-

* One wonders whether at some time the Chorus may not have carried on throughout the play.

† See Autrey N. Wiley, " The English Vogue of Prologues and Epilogues," *Modern Language Notes*, XLVII (1932), pp. 255–257, for a reasonable explanation of the popularity of these appendages after 1660.

lind, doing so, becomes pert; Prospero, humble;
Feste sings " When that I was and a little tiny boy."
The epilogue to the *Second Part of King Henry IV* is
recited by a Dancer who makes misleading promises
about Falstaff and, at the end, drops on his knees to
pray for the Queen. The Chorus concludes *Henry
V*, and poor Gower, *Pericles*.

Of these forms, the Induction is used by Shakespeare only in *The Taming of the Shrew*, where the
sadly incomplete account of Christopher Sly is not
much more than a curtain-raiser. Sly is seated,
properly enough, on the upper stage when the play
itself begins. He is still there at the end of the first
scene.

First Servant. My lord, you nod; you do not mind the play.
Sly. Yes, by Saint Anne, I do. A good matter, surely: comes
        there any more of it?
Page. My lord, 'tis but begun.
Sly. 'Tis a very excellent piece of work, madam lady: would
        'twere done!

There is not a word more of him in Shakespeare.
Perhaps the Elizabethans were enough like some of
us to have insisted on knowing what became of him.
If so, what they got may have been the last pages of
the parallel farce, *The Taming of A Shrew*. In that,
Sly is lugged off, sound asleep, and deposited, in his
own clothes once more, outside the alehouse where
we first saw him. He is awakened by a tapster. He
has had, he says wistfully,

> The bravest dream to-night, that ever thou
> Heardest in all thy life.

The tapster warns him that his wife may make it hot for him. " Will she? " he replies:

> I know now how to tame a shrew!
> I dreamt upon it all this night till now. . . .
>
> But I 'll to my wife presently
> And tame her too, and if she anger me.*

Delightful as this Induction is, it has no tangible value as exposition. The three remaining forms, the prologue, epilogue, and chorus, all have: choruses and prologues consistently; epilogues, when spoken by a chorus. They are extra-dramatic forms, coming to us straight from the author, or the author's chosen intermediary, and their testimony on any point is conclusive. By comparison, even the Butler and the Housemaid, even the First and Second Gentlemen, lapse into unreliability. Samuel Daniel did, indeed, avow that the chorus to his neo-classical tragedy *Philotas* (1604) represented " the multitude and body of a people, who vulgarlie according to their affections . . . censure what is done." † But no public theatre audience of the time would, I am sure, have taken kindly to the distinction — even if they understood it.

---

* *The Taming of A Shrew*, ed. F. S. Boas (" The Shakespeare Classics "), 1908, pp. 64, 65. Though Shakespeare's fifth act is noticeably short, the play is pretty elaborately wound up as it is — without the Epilogue.

† Ed. 1605, sig. A7.

Turning now to particular plays, one finds that
the sonnet-prologue declaimed by a chorus at the
beginning of *Romeo and Juliet* interprets the tragedy.
It is a tragedy of youth arrayed against age, of love
against hate: the " ancient grudge " of the Houses;
the " death-mark'd " love which at length extin-
guishes it. Romeo and Juliet are wholly estimable.
They are " star-cross'd lovers,"

> Whose misadventur'd piteous overthrows
> Do with their death bury their parents' strife —

the " rage " which could be removed only by their
immolation. The interpretation, which is perfectly
unequivocal, may be accepted without misgiving.
That it has not always been accepted, we shall see
presently. The Prologue to *King Henry VIII* is again
concerned with the play as a whole. It is to be
something more than the old-fashioned chronicle
plays, all " fool and fight," of twenty years before —
a dignified representation of national history,

> Sad, high, and working, full of state and woe.

So much is said, indeed, about the seriousness with
which what follows is to be taken that the Prologue
itself has been called misleading, " since the last
lines . . . promise us a tragedy, and the Fifth Act is
far from tragic." * Rumor, on the other hand, who
acts as Prologue to the *Second Part of King Henry IV*,

---

* *King Henry VIII*, ed. Berdan and Brooke (" The Yale Shakespeare "), 119.

confines himself to sounding the note of preparation for the opening scene.

It is but a step from Rumor's picture of the " worm-eaten hold of ragged stone " where " old Northumberland/Lies crafty-sick," to the choral preludes which are introduced before the successive acts of *King Henry V*. " In their sublimity and lyric fervour, these monologues," Professor Mackail writes, " are unique . . . the voice of Shakespeare speaking for himself, for his colleagues, and for his profession." * By an understandable train of reasoning, they are sometimes explained as serving a merely utilitarian purpose, or, in other words, as originating in the very inadequacies of the Elizabethan stage against which they protest. Protest they assuredly do. But it is, perhaps, only in the nature of things that a great creative artist should at moments become dissatisfied with his métier. In spite of its makeshifts, its inadequacy — partly, indeed, because of them — the Elizabethan stage partook in large measure of the ideal. Shakespeare complains, it is true, of the four or five " ragged foils " who must do duty for him as Agincourt armies. But even today, after three centuries, do we ever see on our stage battle scenes (with or without horses) which are much more than a makeshift? I recall one such scene, I admit, but only one — and that in a performance of Rubinstein's *Démon* by a

* *The Approach to Shakespeare*, Oxford, 1930, pp. 56, 57.

small and impoverished opera troupe from the
Russian provinces! Marlowe dreams of " one
poem's period " which should express, what must
remain inexpressible, the poet's sense of beauty.
Shakespeare dreams of " a Muse of fire,"

> A kingdom for a stage, princes to act
> And monarchs to behold the swelling scene.

As a matter of fact, he did not have to write
these choruses at all. The " abuse of distance "
and " the jumping o'er times " are no greater in
Henry V than they are in some of his other histories,
not to mention *Antony and Cleopatra*. If on occasion
he descends to writing programme notes — the
naming of the conspirators, in the Second Chorus,
and the curious indication of place,

> But, till the king come forth and not till then,
> Unto Southampton do we shift our scene —

he writes, too, of the splendor of King Harry's fleet
at sea, describing things which a novelist might describe, or a narrative poet, but which lay beyond his
immediate concern as a playwright. Moreover,
though few nocturnal descriptions in English sur-
pass his Fourth Chorus, there is vivid suggestion of
the night before Agincourt in the text of the play, as
well. In particular, here are once more the definite
time notes which we have come to think of as
Shakespearean. " It now draws toward night,"

Henry says at the end of Act Three, Scene Six:

> Beyond the river we 'll encamp ourselves.

The next scene shows us the French nobles waiting impatiently for morning; but it is still only " midnight," after a hundred lines, and " two o'clock," at the end.   " By ten," Orleans boasts,

> We shall have each a hundred Englishmen.

Darkness continues through the long opening scene of Act Four.   Henry, unrecognized in a borrowed cloak, goes the rounds of the English camp, the effect being gained by means of a series of reversed entrances instead of a series of short scenes (thus, Pistol enters to challenge the King instead of the King's reentering to be challenged by Pistol).   At the beginning, Henry comments on how early they are all up, and he salutes Erpingham with a cheerful " Good Morrow."   Court asks Bates:

Court.   Brother John Bates, is not that the morning which breaks yonder?
Bates.   I think it be so; but we have no great cause to desire the approach of day.
Williams. We see yonder the beginning of the day, but I think we shall never see the end of it. Who goes there?

> (IV, 1, 88)

But Bates, a few lines later, drops the phrase, " as cold a night as 'tis," and at the end Henry recognizes Gloucester by his voice.   It is only in the sec-

ond scene that the sunshine gilds the armor of the
Frenchmen and they move to the field with

> The sun is high, and we outwear the day.

That at times these *Henry V* choruses serve the
prosaic function of supplying information is perhaps
the least essential thing about them. Far from
being, in any true sense, a reflection on the ade-
quacy of the Elizabethan stage, they appeal
throughout for just the quality in their hearers
which that stage peculiarly fostered. We in
the audience, Shakespeare says, are not exempt
from obligation. We must ' work, work our
thoughts,' ' piecing out ' the imperfections of his art
by the completeness of our surrender to it —

> Minding true things by what their mockeries be.

Shakespeare, if we are to believe some of his critics, is never Shakespeare unless he is at his best. So
because Time, in *The Winter's Tale*, is a dull old dog,
meanly endowed poetically as compared with his
brother chorus in *Henry V*, the legitimacy of his
descent has often been questioned. He is quite indispensable, however. Creizenach, describing the
temporal continuity characteristic of Elizabethan
drama — a continuity which, as we have seen, led
to such bizarre manifestations as the phenomenon of
" double time " — says sweepingly that he knows of

no English drama of this period where there is any necessity, as
there is in so many modern plays, to announce specifically that

" Two years elapse between the fourth and fifth acts," or something similar. . . . *The Winter's Tale* [is] the only one of Shakespeare's dramas where anything of the kind occurs.*

The Winter's Tale belongs, furthermore, to the
period of

> Myself, Belarius, that am Morgan call'd,

and of

> Twelve year since, Miranda, twelve year since,†

a period when the master sometimes nods — secure
in his accomplishment, bored, seemingly, with
technical details. A chorus was, in this instance,
such an obvious way out! And, having chosen
Time, Shakespeare may have found him no more
exhilarating than we do.

The most comprehensive of the extra-dramatic
parts is, however, that of Gower in *Pericles*. In some
three hundred lines of bald octosyllabics (the verse
of the real Gower, relieved on three occasions by
pentameters) he performs a truly astonishing variety of functions. He introduces himself and his
story; pleads for a quiet and attentive hearing; urges
the audience, also, to use their imagination and
" hold," if need be, " this stage the ship" (III, prol.,
58). He apologizes for the liberties taken with time
and place, and goes out of his way to ask pardon for
the use of one language throughout the play —

---

* *The English Drama in the Age of Shakespeare*, 251.
† See pages 72, 73, 115, above.

" one language in each several clime / Where our scenes seem to live " (IV, 4, prol., 6) — a convention which even realists seldom boggle at.* *Pericles* is conceived of as a story, Gower ' standing i ' the gaps ' to narrate the less actable chapters:

> And what ensues in this fell storm
> Shall for itself itself perform.
> I nill relate, action may
> Conveniently the rest convey,
> Which might not what by me is told.
>
> (III, prol., 53)

Usually, he brings us exactly to the point where we are to resume.† Thus the " cursed Dionyza " (he never hesitates to take sides) has feed an assassin to do away with Marina, and Gower concludes:

> Dionyza doth appear,
> With Leonine, a murderer —

whereupon " *Enter* Dionyza *and* Leonine," and Dionyza says:

> Thy oath remember; thou hast sworn to do 't.
>
> (IV, 1, 1)

At times, indeed, the story proceeds by still a third method. Gower will suddenly break off his narrative to introduce the representation of some important transitional episode in dumb show, acting himself as Presenter. As such, he appears in a rôle

---

* *Cf.* page 60, above.
† In some respects, Gower's function is thus precisely like that of the announcer in our radio plays.

which respectable Elizabethan choruses now and
then condescended to assume, not, however, without some loss of prestige. " What 's dumb in
show," says Gower, bravely, " I 'll plain with
speech " (III, prol., 14).* After all, he has only to
wait. The epilogue is a choice morsel, all solemnity
and edification. ' You have attended,' he says in
effect, ' a play in which the virtuous prosper and
the wicked miscarry.'

> In Antiochus and his daughter you have heard
> Of monstrous lust the due and just reward:
> In Pericles, his queen, and daughter, seen —
> Although assail'd with fortune fierce and keen —
> Virtue preserv'd from fell destruction's blast,
> Led on by heaven, and crown'd with joy at last.

As for Cleon and " cursed Dionyza," they came to a
bad end too:

> The gods for murder seemed so content
> To punish them; *although not done, but meant.*

*　　*　　*

" Les prétendus *choeurs* de Shakespeare," writes
Stapfer with a touch of Gallic condescension, " ne
sont que des prologues; mais il y a dans son théâtre

---

* *Cf.* Miss M. G. McCaulley, " Non-Organic Elements in
English Drama," *Studies in English Drama*, ed. Allison Gaw, University of Pennsylvania, 1917, pp. 177, 178; Miss F. A. Foster,
" Dumb Show in Elizabethan Drama," *Englische Studien*, XLIV
(1911). The *Hamlet* dumb show, presenting in straight pantomime
everything that is to follow in the play, is altogether exceptional.
Hamlet puts the screws on the King from the very beginning!

d'autres personnages qui . . . réalisent en partie le rôle idéal du choeur antique." * Such a personage, the so-called " chorus character," is quite distinct from the figures we have just been considering. They are extra-dramatic, he is dramatic. Although his testimony is at times inspired, it comes to us less directly than that of Chorus or Prologue. He has his own life to live, such as it is, his own soul to save, in the little world of the dramatist's making. And mingling familiarly with the other persons in the play, he is on occasion subject like them to the criticism of the extra-dramatic figures speaking for the author. Macilente, for instance, in *Every Man Out of his Humor*, is a recognized sort of chorus character — the Jonsonian " demonstrator " who explains and tickets the eccentricities of the comic butts — † but he is exposed, in his turn, to the comments of Cordatus and Mitis. For Cordatus, who is " the author's friend; a man inly acquainted with the scope and drift of his plot," and Mitis, who confines himself to asking Cordatus the right questions, are Ben's " Grex or Chorus," personages carried forward from the Induction to serve as a frame to the play.

---

* *Shakespeare et L'Antiquité*, Paris, 1880, II, 106.

† See Miss E. Woodbridge, *Studies in Jonson's Comedy*, " Yale Studies in English," 1898, pp. 31–33; Albert S. Borgman, *Thomas Shadwell*, New York, 1928, pp. 130, 251. Shakespeare has, I think, no example of the " demonstrator " pure and simple. The Boy's exposure of Pistol, Nym & Co. in *Henry V* (III, 2, 30 ff.) may, however, be compared.

When we discuss the chorus character it is usually as part of a larger subject. What corresponds, we ask, in Shakespearean drama to the tragic chorus of the Greeks? Many and subtle have been the answers. Coleridge found one in " the exquisite lyric intermixtures " of Shakespeare and in his practice of " making general truths the outburst of passion." * Morgann limited his " censure of the Chorus to its supposed use of comment and interpretation." This, he says, is paralleled in Shakespeare, who

seldom trusts to the apprehensions of his audience; his characters interpret for one another continually, and when we least suspect such artful and secret management. . . . I could point out a thousand passages which might put to shame the advocates of a formal Chorus, and prove that there is as little of necessity as grace in so mechanic a contrivance.

And Morgann boldly cites Enobarbus as " in effect " the Chorus of *Antony and Cleopatra*, " as Menenius Agrippa is of *Coriolanus*." † " If the popular Elizabethan playwright had no chorus," writes Mr. Lucas,

on the other hand he could have on the stage at once not three characters only, but almost as many as he chose. And a single one of these, like Enobarbus in *Antony and Cleopatra*, might suffice by himself to do much of the work the chorus once performed.

---

* *Shakespearean Criticism*, ed. T. M. Raysor, I, 230; *cf*. II, 16.
† *Essay on the Dramatic Character of Sir John Falstaff*, 77, 78.

Moreover, " where the Greek Chorus served as a foil," Shakespeare " has his meaner characters, his citizens, his crowds, his clowns." He too employs " lyric relief " and " dark presentiment."

> In *Hamlet*, again, the work of the ancient Chorus is divided between Horatio, and the gravediggers, and Fortinbras . . . and, above all, Hamlet himself, whose " To be or not to be? " might be a chorus of Euripides.*

There is, finally, the answer of Raleigh:

> Shakespeare had no Chorus, but he attains the same end in another way. In almost all his plays there is a clear enough point of view; there is some character, or group of characters, through whose eyes the events of the play must be seen, if they are to be seen in right perspective. Some of his characters he keeps nearer to himself than others. The meaning of *Love's Labour's Lost* cannot be read through the eyes of Armado, nor that of *Twelfth Night* through the eyes of Malvolio.†

The chorus character may also be studied without reference to Greece or Rome. Shakespeare when he was writing a play did not, presumably, give much thought to devising equivalents for the classical chorus — whether of Sophocles, whom he may not have read, or Seneca, whom he never directly imitated. He did give thought, we know, to making important points as clear as possible. Enobarbus and the other chorus characters served him admirably here. And if they are Elizabethan in immediate origin, their counterparts still flourish

---

* *Tragedy*, "Hogarth Lectures on Literature," 1927, pp. 67–71.
† *Shakespeare*, 152.

today. But it is time to attempt a definition. A chorus character is one of the *dramatis personae* — often not a principal — who sums up a number of episodes in the play or whose remarks have obvious appropriateness as an interpretation of the play as a whole. This interpretation, when we get it, may be regarded as the author's clue to how his play is to be taken: it is artistic; not necessarily personal.* Thus, Thersites, in *Troilus and Cressida*, and Kate, at the end of *The Taming of the Shrew*, are chorus characters, but their opinions on heroism and conjugal felicity are quite possibly not those of Shakespeare, who yet asks that they be accepted in a bitter comedy and a farce. Finally, a chorus character is not dependent on either the length or the dignity of his rôle.

A principle of Elizabethan dramatic technique is, as we have seen, that the audience should always be kept informed of what is going on. No wonder, then, that the contemporary relationships of this arch-expositor, the chorus character, are wide, the degrees of kinship difficult to determine. There is the Presenter, for instance. Gower, interpreting the dumb shows in *Pericles*, is extra-dramatic; so in his way is Quince, interpreting the dumb show in the " tedious brief scene " of *Pyramus and Thisbe*.

* One may guess that the Chorus at the end of *Faustus* is not expressing Marlowe's own sentiments — nor is it called upon to do so! Ardsley, at the end of *For Services Rendered* (1932), is Mr. Maugham's bitterly ironic variation on the chorus character.

But, in *King Henry VIII*, the Coronation Procession (one of those many " shows " promised by the Prologue) is interpreted in full by our old friends the First and Second Gentlemen; * and is not Macbeth himself very much like a Presenter to Banquo's spectral " Show of Kings" ? † There is also the epilogue by one of the actors, who drops out of his part to speak it. So the actor who did Prospero has these lines:

> Now my charms are all o'erthrown,
> And what strength I have 's mine own;
> Which is most faint: now, 't is true,
> I must be here confin'd by you,
> Or sent to Naples. Let me not,
> Since I have my dukedom got
> And pardon'd the deceiver, dwell
> In this bare island by your spell;
> But release me from my bands
> With the help of your good hands. . . .

Richard Grant White could make nothing of them, and of course set them down as apocryphal. Why, he asks, should Prospero beg to be freed " from the bands of necromancy" when he is a mighty ma-

* As if the omniscience of the Gentlemen needed excuse, the First is furnished with a list, the Second knows the court ceremonial and can do without one (IV, 1, 13 ff.).

† Another kinsman of the chorus character's — a distant cousin perhaps — is the " Interpreter " in puppet shows. Hamlet refers to him during the acting of *The Mouse-trap*: " You are a good chorus, my lord," Ophelia says; and he snaps her up with, " I could interpret between you and your love, if I could see the puppets dallying " (III, 2, 259).

gician, and is " no longer a magician " ? But Prospero is not speaking now — only the actor who had been Prospero. . . .* As for Mrs. Page, she cannot wait for the end of *The Merry Wives of Windsor* but declaims what is very like an epilogue while poor Sir John is still disguising himself as the fat woman:

> We 'll leave a proof, by that which we will do,
> Wives may be merry, and yet honest too:
> We do not act that often jest and laugh;
> 'T is old, but true, " Still swine eats all the draff."
>
> (IV, 2, 109)

There are, finally, the concluding speeches of recapitulation and dismissal. These are sometimes clearly choral. The references, at the end of *Romeo and Juliet*, to love and hate and sacrifice echo the choral prologue to the tragedy. Richmond, closing *King Richard III*, dwells on the long years when England was mad, and on the lasting cure which has come with the union of " the white rose and the red." When Faulconbridge, a thoroughgoing chorus character, sounds his note of Elizabethan patriotism at the end of *King John*, distinctions seem altogether obliterated, and one recalls with effort that the final speech in Shakespeare is sometimes *not* choral and that it has perceptible characteristics of its own.†

* Furness, *Variorum Shakespeare*, 267, 268.
† See pages 130–132, above.

So much for the Elizabethan relationships of the chorus character. His ancestry, fortunately, needs no tracing; is conterminous, even, with the very beginnings of drama. The chorus character has always been. It is true that the rigorous impositions of the dramatic form — personation and the telling of the tale through dialogue and action alone — have continually threatened his existence. He survives because writers of plays have insisted on his survival; at best, respecting his integrity while they exploit him, at worst, turning him into a stalking-horse for their own sermonizing. Thus, Walter sums up the significance of Mr. Granville-Barker's *Waste* in a speech which gains impressiveness by its position * and is made unmistakably " choral " by its echoing of the title: " Grief is no use. I 'm angry . . just angry at the waste of a good man. Look at the work undone . . think of it! Who is to do it! Oh . . the waste . .! " And there is Jones, speaking no less certainly for Galsworthy, near the end of *The Silver Box*: " Call this justice? What about 'im? 'E got drunk! 'E took the purse — 'e took the purse but [*in a muffled shout*] its 'is *money* got '*im* off — *Justice!* " And naming at random now: Peter Mottram in *Mid-Channel* (a familiar type in Pinero's plays); and Dr. Relling, in *The Wild Duck*; and

* Walter's speech is quoted by Rupert Brooke in a suggestive passage on modern parallels to the classical chorus (*John Webster and the Elizabethan Drama*, 142, 143).

Henry Smithers, in *The Emperor Jones*; and Cokeson, in *Justice*; and Mortimer Quinn, in *Point Valaine*; and both Horn and MacPhail, in *Rain* — all are chorus characters. Mr. Shaw makes no bones of violating the rules. But I do not remember that many persons squirmed when, at the première of *Too True to Be Good*, a character casually strolled down to the footlights, just before the end of the first scene, to tell us that ' the play was now over ' — in the two acts to follow there would only be Bernard Shaw philosophizing.

As defined, the chorus character is not dependent on either the length or the dignity of his rôle. Often, indeed, he is kept a bit removed emotionally from the full brunt of the conflict, and Coventry Patmore in a notable essay, "The Point of Rest in Art," makes this removal attractive. The point of rest, he writes,

is not in itself the most but the least interesting point in the whole work. It is the *punctum indifferens* to which all that is interesting is more or less unconsciously referred. . . . In proportion to the extent and variety of points of interest in a painting or a poem the necessity for this point of rest seems to increase. . . . It is accordingly in the most elaborate plays of Shakespeare that we find this device in its fullest value.

From these plays he draws his illustrations:

In *King Lear* it is by the character of Kent, in *Romeo and Juliet* by Friar Laurence, in *Hamlet* by Horatio, in *Othello* by Cassio, and in the *Merchant of Venice* by Bassanio, that the point of rest is supplied. . . . Each of these five characters stands out of the stream of the main interest, and is additionally unimpressive in itself by reason of its absolute conformity to reason and moral order from which every other character in the play departs more or less. Thus Horatio is the exact *punctum indifferens* between the opposite excesses of the characters of Hamlet and Laertes — over-reasoning inaction and unreasoning action.

Now Horatio is clearly a chorus character and Friar Laurence is often mistaken for one. Moreover, we are apt to think of the chorus character in terms of the Greek tragic chorus, which surely offers just such a point of rest. But, on the other hand, no one would call Bassanio and Cassio chorus characters; * and some chorus characters, notably Antony in *Julius Caesar*, are neither removed from passionate participation in the action nor furnish a *punctum indifferens* or point of rest. † Patmore's idea remains a valuable one, and it is beautifully exemplified in Banquo and one or two other personages presently to be considered. It has, yet, no essential connection with our definition. ‡

The part of the chorus character may be long or short. That the significance of one of yesterday's thesis plays could be suggested, however, in a single clean-cut phrase like " Oh . . the waste . .! " or " 'Is *money* got '*im* off," does not help us much with

---

* Sir Arthur Quiller-Couch, who makes much of Patmore's theory, would substitute Antonio for Bassanio (*Shakespeare's Workmanship*, 45 ff.).

† In *Bussy D'Ambois*, v, 2, Chapman allows two villains, Monsieur and the Guise, to sum up the tragedy.

‡ Something very like the point of rest may be found in comedy as well as tragedy. One remembers, for instance, those distressingly ordinary beings, the Carvers, in Mr. Coward's *Design for Living*.

Shakespeare, since no play of his — not even *Measure for Measure* — is strictly speaking a thesis play. Yet all are strewn, chorus-like, with moral sentences, with " precepts and axioms." Historical criticism is ready enough to explain their presence. The audience — an English audience, mind, though an Elizabethan one — liked them. They were encouraged, too, by stage conditions which made the rhymed " tag " convenient for an actor to spout before his exit — just as, somewhat later, stage conditions encouraged that analogous abomination, the sententious curtain line. The temptation remains to seize upon some single generalization — removing it from its speaker and the context in which it appears — and call it Shakespeare's own interpretation of his play. Thus, two lines,

> As flies to wanton boys, are we to the gods;
> They kill us for their sport, (IV, 1, 36)

have been taken as summing up all the diffused significance of *King Lear*. For answer, there is Bradley's *Shakespearean Tragedy*. The lines remain Gloucester's lines, and they are spoken just before his attempt at self-destruction. Mr. J. Dover Wilson, who does not accept their broader import, jumps at a grim remark of Edgar's in the last scene:

> The gods are just, and of our pleasant vices
> Make instruments to plague us:
> The dark and vicious place where thee he got
> Cost him his eyes. (v, 3, 172)

This he calls " much more likely to express Shake-speare's own sentiments," coming as it does from " the son who loves Gloucester," and it brings out at least " one point which is vital to grasp . . . the idea of expiation." * Of a contrary opinion is Creizenach, who points out that Edmund treats Gloucester no worse than the legitimate children of Lear treat him.† Edgar, by the way, might with his reflective habit have made a very good chorus char-acter; and the fact that he is not has of course noth-ing to do with the length of his part. A last instance of the singling out of a few words as an open sesame to the meaning of a whole Shakespearean play (this time a comedy) comes from Dowden. In the third scene of *All's Well*, the Countess of Rousillon orders the Clown from the room:

Countess. You'll be gone, sir knave, and do as I command you!
Clown. That man should be at woman's command, and yet no
     hurt done!   (I, 3, 95)

Dowden picks up the Clown's speech and makes much of it, but rather as a motto, or starting point, for his own delicately impressionistic critique. For him, the words ' man at woman's command and yet no hurt done ' describe *All's Well*; he does not intimate that they were intended to do so.‡

Before we come to consider the individual chorus

* *Six Tragedies of Shakespeare*, London, etc., 1929, p. 37.
† *The English Drama in the Age of Shakespeare*, 123.
‡ *Shakspere: A Critical Study*, 76.

characters, it is perhaps worth noting that they are not clustered in any single period of Shakespeare's career. Berowne belongs to its very beginnings; Cranmer, to its very end. Chorus characters abound in the tragedies and in the histories. They are proportionately less numerous in the comedies. But though *Twelfth Night*, and the high comedy group as a whole, can get along without them, to the accompaniment of strains of music and the laughter of the Fool, in the dark comedies, so much less easy of comprehension, chorus characters reappear, and among others Thersites, a shining light. No one of them all, however, has gained more general recognition than Domitius Enobarbus, in *Antony and Cleopatra*.

Enobarbus is, of course, intensely interesting in himself — a fine example of the way Shakespeare can wipe out the distinction between major and minor characters. That first Jacobean audience found him, one may suppose, a bit enigmatic at the outset. Antony is very serious in the second scene of the tragedy; Enobarbus speaks lightly. But there is a sting in his words, too, which some in the audience would perceive. If we leave Alexandria, he says, it will be the death of our women:

Antony. I must be gone.
Enobarbus. Under a compelling occasion let women die; it were pity to cast them away for nothing; though between them and a great cause they should be esteemed

> nothing. Cleopatra, catching but the least noise of this, dies instantly; I have seen her die twenty times upon far poorer moment.   (I, 2, 145)

His rôle of chorus character begins, really, only in the second scene of Act Two. There we see him, at the beginning, putting off Lepidus, who would have him aid in establishing friendly relations between Antony and Octavius. Enobarbus, like Menas in the expository scene just before, takes the realistic view that such relations cannot last — so why encourage them?

> *Lepidus.*   'T is not a time
> For private stomaching.
> *Enobarbus.*   Every time
> Serves for the matter that is then born in 't.
> *Lepidus.*   But small to greater matters must give way.
> *Enobarbus.* Not if the small come first.   (II, 2, 8)

He speaks up once during the conference, cutting through its pretences, but he is promptly checked by Antony: " Thou art a soldier only; speak no more." " That truth," he grumbles, " should be silent I had almost forgot." Up to this point, he is, in Mr. Granville-Barker's words, " a simple variant of the outspoken, honest, disillusioned fellow, a type very useful to the dramatist lacking a chorus." But he " is not all prose and fault-finding." * Left with Mecaenas and Agrippa, he describes, with all conceivable gorgeousness, the meeting of Antony and Cleo-

---

* *Prefaces to Shakespeare,* 2nd Series, p. 225.

patra on the river Cydnus, then, by the easiest of
transitions, comes to Cleopatra herself and the spells
which she casts over all who see her. As if application were needed, Mecaenas remarks, with the conference still in mind: " Now Antony must leave her
utterly." " Never; he will not," Enobarbus replies.
Four scenes later, he is talking with Pompey, who
praises his courage:

Pompey.   Let me shake thy hand;
    I never hated thee. I have seen thee fight,
    When I have envied thy behaviour.
Enobarbus.   Sir,
    I never lov'd you much, but I ha' prais'd ye
    When you have well deserv'd ten times as much
    As I have said you did.
Pompey.   Enjoy thy plainness,
    It nothing ill becomes thee. (II, 6, 73)

No audience could resist that sort of thing! From
now on, he would be trusted implicitly.

Mr. Lucas has shown that the chorus-like testimony of Enobarbus has a threefold bearing:

Is the past to be recalled [he writes]? Enobarbus will describe in poetry as vivid as an ode of Aeschylus how Cleopatra
first came to the arms of Antony. . . . Is comment needed
on the present? Enobarbus will reflect on the infatuation of
his master. . . . And if a hint of the future is required, Enobarbus can forebode it.*

There is an instance of such foreboding in the talk
with Menas, at the end of the scene (II, 6). Enobar-

* *Tragedy,* 67–69.

bus is quite explicit now. The friendship of Antony and Caesar will be destroyed by the very means they have adopted to insure its continuance. " Octavia is of a holy, cold, and still conversation "; Antony "will to his Egyptian dish again," and Octavia's sighs will " blow the fire up in Caesar." * By the fifth scene of the following act events have almost caught up with the prediction, and Enobarbus (this time talking with Eros) is ready to take account of them:

> Then, world, thou hast a pair of chaps, no more;
> And throw between them all the food thou hast,
> They 'll grind the one the other.   (III, 5, 14)

The disaster at Actium is foreshadowed in his expostulations: he urges Cleopatra not to accompany Antony, and Antony not to fight at sea (III, 7). When it comes, Enobarbus perceives at once that Canidius will desert to Caesar. But his own thoughts are by no means at one: " I 'll yet follow," he says,

> The wounded chance of Antony, though my reason
> Sits in the wind against me.   (III, 8, 44)

We are ready now for the two very remarkable scenes (III, 11 and IV, 2) to which, perhaps, Enobarbus chiefly owes his eminence among chorus characters. He is wavering in his allegiance; undecided

---

* As for Lepidus — the " poor third " in the triumvirate — Enobarbus of course perceives that he is a nonentity (*cf.* III, 2, 1–20).

whether Antony is worthy of his devotion — for he
knows, or believes, that

> The loyalty well held to fools does make
> Our faith mere folly. (III, 11, 42)

So he watches critically, with all his natural acuteness of observation sharpened by his need of observing. Nothing escapes him. Nothing must! And all
the while, by means of the aside convention we are
seeing through his eyes. But first, replying to Cleopatra's straight question as to the responsibility for
Actium —

> Is Antony or we, in fault for this? —

he gives a straight answer:

> Antony only, that would make his will
> Lord of his reason. (III, 11, 3)

His words are interrupted by the entrance of Antony, who has just received Caesar's message. Antony will reply to it (as Hotspur might) with a challenge to single combat. And Enobarbus says, aside:

> Yes, like enough, high-battled Caesar will
> Unstate his happiness, and be stag'd to the show
> Against a sworder! . . .
>
>   Caesar, thou hast subdu'd
> His judgment too. (III, 11, 29)

Thyreus comes from Octavius. Enobarbus watches
Cleopatra with him, and draws the obvious conclusion that she is playing a double game:

> Sir, sir, thou 'rt so leaky,
> That we must leave thee to thy sinking, for
> Thy dearest quit thee.*

Then comes Antony's order to whip the messenger, and Enobarbus comments again:

> 'T is better playing with a lion's whelp
> Than with an old one dying.
>
> (III, 11, 94)

At the end of the scene he has made up his mind:

> Now he 'll outstare the lightning. To be furious
> Is to be frighted out of fear, and in that mood
> The dove will peck the estridge; and I see still,
> A diminution in our captain's brain
> Restores his heart. When valour preys on reason
> It eats the sword it fights with. I will seek
> Some way to leave him.

Early in the fourth act, Antony assembles his household servants, speaks to each in turn, takes their hands. Cleopatra turns quickly to Enobarbus:

Cleopatra.   What means this?
Enobarbus. 'T is one of those odd tricks which sorrow shoots
                Out of the mind.   (IV, 2, 13)

Antony goes on:

> Well, my good fellows, wait on me tonight,
> Scant not my cups, and make as much of me
> As when mine empire was your fellow too,
> And suffer'd my command.

Cleopatra.   What does he mean?
Enobarbus. To make his followers weep.

---

* III, 11, 63. How nearly right he is, at this point, it is perhaps impossible to determine.

Soldier-like, he is still trying to be cynical.* A few lines more, and he has broken down:

> What mean you, sir,
> To give them this discomfort? Look, they weep;
> And I, an ass, am onion-ey'd. (IV, 2, 33)

When next we see him, he is in Caesar's camp, and his rôle as chorus has come to an end.†

This running commentary of his, on the tragic action, sets off Enobarbus from two other chorus characters, Horatio and Banquo. Horatio, who besides being Hamlet's official apologist, at the end of the play, is his confidant through much of it, does indeed drop remarks along the way which have value as an explanation of what is happening; Banquo is a chorus character partly by virtue of what he is and does, partly by virtue of a single speech of his, which may be supposed to have reference to the tragedy as a whole. Over and above the gift of quiet humor which (as Professor Kittredge has shown) they both possess, there are marked similarities between them. Thus, in *Hamlet* and *Macbeth* alike, one finds the sudden intrusion of the supernatural. A secret is imparted, which profoundly affects the protagonist, and Banquo in the one case,

---

* *Cf.* MacCallum, *Shakespeare's Roman Plays*, 408.

† As if missing him, Shakespeare turns later to Scarus, who has one expository speech of the same sort as those of Enobarbus (IV, 10, 16 ff.; *cf.* also III, 8, 16–18). Dryden uses the comments of Alexas and Ventidius very similarly in the *All for Love* persuasion scenes.

Horatio in the other, shares in the knowledge of it. Each is, moreover, as Patmore defined it, a " point of rest." Hamlet's praise of Horatio as one who is not " passion's slave,"

> A man that fortune's buffets and rewards
> Hast ta'en with equal thanks,*

is obviously pertinent here, throwing light on Horatio, as it does also, indirectly, on Hamlet himself. As for Banquo, he supplies just this " sense of the norm ":

> He is — though on an enlarged scale, having to stand beside the " hero " — the Ordinary Man. Like Macbeth, he is a thane, a general, a gallant soldier. . . . They are brought upon the stage together, two equal friends returning from victory. To Banquo as to Macbeth the witches' predictions are offered. . . . But whereas Macbeth . . . grasps at the immediate means to the end, Banquo, like an ordinary, well-meaning, sensible fellow, *doesn't do it*, and therefore on the fatal night can go like an honest man to his dreams.†

Banquo's dreams are not, from his own account,‡ to be envied him (after all, he too had seen the witches!), nor did the prophecy made to him carry with it quite the same temptation as that made to Macbeth. He is, yet, perfectly clear of evil. Rejecting Macbeth's veiled overtures with the proviso that he ' still keep / His bosom franchis'd and allegiance clear,' he can claim, after the murder, to stand " in

---

* III, 2, 59 ff.
† Quiller-Couch, *Shakespeare's Workmanship*, 46, 47.
‡ II, 1, 6–9, 20.

the great hand of God." " He hath a wisdom,"
Macbeth says of him, " that doth guide his valour /
To act in safety." * Macbeth is hailed as Thane of
Cawdor. " What! " asks Banquo, " can the devil
speak true? " And as the thought grows in his mind,
he adds presently:

> That, trusted home,
> Might yet enkindle you unto the crown,
> Besides the Thane of Cawdor. But 't is strange:
> *And oftentimes, to win us to our harm,*
> *The instruments of darkness tell us truths,*
> *Win us with honest trifles, to betray's*
> *In deepest consequence.*   (I, 3, 120)

That is certainly not all of *Macbeth*, though, as certainly, its reference is to the whole play. It is as near
as we shall get, in Shakespeare, to the simplicity of
" 'Is *money* got '*im* off." . . .

Horatio has one great block of exposition (on the
uninspiring subject of young Fortinbras) in the first
scene. His talk of how signs and omens once
troubled old Rome as now they trouble Denmark,
which fills the interval before the Ghost startles us
for the second time, is of the sort one associates with
the Greek chorus. He checks Hamlet, after the
Ghost's departure —

---

* II, 1, 27; II, 3, 137; III, 1, 53. The absurd idea that Banquo was
a sort of accomplice (" had Banquo told Ross and Angus what he
alone could tell, Duncan would never have been murdered by the
hand of Macbeth," etc.) should be allowed to sleep in peace (see
Furness, *Variorum Shakespeare*, 55, 56, 445 ff.).

These are but wild and whirling words, my lord.

(I, 5, 133)

He watches the King, during the acting of *The Mouse-trap* and, after it is over, agrees that Claudius flinched " upon the talk of the poisoning " (III, 2, 305). Perhaps Horatio gives another check, in the graveyard scene, when Hamlet's excogitations on mortality are becoming fantastic:

Hamlet.   To what base uses we may return, Horatio! Why may not imagination trace the noble dust of Alexander, till he find it stopping a bung-hole?
Horatio.   'T were to consider too curiously, to consider so.

(v, 1, 222)

He certainly tries to prevent the quarrel with Laertes at Ophelia's grave — a quarrel which later Hamlet himself comes to regret.*

So Guildenstern and Rosencrantz go to 't,†

Horatio says dryly, as Hamlet tells him of the forged commission. This time no reproof is implied, seemingly, for a moment later he exclaims, " Why, what a king is this! " and his next remark,

It must be shortly known to him from England
What is the issue of the business there,

leads straight to Hamlet's decisive " the interim is mine." . . . On the other hand, he appears to be

---

* v, 1, 287; v, 2, 75 ff.
† v, 2, 56.

against the fencing bout with Laertes, and when Hamlet tells him of his premonitions (" how ill all 's here about my heart ") Horatio is not sceptical, but says, " If your mind dislike any thing, obey it " (v, 2, 229). He has finally his summary, tantalizing in its conciseness, of the whole tragic story. Hamlet, dying, bids him explain what has occurred:

> Thou liv'st; report me and my cause aright
> To the unsatisfied.   (v, 2, 353)

When Horatio speaks, however, he neither repeats, like Friar Laurence, all that has gone before, nor merely adjourns his narration to a time beyond the limits of the play.* Rather, he gives us the heads of an apology, and leaves us to make what we can of them:

> And let me speak to the yet unknowing world
> How these things came about: so shall you hear
> Of carnal, bloody, and unnatural acts,
> Of accidental judgments, casual slaughters;
> Of deaths put on by cunning and forc'd cause,
> And, in this upshot, purposes mistook
> Fall'n on the inventors' heads; all this can I
> Truly deliver.   (v, 2, 393)

There is so much of the tragedy here: the adulterous relations of Claudius and Gertrude, the murder of old Hamlet, the " incestuous " marriage, the deaths of Polonius, Rosencrantz, and Guildenstern, the ironies of the final carnage! But so much, too, re-

---

* See pages 123 ff., above.

mains unnoticed! * Fortinbras gives Hamlet a soldier's funeral —

> For he was likely, had he been put on,
> To have prov'd most royally. . . .

We are left, at last, with that — and a " peal of ordnance."

Antony in *Julius Caesar* and Aufidius in *Coriolanus*, another pair, are decidedly unlike Banquo and Horatio. Aufidius is, as we have seen, only one of many characters whose testimony contributes to our understanding of the protagonist.† At first glance, it might seem that as a witness the Volscian would be at great disadvantage because of his passionate hostility toward Coriolanus. Looking more closely, one sees that when Aufidius reviews his rival's career he does so under circumstances which make impartiality possible. Coriolanus has deserted Rome. He and Aufidius are joint-commanders of the Volscian army. Aufidius is secretly envious, but for the present he must wait:

> When, Caius, Rome is thine,
> Thou art poor'st of all; then shortly art thou mine.
>
> (IV, 7, 56)

It is at this moment, when it behooves him to reckon up with the utmost exactness the strength and weakness of his enemy, that Aufidius looks back at what

---

* On Horatio, see also J. D. Wilson, ed., *Hamlet*, XLVIII, XLIX.
† Pages 167–172, above.

has happened in Rome. " For once," writes Sir
E. K. Chambers, " the dramatist, not the puppet,
speaks. On the eve of the catastrophe Shakespeare
pauses to sum up his hero's career so far." * Even
so, the speech is placed, and adjusted, with singular
propriety. As for Antony, though he too is very far
from that " absolute conformity to reason and moral
order " which was to distinguish characters who
supply the point of rest, there is no doubt of his
choral function in *Julius Caesar*. Brutus and the
other conspirators have at length quit the stage,
leaving him alone with the body of the murdered
Caesar. He speaks (in soliloquy) with ever mounting emotion. First, there is apology for his seeming
compliance; then, as curse and prophecy mingle, he
foretells the horrors of civil war:

> Domestic fury and fierce civil strife
> Shall cumber all the parts of Italy; . . .
>
> And Caesar's spirit, ranging for revenge,
> With Ate by his side come hot from hell,
> Shall in these confines with a monarch's voice
> Cry " Havoc! " and let slip the dogs of war;
> That this foul deed shall smell above the earth
> With carrion men, groaning for burial.
>
> (III, 1, 263)

Julius Caesar is, when all is said, an imperfectly
unified play. Nevertheless, Antony's soliloquy is
more than a link between parts. The motive of

* Furness, *Variorum Shakespeare*, 475.

vengeance for Caesar, which is sounded here for the
first time, will be heard over and over again before
irony has at last had its way and, as Brutus wished
that they might, the conspirators have indeed
" come by Caesar's spirit." *

When to these five chorus characters in the tragedies — Enobarbus, Brutus, Horatio, Aufidius, and
Antony — is joined a sixth, Lear's Fool, we have
reached the most interesting of them all. Like
Enobarbus, he looks three ways. In his acid jokes
and untuneful fag-ends of song the same story is told
again and again: the realities of the present, the mis-
takes of the past, the promised woes of the future —
all are there. At times, it is true, he slips into mere
jesting and nonsense, partly for the sake of relief,
partly to keep up his professional character. How
freely those early audiences laughed at him is matter
for conjecture — freely enough, I suppose. Shakespeare gave them, none the less, hint after hint that *this*
fool was different. At Goneril's, he is called for thrice
before he comes, and while we are waiting something
is said of him which could scarcely go unnoticed:

Lear. But where 's my fool? I have not seen him this two days.
Knight. Since my young lady's going into France, sir, the fool
     hath much pined him away.
Lear. No more of that; I have noted it well.   (I, 4, 77)

---

* *Cf.* IV, 3, 273 ff.; V, 3, 45, and 94–96; V, 5, 17–20 and 50.
Antony's eulogy over Brutus represents another aspect of the tragedy, since Brutus is technically the hero.

After one of the Fool's first sallies Kent remarks,
" This is not altogether fool, my lord "; Lear calls
him " a bitter fool "; Goneril says he is " more
knave than fool "; and he himself insists that he
tells the truth — " Prithee, nuncle, keep a school-
master that can teach thy fool to lie: I would fain
learn to lie." * Stripped of its elusiveness and of its
poetry (there is much of both in the part), what he
says in his first scene amounts to this: Kent is taking
the losing side in following Lear; Lear was a fool in
treating his daughters as he did; he has nothing; he
can get nothing from his daughters; they are the
masters now, and they will treat him with cruel ingratitude. In the next scene (1, 5) he continues to call
Lear a fool. Regan will be as bad as Goneril, he
says, and Lear is a houseless dependent. At Gloucester's, the sight of Kent in the stocks starts the
Fool on one of his old themes, the folly of siding with
the losers; but the scrap of song beginning " That
sir which serves and seeks for gain " sounds as if he
saw, already, exactly what was coming, and there
is the ominous vagueness of

Winter's not gone yet, if the wild geese fly that way.
> Fathers that wear rags
> Do make their children blind,
> But fathers that bear bags
> Shall see their children kind.

---

* I, 4, 151, 166, 196, 339 (*cf.* 124–126).

Fortune, that arrant whore,
Ne'er turns the key to the poor.
But for all this thou shalt have as many dolours for thy daughters
as thou canst tell in a year.   (II, 4, 46)

His last speech — that about the eels — touches the
acme of horror. On the heath, he helps to make the
storm real to us.* At the farmhouse, it is enough
that he plays his part in the mad trio with Lear and
Edgar. Thereafter, of course, he disappears.

Finally, *Timon of Athens* is remarkable for the fact
that its choral speeches are distributed among at
least three different characters. Before the introductory exposition is fairly brought to a close, the
Poet, describing the verses he is presenting to
Timon, charts the course of the drama — fall from
greatness, with the desertion of the hero by his false
friends. The betrayal of great men by fawning
parasites is dwelt on by Apemantus in the second
scene, where his misanthropic sermons are tinged
with prophecy —

Who lives that's not depraved or depraves? . . .

I should fear those that dance before me now
Would one day stamp upon me: it has been done.
                    (I, 2, 147)

Flavius, when his turn comes, throws the emphasis
on the hero's tragic fault:

* *Cf.* pages 31 ff., above.

> Poor honest lord! brought low by his own heart,
> Undone by goodness. Strange, unusual blood,
> When man's worst sin is he does too much good!
> Who then dares to be half so kind agen?
> For bounty, that makes gods, does still mar men.
>
> (IV, 2, 37)

And again:

> O monument
> And wonder of *good deeds evilly bestow'd!*

Then, with a return to the idea of betrayal:

> How rarely does it meet with this time's guise,
> When man was wish'd to love his enemies!
>
> (IV, 3, 475)

As we shall see, a similar distribution of the choral speeches occurs in two of the histories, *Richard II* and *Henry VIII.*

In the comedies, Berowne, the Duke (in *Measure for Measure*), Kate the Shrew, and Thersites stand out with some distinctness as chorus characters. At the beginning of *Love's Labor's Lost,* Berowne raises his voice in expostulation and prophecy: these " strict observances," he says, are " barren tasks, too hard to keep," and

> Necessity will make us all forsworn. . . .
> But I believe, although I seem so loath,
> I am the last that will last keep his oath.   (I, 1, 148)

When, in the fourth act, he finds himself fairly caught, there is a moment of vexation in which he calls Costard a " whoreson loggerhead "; then he is himself again:

Sweet lords, *sweet lovers*, O! let us embrace . . .

We cannot cross the cause why we were born.

(IV, 3, 214)

And he proceeds to prove eloquently that ' their loving is lawful, and their faith not torn.' In Berowne, writes Alden, " the satiric perception of the folly is incarnated, as well as the experience of it." * The Duke, in *Measure for Measure*, presides over the destiny of a dark comedy which from time to time he condescends to interpret. Thus, even before we first see Isabella, he puts us on our guard against the Deputy.   Lord Angelo is precise,

> scarce confesses
> That his blood flows, or that his appetite
> Is more to bread than stone: *hence shall we see,*
> *If power change purpose, what our seemers be.*
>
> (I, 3, 51; *cf.* III, 2, 40)

Pater finds that the Duke's " quaint but excellent moralising " on Death, at the beginning of Act Three, expresses, " like the chorus of a Greek play, the spirit of the passing incidents." † Later the hootings of Lucio lead the Duke to discourse on calumny (III, 2, 200 ff., *cf.* IV, 1, 61). And in the lines beginning

He, who the sword of heaven will bear . . .

---

* *Shakespeare*, " Master Spirits of Literature," New York, 1922 p. 196. Note also Berowne's epilogue-like comments, v, 2, 882 ff
† *Appreciations*, 181.

at the close of the act, we get at last something like a full-length choral speech. Crabbed as these lines are, their general drift is plain enough; and it is echoed, two scenes later, as the Duke talks with the Provost about Angelo:

> His life is parallel'd
> Even with the stroke and line of his great justice:
> He doth with holy abstinence subdue
> That in himself which he spurs on his power
> To qualify in others: *were he meal'd with that*
> *Which he corrects, then were he tyrannous.*
>
> (IV, 2, 82; cf. 111–116)

As for Katharina's homily, it would be there anyhow, at the end of the fifth act, because of the plot and because of the good old principle of reversal: Kate the Shrew preaching the submission of wives is like Johan Johan (and how many other henpecked husbands in farces!) rising in revolt. On the other hand, the speech is in part retrospective —

> My mind hath been as big as one of yours,
> My heart as great, my reason haply more —

and it expresses with appropriate violence some of the ideas about marriage which the hearers were expected to hold, at least within the theatre. John Fletcher's sequel and antidote, *The Tamer Tamed*, shows that Kate was not taken too seriously.

Enobarbus and Lear's Fool are Shakespeare's greatest chorus characters, Thersites taking rank just below them. Enobarbus has his own tragedy to live; Lear's Fool makes pitiful attempts to cheer his master; both are to such a degree " sympathetic " characters that their expository function is almost wholly concealed. By comparison Thersites is machine-like; his " gall coins slanders like a mint " (I, 3, 192). Envy moves him — the devil whom he invokes in his prayer — envy, and " intellectual pride," * but his motives are as abstract as his abuse is impartial. Somewhat as in *King Lear*, the two plots of *Troilus and Cressida* are in effect one and the same: Cressida is merely a variation on the theme of Helen. Thersites perceives this. " Here is such patchery, such juggling, and such knavery!" he says of the Ten Years' War:

> All the argument is a cuckold and a whore; a good quarrel to draw emulous factions and bleed to death upon. Now, the dry serpigo on the subject! and war and lechery confound all!
>
> (II, 3, 78)

And in the betrayal scene (where his presence, daringly introduced, accords perfectly with the prevailing spirit of the play):

> *Thersites.* Would I could meet that rogue Diomed! I would croak like a raven; I would bode, I would bode.... Lechery, lechery; still, wars and lechery: nothing else holds fashion. A burning devil take them!
>
> (v, 2, 187)

---

* Wyndham Lewis, *The Lion and the Fox*, New York and London [1927], p. 258.

The authenticity of his croakings is really not to be questioned. If it is, turn but to Diomed on Helen, at the beginning of the fourth act, or to Hector before Hector's reason is silenced by his love of glory:

> But value dwells not in particular will;
> It holds his estimate and dignity
> As well wherein 't is precious of itself
> As in the prizer. 'T is mad idolatry
> To make the service greater than the god;
> And the will dotes that is inclinable
> To what infectiously itself affects,
> Without some image of the affected merit.
>
> (II, 2, 53)

As for Prospero in *The Tempest*, he has frequently been identified with Shakespeare — but the personal identification of a chorus character with the author is not, I maintain, essential. Prospero's words, " The rarer action is / In virtue than in vengeance," express something of the benign mood of the play, just as the great passage beginning " Our revels now are ended " seems to have a peculiar rightness where one finds it.* More even than the Duke in *Measure for Measure*, Prospero is a directive force, shaping the plot to his will, and pausing from time to time to comment on its progress. Yet, when all is said, I find it a little difficult to associate him with characters like Horatio and Enobarbus.

There is a good deal to be said for reading Shakespeare's histories in the order in which they stand

* v, 1, 27–28; IV, 1, 148 ff.

in the Folio: *King John* first, then in an unbroken
sequence the York and Lancaster plays from *Richard II* through *Richard III*, and last, *Henry VIII*.
When read in this order, which corresponds, to be
sure, only occasionally with the order of their composition, the histories will be found to contain a
series of very great speeches setting forth, on the one
hand, the miseries of civil strife, on the other, the
splendors of the new nationalism. Faulconbridge,
at the end of *King John*, sums up the lesson in words
which still have life in them despite their familiarity:

> This England never did, nor never shall,
> Lie at the proud foot of a conquero¬,
> But when it first did help to wound itself. . . .

In *Richard II*, John of Gaunt's dying speeches combine praise of England with recognition of the
viciousness of Richard, ' England's landlord ' (II, I).
The blame is, however, rested squarely on another's
shoulders; for, later in the play, the Bishop of Car-
lisle prophesies the coming of wars which

> Shall kin with kin and kind with kind confound,

making the land another " field of Golgotha " — if
Bolingbroke usurps the throne.* *Henry V* is a tri-
umphant interlude. Then, when we come to the
beginning of the next reign, Exeter warns us of the
fruits of dissension, and cites the prophecy that

* IV, I, 114 ff.; *cf.* 322–323.

" Henry born at Windsor " should lose all that " Henry born at Monmouth " had won.* Henry VI is himself the chorus in the last of the plays which bear his name. Act Two, Scene Five, is indeed symbolic rather than dramatic. The Son mourning for his father, the Father for his son, are like a picture out of an emblem book with Henry's lamentations as the explanatory text. To Henry also are given not only a prophecy of the woes to come, under another Richard, but " divining thoughts " of the passing of strife under the " peaceful majesty " of the first Tudor.† His lamentations and prophecies call to mind the customary lamentations and prophecies of the Greek chorus. The conception of Margaret in *Richard III* is even more strikingly Greek,‡ but in her case it is of the Furies or of Nemesis that one is first reminded. Unlike Henry, she looks back rather than forward. Her lamentations, her curses so inexorably fulfilled, well up out of the past; and if *Richard III* is kept tragic, it must never be dissociated from what has gone before. Let that happen and one gets Colley Cibber's version, mere melodrama and actor's vehicle. Nevertheless, it is not Margaret who closes, but Rich-

---

* *1 Henry VI*, III, 1, 186 ff.; *cf*. IV, 1, 182 ff.
† *3 Henry VI*, v, 6, 37 ff.; IV, 6, 68 ff.
‡ Of the beginning of IV, 4, Schelling writes that " it would be difficult to find in the whole range of the English drama a scene reproducing so completely the nature and the function of Greek choric ode " (Furness, *Variorum Shakespeare*, 316).

mond; and in Richmond's speech the past yields to the future — to the days of peace and plenty which Cranmer also promises at the end of *Henry VIII*.

The histories contain, then, chorus characters whose province is not that of any single play, whose thesis —

England is safe, if true within itself * —

is kept before us with insistence. Side by side with these are a few chorus characters of the ordinary sort. Thus, York, before he becomes " neuter," speaks home truths to both Richard and Bolingbroke; † and Norfolk is at least busily informative through part of *Henry VIII*, though the final appraisement of Wolsey is left to Katharine and Griffith (IV, 2). Far more interesting is the Bastard Faulconbridge. " With the exceptions of Sir Toby Belch and Justice Shallow," writes Mr. Masefield, " the Bastard is the most English figure in the plays "; and Mr. Logan Smith calls him " not only full of vitality " but " Shakespeare's first fully-alive creation." ‡ As a chorus character, whether he discourses on " Commodity " or points out the evils attendant on young Arthur's death, whether he expresses the Englishman's traditional contempt of French arms or rejoices at the healing of his country's wounds, Faulconbridge is trustworthy and

---

* *3 Henry VI*, IV, I, 40.

† *R. II*, ii, I, 164; II, 3, 83 ff.; *cf.* III, 3, 7–17.

‡ *William Shakespeare*, 82; *On Reading Shakespeare*, 42.

engaging.* I like to think of him in connection with a passage in Tom Heywood's *Apology for Actors* (1612):

> What English blood, seeing the person of any bold English-man presented, and doth not hugge his fame, and hunnye at his valor, pursuing him in his enterprise with his best wishes, and as beeing wrapt in contemplation, offers to him in his hart all pros-perous performance, as if the personator were the man personated? †

The foregoing enumeration of Shakespeare's chorus characters is admittedly tentative. The complexities — the simplicities — of Elizabethan dramatic practice stand in the way of dogmatism. Norfolk, in *Henry VIII*, I have called a chorus char-acter, but is he really much more than a glorified " First Gentleman "? On the other hand, it is quite conceivable that I have overlooked some chorus characters of sorts. Albany, in *King Lear*, seems rather like one of Patmore's " points of rest " — Mr. Mackail finds him " central," the one figure in the tragedy " who is from first to last completely sane, balanced, and normal." ‡ But Albany is not quite blameless while Lear is at his house, and a good deal is made of his subsequent conversion.§ In any case, " point of rest " and " chorus char-

---

* *K. J.*, II, 1, 561 ff.; IV, 3, 140 ff.; V, 2, 128 ff.; V, 7, 110 ff.
† Shakespeare Society Ed., 1841, p. 21.
‡ *The Approach to Shakespeare*, 78 ff.
§ Bradley calls attention to the Knight's speech, I, 4, 61 ff. (*Shakespearean Tragedy*, 297); *cf.* lines 297–298.

acter " are not, as we saw, interchangeable terms. Theseus, again, in the last act of " *A Midsummer Night's Dream*, may have that graceful comedy itself in mind as he talks of fancy:

> The poet's eye, in a fine frenzy rolling,
> Doth glance from heaven to earth, from earth to heaven;
> And, as imagination bodies forth
> The forms of things unknown, the poet's pen
> Turns them to shapes, and gives to airy nothing
> A local habitation and a name.
>
> (v, 1, 12)

Taken in their context, however, the lines become rather an expression of sturdy incredulity — or what Oberon prepared us for when he said that the night's accidents would seem to mortals no more than " the fierce vexation of a dream." * Finally, the comparative detachment of Friar Laurence, his counsels of moderation, the grave benignity of his manner, are so like those of the classical chorus that one can understand why a good deal of ink has flowed in maintaining that he was (or was not) a chorus character. So Gervinus, for the affirmative, writes that by Friar Laurence

the leading idea of the piece is expressed in all fulness . . . that excess in any enjoyment however pure in itself, transforms its sweet into bitterness . . . that love can only be a companion to life. . . . These ideas are placed by the poet in the lips of the wise Laurence in almost a moralizing manner, with gradually increasing emphasis, as if he would provide most circumspectly

---

* iv, 1, 75. Dowden (*Shakspere*, 60–62) compares lines 215 ff. " The best in this kind are but shadows. . . ."

that no doubt should remain of his meaning. He utters them in
his first soliloquy . . . in a manner merely *instructive* and as if
without application; he expresses them *warningly*, when he
unites the lovers, at the moment when he assists them, and
finally he repeats them *reprovingly* to Romeo in his cell, when he
sees the latter undoing himself and his own work, and he pre-
dicts what the end will be.*

Edward Dowden did good service to Shakespearean
criticism by returning time after time to attack this
interpretation of the Friar's rôle.

These violent delights have violent ends †

might well have been the central idea of the tragedy. Dowden realized that it is not. " The rap-
ture of the lovers," he writes, " does not of itself
cause the tragic ending of their joy "; they " die as
sacrifices . . . therefore shall their statues be raised,
and in ' pure gold.' " ‡ It is after all only natural, in
view of Friar Laurence's profession and his relation
to the lovers, that he should caution them against
haste, against violent passion. The last speeches in
the play strike a very different note. So does the
introductory chorus — and it is a safe principle in
matters of this sort that the more dramatic should
give place, as evidence, to the less.

*　　　*　　　*

* *Shakespeare Commentary*, 1, 293 ff.
† II, 6, 9.
‡ Shakespeare's *Tragedies*, ed. Craig, Oxford, 1924, p. 300;
Romeo and Juliet, ed. Dowden, London, 1900, p. xxxiii.

There are, of course, at least three parties to the performance of a play, the actors, the author, and the audience. Of these three, the actors are not merely the most conspicuous group concerned, but also — with allowance made for the possibility of improvization, on the one hand, of private performance, on the other — possibly the only essential one. The author is, ideally, everything and nowhere, an invisible magician or master of the revels speaking, within the play, only indirectly, or perhaps through a chorus character. The audience, finally, are virtually inarticulate. Not that their presence, and the very degree of their responsiveness, are unfelt — ask any actor about that! An audience, too, may applaud the " sentiments " of one of the characters or a happy turn of the plot (such applause, though rare, is still to be heard in our theatres); they might, until recently, hiss the villain in good earnest. Another kind of applause, actually more disturbing to dramatic illusion, still greets the first entrance of Mr. Leslie Howard, or Mr. Hampden, or of Miss Cornell. The Elizabethans, Dekker implies, were capable of ' mewing at passionate speeches.' These are but makeshifts when all is said, and playwrights have tried now and again to supplement them by strictly dramatic means. So, at any rate, I explain the presence in some plays of characters who seem designed to say, at moments of stress, what the audience need to have said, or would like to say themselves. A character of this sort, who stands in approximately the same relationship to the spectators as the chorus character to the author, may be designated, for want of a better term, the " spokesman for the audience." As a witness, by the by, he cuts a rather poor figure.

Though he has an august counterpart in Greek tragedy,* it is in popular plays of great emotional tension — plays in which sides are clearly defined so that the sympathy of the spectators may be given whole-heartedly — that the spokesman for the audience is most easily recognized. Thus, in melodrama where the characters are aligned like pieces on a checkerboard, black against white, he flourishes. I recall vividly a scene in Dion Boucicault's *Octoroon*, at a revival some years ago. M'Closky, the villain, has committed a murder. He attempts to put the blame on Wahnotee, a worthy Indian, and incites the mob against him. Fortunately, Scudder (the hero) has discovered evidence pointing to M'Closky as the real murderer. At the critical moment, Scudder produces this evidence. M'Closky is seized and searched, while Pete, a negro, Scudder's faithful servant, stands

* Though some authorities on Greek drama would have the chorus speak for the author, at all events in the choral odes, the usual view is that it stands in some sort as an " ideal spectator." Yet the Spokesman for the Audience seems to me rather less intimately related to the chorus than the chorus character.

watching. As played, the dialogue then proceeded
as follows:

Scudder [*opening the pocket-book*]. What 's here? Letters? Umm, I
    smell a rat!

Pete. Catch him, Mass' Scudder!

Scudder. Hello! To " Mrs. Peyton, Terrebonne, Louisiana,
    United States." Liverpool postmark. Ho! I 've got
    hold of the tail of the rat!

Pete. Hold him tight, Mass' Scudder!

Scudder [*reads*]. What's this? A draft for eighty-five thousand
    dollars. . . . Aha! The rat's out!

Pete. Make him squeak, Mass' Scudder!

Scudder. Jacob M'Closky, you killed that boy. . . .*

Pete is, of course, the spokesman for the audience,
saying what the audience needed to have said, crow-
ing over M'Closky as they would like to have
crowed, themselves. Half the relish of the scene lay
in those three exhortations. . . . Or there is Jarvis
Williams, in *Sweeney Todd, the Demon Barber of Fleet
Street*, who, when Sweeney is at last cornered, fairly
bursts out with " St. George for England! " In
Shakespeare one need not go beyond the trial scene
in *The Merchant of Venice*:

Shylock. Most learned judge! A sentence! come, prepare!

Portia. Tarry a little: there is something else. . . .

And, as she turns the tables on the Jew, Gratiano
cries:

---

* I am indebted to Miss Marian Lee Winkler, who appeared in
the revival (at the Repertory Theatre, Boston, January 21, 1929)
for a transcript of the acting version at this point. It differs strikingly from any of the printed texts I have been able to see, and
Pete's lines are quite possibly the actor's gags.

O upright judge! Mark, Jew: O learned judge! . . .

A second Daniel, a Daniel, Jew!
Now, infidel, I have thee on the hip.*

On the printed page, Gratiano's words may sound crude enough today. When one remembers, however, the intimacy of the Elizabethan theatre, the tenseness of the situation a moment before followed by the brilliancy of Portia's *coup*, one realizes that the same words must once have been electrifying.

The spokesman for the audience expresses our elation as the tide of fortune turns and the characters with whom we sympathize triumph. He is there, too, in those dark moments when the virtuous are oppressed and our adversaries have (or seem to have) everything their own way. Then, when otherwise the situation might become unendurable, he speaks up for us, and " the losers have their words." So Caroline, the plucky soubrette in *Secret Service*, takes the villain down a peg:

Arrelsford. I give my reasons to my *superiors* Miss Mitford!
Caroline. Then you 'll have to go 'round givin' 'em to everybody in *Richmond*, Mr. Arrelsford! (*Saying which* Caroline *makes a deep courtesy and turns and sweeps out through doors up* R. C.).†

---

* IV, I, 305 ff.; *cf.* also *12 N.*, v, 1, 382 ff. Falstaff's urging on of the Prince at Shrewsbury (" Well said, Hal! to it, Hal! Nay, you shall find no boy's play here, I can tell you," *1 H. IV*, v, 4, 75) is calculated to influence our feelings as well as express them.
† Ed. Quinn, *Representative American Plays*, New York, 1925, p. 521.

Or there is Harry Herbert, in Thomas Morton's *Columbus*, who turns on the wicked Roldan with:

> Hands off, reptiles! *(to Roldan)* That you are the most infernal scoundrel the devil ever made a friend of, all your worthy associates about you will, I dare say, allow — but I brand you with the name of fool, for enabling an humble man like me, thus to triumph over you, to defy you — scorn you — laugh at you — Hands off, reptiles! *

Flaminius, as he flings back Lucullus's tip, in *Timon of Athens*,[†] is a spokesman for the audience; so, in *King Lear*, is the Fool, singing derisively at Goneril, and Kent, soaring to a climax of invective against Oswald and finally beating him — a chance to kick your adversary's dog is something![‡] Volumnia and Virgilia have a moment of the same sort, in *Coriolanus*, as they rail at the Tribunes.[§] And Mr. Wyndham Lewis writes of the last scene in *Othello*:

> It is *we* who are intended to respond to these events, as the Venetian, Lodovico, does, when he apostrophizes Iago, describing him as:
>
> > More fell than anguish, hunger or the sea![‖]

Moral squeamishness has found fault with one of these characters. Kent, says Richard Grant White, " rails us into something like sympathy with Os-

---

* Ed. 1792, p. 22. Lydia has the same function in *Saints and Sinners* — the melodrama which Matthew Arnold took so seriously.
† III, 1, 49–67.
‡ I, 4, 339 ff. (*cf.* 216–219), and II, 2, 1 ff.
§ IV, 2, 11 ff.
‖ *The Lion and the Fox*, 192.

wald." * Though Kent's outburst was certainly not intended to produce the effect White attributes to it — is, in point of fact, an unalloyed consolation — the violence of the spokesman for the audience does at times call forth, or restore, our sympathy for the person he scolds. Aware of this, a practiced playwright, when he sets about the rehabilitation of one of his characters, will sometimes make an under-dog of him, trusting to the reaction which excessive abuse is bound to evoke. A pretty instance of the sort occurs in the Elizabethan play, *Patient Grissell* (1600). The authors, Dekker and others, showed tact. Their source, the story told by Chaucer's Clerk, was all very well where they found it, and nicely adjusted to the scheme of the *Canterbury Tales*. Once this story was detached, however, and dramatized, there was danger that the spectators might revolt at having to witness Griselda's unmerited sufferings, and might turn in disgust against the tyrannical husband who was the cause of them. So the authors did three things: they gave a lyrical tone to the whole play, and strewed it with songs; they supplied appropriate and abundant comic relief; and they introduced in Lucio, Griselda's brother, a character who says everything against the husband an audience could want said, and more besides.†

* *The Riverside Shakespeare*, VI, 641, note; *cf.* Lily Campbell, *Shakespeare's Tragic Heroes: Slaves of Passion*, Cambridge (England), 1930, p. 207.
    † Lucio is " a kind of chorus character . . . provided to speak for

Shakespeare's use of Paulina, in *The Winter's Tale*, is very similar. Hermione's lord and master must have been almost as trying as Griselda's — and Paulina lays it on. In the second scene of Act Two, she explains what is coming:

> He must be told on 't, and he shall: the office
> Becomes a woman best; I 'll take 't upon me.
> If I prove honey-mouth'd, let my tongue blister,
> And never to my red-look'd anger be
> The trumpet any more.   (II, 2, 31)

And, to make all sure, Emilia praises Paulina for her " free undertaking," and says that " there is no lady living / So meet for this great errand." Through a hundred lines of the next scene, Leontes bears the brunt of her reproaches. She renews them, after the reading of the oracle, and comes at length to a climax:

> But, O thou tyrant!
> Do not repent these things, for they are heavier
> Than all thy woes can stir; therefore betake thee
> To nothing but despair.   A thousand knees
> Ten thousand years together, naked, fasting,
> Upon a barren mountain, and still winter
> In storm perpetual, could not move the gods
> To look that way thou wert.
>
> *Leontes.*   Go on, go on;
> Thou canst not speak too much: I have deserv'd
> All tongues to talk their bitterest.   (III, 2, 208)

" Into Paulina's lips," writes Lady Martin (Helen Faucit, the actress), " Shakespeare seems as if he

---

the audience " (Willard Thorp, *The Triumph of Realism in Eliza-bethan Drama*, Princeton, 1928, pp. 89, 90).

wished to put, as the Greek tragedians put into those of the Chorus, the concentrated judgement of every man and woman in his kingdom." * By the fifth act, however, when Paulina begins again, the audience have had enough, and are ready to forgive a humbled and very penitent Leontes.† Claudio, in *Much Ado*, undergoes much the same castigation, at the hands of the old men (v, 1), and even Othello is not exempt from it. Emilia's outbursts against him, after the murder —

even that most characteristic one

She was too fond of her most filthy bargain —

lift the overwhelming weight of calamity that oppresses us. . . . Terror and pity are here too much to bear; we long to be allowed to feel also indignation, if not rage; and Emilia lets us feel them and gives them words.‡

With these three sorts of spokesmen for the audience we have been, I believe, on reasonably firm ground. Further inquiry would, doubtless, disclose others. The tirades of Apemantus in the fourth act of *Timon*, Horatio's incredulity about the Ghost, the earthiness of Mercutio and of the Nurse, might all be found pertinent. It is even possible, going outside the drama, that something could be made of our old friend, Dr. Watson, as both a point of rest and a spokesman for the audience.

* Furness, *Variorum Shakespeare*, 133.

† Professor Kittredge calls my attention to the fact that Paulina herself realizes that she has gone too far (iii, 2, 221 ff.).

‡ Bradley, *Shakespearean Tragedy*, 241, 242. See also Gervinus, *Shakespeare Commentaries*, ii, 476.

Chapter VIII

THE VILLAIN AND THE HERO

Bradley's Distrust of Iago — The Villains accused of
Excessive Candor — Shakespeare's Frenchmen — And
Minor Murderers — Testimony of Villains about Themselves — And about the Good Characters — Testimony
of the Good Characters — Julius Caesar — Hal's Soliloquy — " Now might I do it pat."

" AN EVIL crow, an evil egg." Shakespeare's
villains are sometimes accused of lying merely
because they are villains. Thus, Bradley warns us
not to believe Iago's " statement that there was a
report abroad about an intrigue between his wife
and Othello " —

> I hate the Moor,
> And it is thought abroad that 'twixt my sheets
> He has done my office. (I, 3, 392) *

But Iago's statement is part of a soliloquy; and
soliloquy, as we saw, represents the actual thoughts
of the character externalized in words. Some such
scandalous report must, therefore, have come to
Iago's ears, wholly unfounded as we may be certain it was. Bradley even distrusts the first part of
the quotation: " The only ground for attributing "
to Iago "anything deserving the name of hatred a

* *Shakespearean Tragedy*, 215, note.

all, is his own statement, 'I hate Othello'; and we
know what his statements are worth." * But the
horrible reality of Iago's hatred is beyond question.
In another soliloquy, he says of Desdemona:

> Now, I do love her too;
> Not out of absolute lust, — though peradventure
> I stand accountant for as great a sin, —
> But partly led to diet my revenge,
> For that I do suspect the lusty Moor
> Hath leap'd into my seat; the thought whereof
> Doth like a poisonous mineral gnaw my inwards.† . . .

The same fear that Shakespeare's villains may, at
some point, be fooling us prompted the Cowden-
Clarkes to suggest that minor inaccuracies in
Iachimo's recapitulation, near the end of *Cymbeline*,
were due to the speaker's " innate untruthfulness "
(in other words, even the fruits of a villain's conversion are to be suspected!) and led Sir Arthur
Quiller-Couch to question the right of the witches in
Macbeth to call themselves " Weird Sisters." ‡

Of late, however, critics have been less troubled
by the mendacity of the villains than by their extreme candor. Shakespeare's characters, it is asserted, are given to self-exposition. They say of
themselves things which would come with dramatic
propriety only from somebody else. And the vil-

* *Ibid.*, 224.
† II, 1, 303 ff.; *cf.* IV, 2, 145 ff.
‡ *Cymb.*, v, 5, 143 ff.; Furness, *Variorum Shakespeare*, 405; *Shake-
speare's Workmanship*, 28 ff.

lains, in particular, are charged with recognizing, what they would be unlikely to perceive, their own wickedness and the virtues of the good characters. So the villain of a minor Elizabethan play — Lorenzo in the *First Part of Jeronimo* — soliloquizes as follows:

> Andrea's gone embassador;
> Lorenzo is not dreamt on in this age.
> Hard fate,
> When villains sit not in the highest state!
> Ambition's plumes, that flourished in our court,
> Severe authority has dashed with justice;
> And policy and pride walk like two exiles,
> Giving attendance, that were once attended;
> And we rejected, that were once high-honoured.
> I hate Andrea; 'cause he aims at honour,
> When my purest thoughts work in a pitchy vale,
> Which are as different as heaven and hell.
> One peers for day, the other gapes for night.*

Here the dramatic method is one of simple reversal. Right is still right to Lorenzo, and wrong, wrong. The facts of the play stand unchanged before his eyes. He refers to them not impartially, however, for he shares our notions of them though he has taken sides against us. He is *our enemy*, that is all, and speaks as such.

Professor Schücking in his important book, *Character Problems in Shakespeare's Plays*, makes out a case for the survival of primitive methods in Shakespeare's portrayal of villains. Lady Macbeth, he

---

* Dodsley's *Old Plays*, ed. Hazlitt, IV, 353.

discovers, " looking at her own behaviour from an outside point of view, calls it ' cruelty,' and describes her murderous intentions as ' fell.' " To Schücking, this is not realism: it " flatly contradicts the facts of life." " We clearly see," he asserts, " that the villains in Shakespeare are not allowed to appear as honest characters even in their own eyes, and that the noble characters must be noble even in the eyes of their wicked enemies." The reason is simple.   It lies

in the careful regard which Shakespeare everywhere pays to the limited mental capacity of the public. The poet desires above all to avoid misapprehension of the main outlines of the action and :he characters, to prevent the spectators from confusing the ethical values and from taking pleasure in the vices represented and the situations produced by them. . . . The villain is to be a villain, the noble character is to appear noble, from whichever side we look at them.*

Although Professor Stoll is, in effect, equally insistent upon the flaws in Shakespeare's portrayal of villainy, he does not accept Schücking's explanation of them. " There is much plain-speaking that is unnecessary," he points out. " Comment by others, together with his own conduct and the irony of the fate that befalls him (with appropriate comment again), would sufficiently reveal the wickedness and duplicity of an Iago." † Therefore, it is not the stupidity of the audience which is to blame.

* Pages 36, 37, 65, 66.
† *Shakespeare Studies*, 369.

No doubt Shakespeare could take a character's point of view, and shift his speech accordingly, if ever dramatist could; but he was not careful to keep it when morals and conscience were at stake or the villain was on parade — did not bear in mind the psychological necessity or esthetic propriety of keeping it.[*]

This failure he shared with his fellows. In Elizabethan drama, Stoll continues, " the influence of Senecan technique prevails, which had not yet been sufficiently developed out of the epical and lyrical to permit the character quite to keep his own point of view." No dramatist yet had fully realized that " a character is not one who tells his story but acts it."[†]

In reply, it must be urged that Shakespeare was not attempting to depict the criminal type, as such, in his major villains. They are creatures of the Renaissance, great individual characters, brilliant and daring, who were designed to startle us, as on occasion they startle themselves. To make. generalizations about the common run of real criminals is one thing; to deny that Lady Macbeth could have perceived the cruelty of her own purpose is quite another. Though meaner minds take refuge in self-deception, it does not follow that hers would. Statistics, however impressive, only indicate — what we knew before — that she is exceptional. Anticipating

---

[*] *Ibid.*, 375, 376.

[†] *Ibid.*, 75, 364. It is impossible to do justice to Mr. Stoll's arguments here. His chapter on the criminals should be read in its entirety.

the objections of a later generation, Schlegel found a different line of defence. " Richard," he wrote, " as well as Iago, is a villain with full consciousness. That they should say this in so many words, is not perhaps in human nature: but the poet has the right in soliloquies to lend a voice to the most hidden thoughts." * The novelist, working in a less explicit medium, has all the advantage here. Thus, Arnold Bennett can tell us of Gerald, in *The Old Wives' Tale*, that " as in his mind he rapidly ran over " such-and-such matters, " he kept saying to himself, far off in some remote cavern of the brain " — something very different. In Shakespearean soliloquy, the same distinction could be expressed only with difficulty; the " hidden thoughts " have to take their chance of being recognized for what they are. Yet unless we recognize them, we do the author an injustice — as Schlegel saw.

Shakespeare's national villains, the French, certainly do not carry conviction as they are represented in the *First Part of Henry VI*. To them, the English appear "lions," "Samsons," and "Goliases." And if, at times, they are referred to more realistically, as "rascals" and "slaves," the full force of the speaker's phrase is likely to remain complimentary.[†] The French leaders have no sooner escaped

* *Lectures on Dramatic Art and Literature* (1809, 1811), tr. John Black, London, 1883, p. 435.

† I, 2, 25 ff. Aeschylus, in *The Persians*, parts with probability in much the same way.

from Orleans, by jumping off the walls, than they
pause, " all unready " as they are, to pay tribute to
the prowess of their enemies:

Alençon. Of all exploits since first I follow'd arms,
    Ne'er heard I of a war-like enterprise
    More venturous or desperate than this.
Bastard. I think this Talbot be a fiend of hell.   (II, 1, 43)

The Bastard's words promise something more life-
like, but our hopes are dashed by Reignier's answer:

If not of hell, the heavens, sure, favour him.

Besides speaking well of the English, these preposterous enemies of theirs occasionally speak evil of
themselves.

Now for the honour of the forlorn French!

is perhaps an excusable lapse on King Charles's
part; but what are we to think of a Joan of Arc
whose comment on Burgundy's treachery is

Done like a Frenchman: turn, and turn again! *

The Kaiser and the Crown Prince said such things
of themselves, in *Punch*, during the last war. *Henry
VI* is a drum-and-trumpet play for the popular
theatre, and a dash of caricature more or less does
it no great harm. As for the later Frenchmen in
Henry V, they are vain and over-confident, but these
very qualities prevent them, for the most part, from

* I, 2, 19; III, 3, 85.

falling into the undramatic style of their predecessors. Even so, the point of view of Charles VI seems, in the following lines, too much like that of Shakespeare's countrymen:

> Think we King Harry strong;
> And, princes, look you strongly arm to meet him.
> The kindred of him hath been flesh'd upon us . . .
>
> Witness our too much memorable shame
> When Cressy battle fatally was struck
> And all our princes captiv'd by the hand
> Of that black name, Edward Black Prince of Wales;
> Whiles that his mounting sire, on mountain standing,
> Up in the air, crown'd with the golden sun,
> Saw his heroical seed, and smil'd to see him
> Mangle the work of nature, and deface
> The patterns that by God and by French fathers
> Had twenty years been made.   This is a stem
> Of that victorious stock.*

The common murderers hired by Richard III to despatch Clarence and the little Princes are conscious of the horror of their deeds. Tyrrel says that though Dighton and Forrest were " flesh'd villains, bloody dogs," they wept like children as they told him of the " tyrannous and bloody " crime which they had committed (IV, 3, 1). Richard warns the murderers of Clarence not to give him a chance to plead, for Clarence was " well-spoken " and might move them to pity. But before their victim has

---

* II, 4, 48; cf. III, 5, 15-26. The Dauphin is ridiculed even by his own followers (III, 7, 103 ff.)

awakened, the Second Murderer feels qualms of
conscience. His " holy humour " will change, he
hopes: " it was wont to hold me but while one tells
twenty." * The topsy-turvy morality of his arraign-
ment of conscience ("A man cannot steal, but it
accuseth him," etc.) is morality still, though it is
quaintly disguised; he is slack when the moment
comes for performance, and repents immediately
afterwards. It is notable that, meanwhile, the First
Murderer has remained callous. His amusement
at his fellow-ruffian's discourse on conscience finds
expression in irony — " ' Zounds! it is even now at
my elbow, persuading me not to kill the duke " —
and when Clarence bids them relent this scoundrel is
merely disdainful:

> Relent! 't is cowardly, and womanish.　(1, 4, 267)

The Frenchmen, then, and at times Richard's
cutthroats, do seem to transgress the bounds of dramatic propriety. Nor is it possible, in either case, to
defend them as characters of extraordinary acuteness whose " hidden thoughts " are given us in
soliloquy. The point of view of the Frenchmen is
sacrificed in the interests of patriotic feeling. The
qualms felt by the murderers serve to accentuate the
pitifulness of their victims. Shakespeare had reasons
for what he did, though we may not be satisfied with

* *R. III*, 1, 3, 348; 1, 4, 121.

them. After all, neither *Henry VI* nor *Richard III* is
the work of his artistic maturity.

In the following pages I shall consider briefly,
first, the testimony of the major villains about themselves, then, their testimony about the good characters. Aaron, in *Titus Andronicus*, paints his own
picture:

> Madam, though Venus govern your desires,
> Saturn is dominator over mine:
> What signifies my deadly-standing eye,*
> My silence and my cloudy melancholy,
> My fleece of woolly hair that now uncurls
> Even as an adder when she doth unroll
> To do some fatal execution? . . .
>
> Vengeance is in my heart, death in my hand,
> Blood and revenge are hammering in my head.
>
> (II, 3, 30)

A " barbarous " and " misbelieving " Moor, his
villainy springs in part from ambition. His imagination takes fire at the thought of mounting aloft with
his " imperial mistress ":

> Away with slavish weeds and servile thoughts!
> I will be bright, and shine in pearl and gold,
> To wait upon this new-made empress.
> To wait, said I? to wanton with this queen,
> This goddess, this Semiramis, this nymph,
> This siren, that will charm Rome's Saturnine,
> And see his shipwrack and his commonweal's.
>
> (II, 1, 18)

---

* Lucius singles out the same feature, later in the play: " Say,
wall-ey'd slave " (V, 1, 44).

He takes pleasure, too, in looking back at what he has already accomplished, finding that it was " a happy star " which brought him to Rome.* On the other hand, though " it is true that Aaron belongs to a subjected nation . . . this hardly explains either his hatred of the whole human race, or the depth of his malice." † The horrors which he contrives excite in him a frenzy of delight.

> O! how this villany
> Doth fat me with the very thoughts of it,

he chuckles, as he makes off with Titus's hand; and when, peering through " the crevice of a wall," he saw the old man receive his sons' heads in exchange, he laughed (he says) till he cried.‡ Having dedicated himself to the service of evil, he wishes to " have his soul black like his face " and counts that day lost in which he " did not some notorious ill." § The wickedness of Tamora and her sons, he treats in much the same way. The " forest walks," he tells Chiron and Demetrius, are convenient for " rape and villany." Tamora must be taken into their confidence:

> Come, come, our empress, with her sacred wit
> To villany and vengeance consecrate,
> Will we acquaint with all that we intend.
>
> (II, 1, 120)

---

* IV, 2, 32 ff.
† C. V. Boyer, *The Villain as Hero in Elizabethan Tragedy*, London and New York [1914], pp. 106, 107.
‡ III, 1, 202; V, 1, 113 ff.
§ III, 1, 205; V, 1, 125 ff.

" Brave boys," he calls them in conclusion. But they become " murderous villains " — and the words ring with a new sincerity — when they attack his son. For Aaron is not quite the bugaboo which some of the critics would make him.* His love for his child is more than a device in the plot by which he may be caught and, for the child's sake, confess his crimes.

> Look how the black slave smiles upon the father,
> As who should say, " Old lad, I am thine own." . . .
>
> *My son and I* will have the wind of you.   (IV, 2, 121)

The speaker of those lines is a human being, not a monster.

Another early villain, Jack Cade in the *Second Part of Henry VI*, is of a very different sort. York, who describes him before his first appearance, calls him " headstrong " and " stubborn," dwells on his courage, and sums him up as " this devil." † Cade's cruelty and stupidity, qualities which he shares with his followers, are brought out in the insurrection scenes. But instead of recognizing his own villainy, as we might expect him to do, he exults in the possession of an " unconquered soul." Pity touches him momentarily, and when he is hungry he comes to regret his " ambition." ‡ But,

* See especially Stoll, *Shakespeare Studies*, 345.
† III, 1, 356 ff.
‡ IV, 7, 110; IV, 10, 1, 69.

if we took him at his own valuation, he would be a sort of Kentish Worthy rather than the " bloudie wretch " of the chronicles. " Heavens and honour be witness," he exclaims, " that no want of resolution in me, but only my followers' base and ignominious treasons, makes me betake me to my heels " (IV, 8, 65). And dying he bids his slayer " farewell; and be proud of thy victory. Tell Kent from me, she hath lost her best man, and exhort all the world to be cowards; for I, that never feared any, am vanquished by famine, not by valour " (IV, 10, 76). Jack Cade is not a great character, but the steadiness with which he keeps his own point of view deserves more credit than it has received.

Richard, even more than Aaron, is a villain by choice. Brander Matthews could find " no psychologic veracity " in his extended soliloquies of self-revelation.

" It is inconceivable," he writes, " that Richard should so completely admit to himself that he is a villain and confess that he is ' subtle, false and treacherous.' To make him say this to the audience is to put in his mouth, not any opinion that he might possibly hold of himself, but the opinion of every outside commentator on his character." *

Stated in these terms, the case against Richard is a strong one; and there is no pretending that the play which he dominates does not tip toward melodrama. The fullest explanation of his character is

* *Shakspere as a Playwright*, 90.

not the famous monologue at the beginning of
Richard III but a still earlier soliloquy, some seventy
lines long, in the *Third Part of Henry VI.** It begins
with a curse:

> Ay, Edward will use women honourably.
> Would he were wasted, marrow, bones, and all,
> That from his loins no hopeful branch may spring,
> To cross me from the golden time I look for!

But even if Edward were to die without issue, many
lives would stand between Richard and the crown.
Therefore, he is only ' flattering himself with im-
possibilities.'

> Well, say there is no kingdom then for Richard;
> What other pleasure can the world afford?
> I 'll make my heaven in a lady's lap,
> And deck my body in gay ornaments,
> And witch sweet ladies with my words and looks.
> O miserable thought! and more unlikely
> Than to accomplish twenty golden crowns.

And he dwells with disgust on his deformity — his
shrunken arm and the " envious mountain " on his
back.

> Then, since this earth affords no joy to me
> But to command, to check, to o'erbear such
> As are of better person than myself,
> I 'll make my heaven to dream upon the crown;
> And, whiles I live, to account this world but hell,

---

* III, 2, 124–195. For the " continuity of Richard's character,"
cf. E. K. Chambers, *William Shakespeare*, Oxfcrd, 1930, I, 286, 287.
3 H. VI, v, 6, 61 ff., is rather an expression of the speaker's fury than
a description of his character.

> Until my mis-shap'd trunk that bears this head
> Be round impaled with a glorious crown.

But the thought of the difficulties returns. He is, he says,

> like one lost in a thorny wood,
> That rents the thorns and is rent with the thorns,

searching for a way out. His desperation is horribly real. Somehow he must free himself — or " hew " his way out " with a bloody axe." And the knowledge of his intellectual superiority gives him confidence.

> Why, I can smile, and murder while I smile,
> And cry," Content," to that which grieves my heart . . .

> Change shapes with Proteus for advantages,
> And set the murd'rous Machiavel to school.
> Can I do this, and cannot get a crown?

Richard's deformity, then, shuts him off from any conceivable pleasure in life except the gratification of ambition. His " soul's desire " is to become king, and that can be accomplished only through a prolonged course of villainy. The same argument is set forth anew in " Now is the winter of our discontent." The very dogs, he says, bark at him as he limps by. But since he "cannot prove a lover " he is

> determined to prove a villain,
> And hate the idle pleasures of these days.

He has already laid plots,

> And if King Edward be as true and just
> As I am subtle, false, and treacherous,

the plots are likely to thrive. Even when he pos-
sesses the crown, there is no pausing in mischief.
" I am in," he finds,

> So far in blood, that sin will pluck on sin.
>
> > (*R. III*, IV, 2, 63)

Macbeth was to learn much the same lesson.*
Shakespeare, in fact, is following Holinshed, who
describes Richard as " despitious and cruell, not for
euill will alway, but ofter for ambition, and either for
the suertie or increase of his estate." † That Richard takes a certain relish in his own wickedness is
undeniable. And if we accept the rest, this quality
in him is not really disturbing. What is harder for
a modern reader to credit is that so complete an
egotist should not be exempt from remorse. Af-
flicted on the night before Bosworth Field by the
ghosts of his enemies, he attempts to reason away his
terror:

> Is there a murderer here? No. Yes, I am. . . .

> I am a villain. Yet I lie; I am not.
> Fool, of thyself speak well: fool, do not flatter.
> My conscience hath a thousand several tongues,
> And every tongue brings in a several tale,
> And every tale condemns me for a villain.   (v, 3, 185)

---

*   " I am in blood
Stepp'd in so far, that, should I wade no more,
Returning were as tedious as go o'er " (III, 4, 136).
† *Shakespeare's Holinshed*, ed. W. G. Boswell-Stone, London,
1907, p. 423.

It is a measure of his intellectual strength that he is pitiless toward himself. A lesser criminal would, doubtless, have made excuses. He makes none.

Shakespeare, like any other accomplished playwright, is forever doing more than one thing at a time. Thus, Lady Macbeth's first soliloquy is not only a subtle exposition of her husband's character. It is a revelation of herself. " Highly " is set over against " holily ": for " illness," she assumes, is required of one who would be great. Macbeth is not " full o' the milk of human kindness "; he is " too full . . . to catch the nearest way." Instead of labelling her crime, or viewing it impartially, she speaks as one intoxicated with thoughts of " the golden round " which the Weird Sisters have promised. The same exhilaration carries her forward through the invocation, magnificently conceived, which she addresses to the spirits that " wait on nature's mischief." She is deliberately steeling herself, deliberately setting aside her humanity. And if we hesitate, even after the experiences of the last war, to accept the full implications of this, our doubts are silenced by what follows. " Great Glamis! worthy Cawdor! " she cries,

> Greater than both, by the all-hail hereafter!
> Thy letters have transported me beyond
> This ignorant present, and I feel now
> The future in the instant. . . .
>
>   You shall put
> This night's great business into my dispatch;

Which shall to all our nights and days to come
Give solely sovereign sway and masterdom.
                                        (I, 5, 55)

Later, she calls the murder of Duncan " our great
quell," and Macbeth's imaginings, a relaxing of his
" noble strength." *

Macbeth, too, shows that he is dazzled by the
thought of greatness. The fulfilment of the first
prophecies of the Weird Sisters, he speaks of

> As happy prologues to the swelling act
> Of the imperial theme.   (I, 3, 128)

His letter to Lady Macbeth is full of suppressed
excitement. " This have I thought good to deliver
thee," he concludes, " my dearest partner of greatness, that thou mightest not lose the dues of rejoic-
ing, by being ignorant of what greatness is promised
thee." Actual words of his seem echoed in Lady
Macbeth's taunt,

> Wouldst thou have that
> Which thou esteem'st *the ornament of life,*
> And live a coward in thine own esteem?†

Even as late as the time of his second interview with
the Sisters, he is capable of exulting:

> Sweet bodements! good!
> Rebellion's head, rise never till the wood
> Of Birnam rise, and *our high-plac'd Macbeth*
> Shall live the lease of nature.   (IV, 1, 96)

---

* I, 7, 72; II, 2, 46.
† I, 7, 41; *cf.* also I, 3, 117 (" The *greatest* is behind ").

On the other hand, before the murder of Duncan, and almost at the very moment of its accomplishment, Macbeth is keenly sensible of the horror of his act. Shakespeare has brought great forces to bear on him from without. An evil destiny impels him toward the deed, and Lady Macbeth completes what the Sisters began. There was no need, then, to emphasize the criminal in Macbeth, and Shakespeare does not do so. Instead, he makes him a character with whom we can sympathize, the hero of the play as well as the villain. He endows him, moreover, with an imagination as acutely sensitive, perhaps, as his own. To Macbeth the voices on the stairs and the beckoning dagger are terrifying realities. They are also symbolical accompaniments of the crime which he is committing. And as, in another tragedy, Lear has been said to act the storm, so, in this, Macbeth acts the murder.*

Iago will be discussed a little later. When Sebastian and Antonio are conspiring against Alonso in the second act of *The Tempest*, Sebastian recalls that Antonio had supplanted Prospero. " True," Antonio says,

> And look how well my garments sit upon me.

" But, for your conscience," Sebastian begins. Antonio interrupts him:

* *Cf*. Granville-Barker, *Prefaces*, 1st Series, 142; Miss Bradbrook, *Elizabethan Stage Conditions*, 101, 102.

> Ay, sir; where lies that? if it were a kibe,
> 'T would put me to my slipper; but I feel not
> This deity in my bosom.   (II, 1, 284)

Sebastian needs no further encouragement. As if Naples were already his, he assumes the style of royalty:

> Draw thy sword: one stroke
> Shall free thee from the tribute which thou pay'st,
> And I the king shall love thee.

There is no want of dramatic objectivity in that! Shylock usually speaks well of himself — his " sacred nation," and " well-won thrift," and the " sober house " which Jessica found " hell." Launcelot, he is confident, will miss " old Shylock." *
Once, it is true, he refers to his conduct toward Antonio as villainy — the villainy of Christians. He has reached the climax of a bitter denunciation:

> If a Jew wrong a Christian, what is his humility? Revenge. If a Christian wrong a Jew, what should his sufferance be by Christian example? Why, revenge. The villany *you teach me* I will execute, and it shall go hard but I will better the instruction.
> (III, 1, 73)

It is not self-characterization at all, but the same passionate logic which Shylock uses later when he flings out at Antonio:

> Thou call'dst me dog before thou hadst a cause,
> But, since I am a dog, beware my fangs.   (III, 3, 6)

---

* *Mer. Ven.*, I, 3, 49, 51; II, 3, 2; II, 5, 2, 36.

Meanwhile, he has been heaping abuse on the head of his enemy, the good Antonio.

How like a fawning publican he looks!

is Shylock's first comment on him. Antonio refuses to take interest out of " low simplicity " and is a " fool " for doing so. He is a " prodigal," one who used to " come so smug upon the mart," and now is a " beggar," and " that bankrupt there." * As if to avoid the possibility of anyone's believing the Jew, Shakespeare has Antonio earnestly praised by the other trustworthy persons in the play.[†]

The maligning of Antonio by Shylock brings us to the second phase of our inquiry. The villain, we have been told, ceases to be himself when he speaks of the virtuous characters, and, whether for expository, or ethical, purposes — or merely because Shakespeare was nodding — recognizes their good qualities.[‡] So Richard III, in lines recently quoted, speaks of King Edward as " true and just." Clarence he calls " simple, plain Clarence," whose soul he is sending to heaven. And of Anne's Edward, the former Prince of Wales, he says that

A sweeter and a lovelier gentleman . . .

---

* I, 3, 42, 44; III, 1, 49–51; III, 3, 2; IV, 1, 122.

† II, 8, 35 ff.; III, 2, 293 ff.; III, 4, 5 ff., etc.

‡ Aaron says of Lavinia that " Lucrece was not more chaste "— and therefore she must be forced. Tamora, however, refers to the daughter of her enemy as " this trull " (Tit. And., II, 1, 108; II, 3, 191).

> Young, valiant, wise, and, no doubt, right royal,
> The spacious world cannot again afford.*

In the first passage, the seeming compliment to King Edward, Richard, like several of the other villains, practically identifies goodness with gullibility. If Edward, he says is " as just and true " — and, therefore, as simple —

> As I am subtle, false, and treacherous,

then my plots and " inductions dangerous " will succeed. " Simple, plain Clarence " is again contemptuous; and it is followed by a grim joke. In the *Second Part of Henry VI*, Richard had raised a laugh at Young Clifford's expense:

Richard.	Fie! charity! for shame! speak not in spite,
	For you shall sup with Jesu Christ to-night.
Young Clifford.	Foul stigmatic, that 's more than thou canst tell.
Richard.	If not in heaven, you 'll surely sup in hell.

(v, 1, 213)

Now, after seeing his brother led off to the Tower, he says in soliloquy:

> Simple, plain Clarence! I do love thee so
> That I will shortly send thy soul to heaven,
> *If heaven will take the present at our hands.*

The tribute to the little Lancastrian prince whom Richard himself had " stabb'd " in his " angry mood " is harder to explain.

> Was ever woman in this humour won?

---

* *R. III*, I, 1, 36, 118; I, 2, 244.

he asks, summing up in his soliloquy the scene of Anne's sudden capitulation.* In his gloating, he deliberately assumes her point of view. Anne, he recalls, had

> God, her conscience, and these bars against me,
> And nothing I to back my suit withal
> But the plain devil and dissembling looks.

His lauding of the Prince's virtues is, thus, in reality an extolling of his own cleverness, even when, looking at the matter dramatically, as it were, he prefers Edward to himself:

> And will she yet abase her eyes on me,
> That cropp'd the golden prime of this sweet prince . . .
>
> On me, whose all not equals Edward's moiety?

The primary purpose of the monologue is, doubtless, expository. Shakespeare has tried, nevertheless, to reconcile its terms with the mood of the speaker.

" The children of this world are in their generation wiser than the children of light." That might be the favorite text of many a Shakespearean villain! The consciousness of intellectual superiority which Richard enjoys, not only explains, or was intended to explain, most of his comments upon the good characters. It distinguishes him, also, from lesser criminals like Buckingham. Buckingham, at one point in the play, talks just as I suppose he might

---

* For soliloquies of this sort, see page 77, above.

be asked to do by those who object to Richard's
clearsightedness:

> Think you, my lord, this little prating York
> Was not incensed by his subtle mother
> To taunt and scorn you thus opprobriously?

Richard agrees, adding:

> O! 't is a parlous boy;
> Bold, quick, ingenious, forward, capable:
> He 's all the mother's, from the top to toe.
>
> (III, 1, 151)

The impartiality of the comment is a measure of the
speaker's greater intellectual reach. It is only when,
talking with his confidant, Ratcliff, he refers to the
future Henry VII as " shallow Richmond " that his
judgment of men fails him.*

Macbeth is able to perceive the virtues of Duncan
just before killing him. But that need not alarm
those who agree with what has already been said
of Macbeth's character.† His praise of Banquo is
tinged with hostility (" he *chid* the sisters ") and
with a kind of envy. He dwells, nevertheless, on
Banquo's " royalty of nature," on his courage and
wisdom, because it is these qualities which make
Banquo dangerous as an opponent. " Under him,"
Macbeth confesses,

---

* v, 3, 220; *cf.* lines 324 ff. The unconscious irony of these
speeches would not be lost on Shakespeare's audience.

† Lady Macbeth, of course, does not laud their victim.

My genius is rebuk'd, as it is said
Mark Antony's was by Caesar.   (III, 1, 56)

Early in *As You Like It*, Oliver tries vainly to explain to himself his hatred for Orlando:

I hope I shall see an end of him; for my soul, yet I know not why, hates nothing more than he. Yet he's gentle, never schooled and yet learned, full of noble device, of all sorts enchantingly beloved, and, indeed so much in the heart of the world, and especially of my own people, who best know him, that I am altogether misprised. But it shall not be so long.

(I, 1, 173)

That Oliver's villainy was actuated by pure envy is made clear in a speech of Adam's later in the comedy. Why, Adam asks, is Orlando so virtuous; why, so beloved?

Know you not, master, to some kind of men
Their graces serve them but as enemies?
No more do yours. . . .

Come not within these doors; within this roof
The enemy of all your graces lives.   (II, 3, 10)

Oliver, Adam continues, has heard of the praise that his brother has won and is waiting to murder him. There would not seem to be much ground for complaint here, especially if one recognizes Oliver's soliloquy for what it is, a groping attempt to account for his own enmity. Even Professor Schücking admits that the speech might " pass muster " if it were not for two considerations: first, the " exact parallel " which he finds between Oliver's praise of Or-

lando and Edmund's praise of Edgar, in *King Lear*;
and second, the expository value of Oliver's lines.
" Evidently," he concludes, " the dramatist has
thought it necessary at this stage . . . to place before
his audience a clear statement of the whole case.
In comparison with this aim the slight distortion of
the mental physiognomy of the villain was of no
great moment." * Edmund's praise of Edgar will
be discussed presently. Meanwhile, it need scarcely
be emphasized that any part of a play may be good
exposition, and good psychology as well. Oliver's
speech is no exception.

In the same comedy, Duke Frederick makes Rosalind's merits a reason for banishing her. Celia
pleads for her friend. " She is too subtle for thee,"
the Duke replies,

> and her smoothness,
> Her very silence and her patience,
> Speak to the people, and they pity her.
> Thou art a fool: she robs thee of thy name;
> And thou wilt show more bright and seem more virtuous
> When she is gone.   (1, 3, 80).

The sinister suggestion in his first words is strong
enough, it may be,'to keep the rest of the speech in
character.†

Although Cassius, in *Julius Caesar*, is not actually
a villain, he plays, for a time, a villain's rôle, and

---

* *Character Problems in Shakespeare's Plays*, 60–62.
† *Cf.* 1, 2, 294 ff. Don John, the melancholy villain in *Much
Ado*, refers to Claudio only with derision (1, 3, 52 ff.)

one speech of his is of the sort we have been considering. Brutus has just left the stage, at the end of the second scene. Cassius soliloquizes:

> Well, Brutus, thou art noble; yet, I see,
> Thy honourable metal may be wrought
> From that it is dispos'd: therefore 't is meet
> That noble minds keep ever with their likes;
> For who so firm that cannot be seduc'd?
> Caesar doth bear me hard; but he loves Brutus:
> If I were Brutus now and he were Cassius
> He should not humour me.   (I, 2, 313)

And he goes on to outline the means by which he hopes to persuade Brutus to take part in the conspiracy. Professor Stoll cites the monologue with disapproval, italicizing "noble" and "honourable," and insisting, when Cassius draws his moral (" therefore 'tis meet," etc.), that " it would not be like him here to be joking." * But joking is not the word. Cassius has just been described by Caesar as " a great observer," one who looked " quite through the deeds of men." He smiles seldom, and then,

> in such a sort
> As if he mock'd himself, and scorn'd his spirit
> That could be mov'd to smile at any thing.
> (I, 2, 201)

Surely, he is living up to Caesar's description of him now. " Noble" and " honourable" are not contemptuous, but they have just so much of contempt

* *Shakespeare Studies*, 371.

in them as the practical person feels for the idealist
when he sees that at certain weapons the idealist is
no match for him. Brutus should keep with men
like himself, Cassius says — and smiles.

It will be remembered that Schücking found in
Edmund's comments on Edgar an " exact parallel "
to Oliver's comments on Orlando. Both soliloquies
occur near the beginning of their respective plays.
Both serve an expository purpose, though the fact
that they do so need not cast suspicion on their psychological veracity. Edmund's plot against Gloucester and Edgar has opened auspiciously, and when
the villain is left alone he plumes himself:

> A credulous father, and a brother noble,
> Whose nature is so far from doing harms
> That he suspects none; on whose foolish honesty
> My practices ride easy! I see the business.
>
> (I, 2, 201)

" We may be certain," Schücking writes, " that an
abject rascal like Edmund would never make this
confession of admiration, the false impartiality of
which is but little modified " by the concluding
phrases.* But Edmund's thought is complete in the
first line,

> A *credulous* father, and a brother *noble*. . . .

To this coolly intellectual villain, Gloucester's super-
stition and Edgar's unsuspecting honesty amount to

---

* *Character Problems in Shakespeare's Plays*, 62.

the same thing. He looks at them, in fact, quite
without admiration. Against such opponents his
" practices " will " ride easy," that is all. The point
of view is Richard's, not Oliver's, to which it is, in a
sense, directly opposed — envy, on the one hand;
the superiority of a ' child of this world,' on the
other.

> All with me 's meet that I can fashion fit

is Edmund's conclusion.

The testimony of Coriolanus's enemies — Sicinius
and Brutus, the Citizens, and Aufidius, the chorus
character — has already been considered.* Dr.
Arnold found it " rather curious, but obviously expository, that the villains credit the objects of their
hatred with their true merits. . . . The cruel Queen
of ' Cymbeline ' admits Pisanio's constancy." †
So, indeed, she does — but in terms which are perfectly in character. At Pisanio's entrance, in Act
One, Scene Five, she says aside:

> Here comes a flattering rascal; upon him
> Will I first work: he 's for his master,
> And enemy to my son.

At the end of their conversation, Pisanio departs,
and she gives us her opinion of him:

> A sly and constant knave,
> Not to be shak'd; the agent for his master.

---

* Pages 167–172, 228–229, above.
† *Soliloquies of Shakespeare,* 59.

Cloten, in the same play, has been taken to task for talking " quite glibly " of the wicked commands which he has issued.* But, in spite of his viciousness, Cloten is not, strictly speaking, a villain at all. A vainglorious puppy, teased by his own Gentleman, he serves as a mark for ridicule. Thus, in the speech referred to, he addresses Pisanio:

> Sirrah, if thou wouldst not be a villain, but do me true serv-ice, undergo those employments wherein I should have cause to use thee with a serious industry, that is, what villany soe'er I bid thee do, to perform it directly and truly, I would think thee an honest man; thou shouldst neither want my means for thy relief nor my voice for thy preferment.   (III, 5, 108)

The clumsiness with which he manages to give him-self away here is in keeping with his abiding stu-pidity. And it is notable that throughout the play Cloten rails against the " villain Posthumus " — as the unintellectual Caliban rails against Prospero, in *The Tempest* — and brags with little warrant of his own " noble and natural person " and " the adornment " of his " qualities." †

It must be admitted, then, that on occasion Shakespeare's villains do call attention to their own villainy, and do point out the merits of the good char-acters. In a certain number of cases, moreover, this clearsightedness on their part is of obvious con-venience in forwarding the exposition. On the

---

* Schücking, *Character Problems in Shakespeare's Plays*, 36.

† III, 5, 135, 140. Iachimo's abuse of Posthumus is discussed in the next chapter (pages 304, 305).

other hand, some of the villains consistently speak
well of themselves, or evil of the good characters, or
both. And though a few of the " impartial "
speeches — some of Richard's, for instance — seem
scarcely in character, the fact remains that a surprisingly large number of them demonstrably are.
Over-subtlety in the interpretation of debatable
passages is, of course, to be avoided; but this does not
absolve a critic from the duty of giving credit where
credit is due.

Iago, the greatest of the villains, is still to be considered; and from the very beginning Iago is difficult. We have seen that his first speeches might, at
least momentarily, win sympathy for him from an
audience unacquainted with the sequel.* To what
extent, we ask, was he justified in feeling that
Othello had treated him shabbily in the matter of
the lieutenancy? Bradley, who is ever on his guard
against being fooled by Iago, distrusts the whole
story. " It is absolutely certain," he writes, " that
Othello appointed Cassio his lieutenant, and *nothing*
else is absolutely certain." Cassio, he argues, cannot have been an unpractised theorist, for " Othello
chose him for lieutenant " (which neatly begs the
question), the Venetian Senate made him Governor
of Cyprus, and Desdemona once mentions that he
had " shar'd dangers " with her husband (iii, 4,
95). " What is certain," again, is that Othello

* Pages 108, 109, above.

" never dreamed of Iago's being discontented "
at the appointment.* Following a very different
method of approach, Brander Matthews finds that

Shakspere was too experienced a playwright not to know that
the spectator cannot help forming his impression of characters
not yet seen from what is said about them before they appear.
. . . We may rest assured that Shakspere put these speeches in
Iago's mouth for the definite purpose of making clear to the
audience that Iago believes he has reason to detest Othello.
The actual truth of what Iago says does not matter.†

Iago's vindictiveness comes out so plainly, indeed,
before the first scene is over, that we suspend judgment until we can hear —what is never vouchsafed
us — Othello's side. The reality of the Ancient's
desire to supplant Cassio is not, however, to be
doubted. The lieutenancy figures in more than one
of his early soliloquies; ‡ and that it was a definite
incentive is made clear by a speech of Emilia's,
perfect in its unconscious irony. " I will be hang'd,"
she cries,

> if some eternal villain,
> Some busy and insinuating rogue,
> Some cogging cozening slave, *to get some office*,
> Have not devis'd this slander.   (IV, 2, 130)

It is quite true that Iago " takes no particular
pleasure in Cassio's place once he has got it."§ But

---

* *Shakespearean Tragedy*, 211–213.
† *Shakspere as a Playwright*, 249.
‡ I, 3, 399; II, I, 172–174 and 320; *cf.* also II, 3, 128 ff.
§ Stoll, *Shakespeare Studies*, 387. " Having motives," Stoll con-
tinues, Iago " acts as if he had them not."

that is explained by the progressive character of
Iago's plot — when at last he hears Othello say,
"Now art thou my lieutenant," he is deeply in-
volved * — and by the multiplicity of his motives.

Iago, as we have seen, hates Othello. A report
has come to his ears that Othello has had to do with
his wife —

> ' the thought whereof
> Doth like a poisonous mineral gnaw his inwards.'

Though he is unconvinced of the truth of this story,
he has not concealed his suspicion from Emilia;
and he decides, early in the tragedy, to act " as if for
surety" and match his enemy "wife for wife," or, at
least, practice " upon his peace and quiet / Even to
madness." † He also hates Cassio. Cassio was pro-
moted when Iago feels that he himself should have
been, and he ' fears Cassio with his night-cap too.' ‡
His suspiciousness does not stop even there. For he
is ready to believe that Cassio is in love with Desdemona, and tries to lead him into betraying himself.§

Iago is not lying, therefore, when he refers to
himself as " nothing if not critical " (that is, cen-
sorious), or when he says that it is his " nature's
plague / To spy into abuses " and that often his

* III, 3, 479.
† I, 3, 392 ff.; II, 1, 303 ff.; IV, 2, 145–147.
‡ II, 1, 319. The actor should, I think, make something of II, 1,
96–103, where the dryness of Iago's reply is noticeable.
§ II, 1, 298; II, 3, 14 ff. See Schücking, *Character Problems in
Shakespeare's Plays*, 208–210.

" jealousy / Shapes faults that are not." * Such a man would be sure to have many motives for his villainy. To insist upon their reality is not to question the rightness of Othello's final designation of him as " that demi-devil."

In the last chapter, we saw that Shakespeare likes to bedeck the speeches of his characters with moral sentences in the manner of a chorus. Even Iago is permitted to drop out of his part in order to deliver lines of this sort. In the fourth act, after Othello has fallen in a trance, Iago stands over him, gloating:

> Work on,
> My medicine, work! Thus credulous fools are caught;
> *And many worthy and chaste dames even thus,*
> *All guiltless, meet reproach.* What, ho! my lord!
>
> (IV, 1, 45)

" Thus credulous fools are caught," is as right as can be. Then, quite without warning, we are preached at. On two other occasions when dramatic propriety is sacrificed the words form part of a rhymed tag; and in rhymed tags a character is not always himself. So Iago's first soliloquy ends,

> I have 't; it is engender'd: *hell and night*
> *Must bring this monstrous birth to the world's light;*
>
> (I, 3, 409)

and his second,

> 'T is here, but yet confus'd:
> *Knavery's plain face is never seen till us'd.*   (II, 1, 323)

---

* II, I, 119; III, 3, 146–148.

If we forget these undramatic, or rather these extra-dramatic, aberrations of his, the plausibility of Iago's comments on himself need be questioned, I think, at only one point in the play.* He has been urging Cassio to seek Desdemona's help, and Cassio has determined to do so. " You advise me well," he observes. Then Iago speaks in soliloquy:

> And what 's he then that says I play the villain?
> When this advice is free I give and honest,
> Probal to thinking and indeed the course
> To win the Moor again?

Desdemona, he continues, will be sorry for Cassio; and she can do what she likes with Othello.

> How am I then a villain
> To counsel Cassio to this parallel course,
> Directly to his good?   Divinity of hell!
> When devils will the blackest sins put on,
> They do suggest at first with heavenly shows,
> As I do now.   (II, 3, 345)

It *was* good advice; but only the quibbling theologians of the devil would call it so. . . . If the speech offends at all, it offends in expression. The thought, to one of Iago's mental acuteness, is a perfectly natural one. And only dramatic criticism at its prosiest will boggle over such a phrase as " divinity of hell." †

* I, 3, 364 (" all the tribe of hell ") seems no more than a flippant development of the idea of Roderigo's damning himself.

† Exception might be taken to the first line, which may (though it need not) imply recognition of the presence of the audience.

In his conversations with Roderigo, Iago speaks with the utmost bitterness against Cassio and Othello.* In his soliloquies, when we can be certain that no disguise conceals him, he is the complete egotist who identifies " honesty " with folly and triumphs over both. " He holds me well," Iago says of his general, at the beginning,

> The better shall my purpose work on him. . . .
>
> The Moor is of a free and open nature,
> That thinks men honest that but seem to be so,
> And will as tenderly be led by the nose
> As asses are.   (I, 3, 396)

In Othello's affection for Desdemona —

> The Moor, howbeit that I endure him not,
> Is of a constant, loving, noble nature;
> And I dare think he 'll prove to Desdemona
> A most dear husband —

he sees only a means of tormenting him, of " practising upon his peace and quiet / Even to madness." † And it is characteristic of him to refer to Cassio, in soliloquy, not as " a pestilent complete knave " — that is spoken partly for Roderigo's benefit — but as an " honest fool." ‡ The " goodness " of Desdemona is conceived of in the same way; for out of it he will "make the net / That shall

---

* Shakespeare even dares to let Iago describe Othello's courtship of Desdemona (II, 1, 225 ff.).

† II, 1, 300, 322.

‡ II, 1, 253; II, 3, 362; cf. also I, 1, 44 ff.

enmesh them all," and " thus credulous fools are
caught." * At one moment in the tragedy, he even
applies the thought, ironically, to himself. Othello
has borne down on him threateningly, and Iago
cries out:

> O grace! O heaven forgive me!
> Are you a man! have you a soul or sense?
> God be wi' you; take mine office.   O wretched fool!
> That liv'st to make thine honesty a vice.
> O monstrous world!   Take note, take note, O world!
> To be direct and honest is not safe. . . .

> I should be wise; for honesty's a fool.   (III, 3, 374)

That brings us back to the question of Iago's motives. For, how, it is asked, could he possibly have
believed that this Othello, or this Cassio, would be
willing to carry on an intrigue with Emilia? † But
Iago is not coolly logical when he fancies that he has
been wronged. Then his language is the language
of passion, while the thought of ' the lusty Moor's
leaping into his seat ' provokes physical sensations
in him and ' gnaws his inwards.' The character of
his mind is also to be taken into account — the
mind of a brilliant opportunist, quick to seize upon
advantages, content to proceed at all hazards with a
plan but half-formed. Thus, Othello's nobility and
Cassio's honesty he recognizes only as they are
pertinent to the interest of the moment. When he is

---

* II, 3, 348–351, 367–371; IV, 1, 46.
† Iago, Professor Kittredge suggests, " has no belief in anybody's *sexual* morality "— which is, perhaps, a sufficient answer.

suspicious, he simply disregards them, and acts " as if for surety." There is, perhaps, only one passage which is seriously disturbing to this interpretation of Iago. In lines already quoted in another connection, the villain runs over his reasons for disposing of both Roderigo and Cassio.* Roderigo, he says, is growing angry and may call him to account for the gold and jewels which he has " bobb'd from him " ;

> If Cassio do remain,
> *He hath a daily beauty in his life*
> *That makes me ugly;* and, besides, the Moor
> May unfold me to him; there stand I in much peril.
> No, he must die. †

If Cassio confers with Othello, Iago is ruined. That he sees clearly, and for him it is reason enough — he does not hesitate. But also, in a flash of thought, Iago perceives that Cassio has something which he himself has no longer — something, too, which he hates Cassio for possessing — honor. To an ordinary criminal, the thought might never occur; but Iago is not an ordinary criminal.

*   *   *

The testimony of the good characters about others needs little discussion. Except when they are duped

---

* Pages 73, 74, above.
† v, 1, 18. There is just a possibility, 1 think, that Iago means *ugly to others*. Then Cassio's " beauty " need no longer be moral beauty, as his own ugliness would no longer be moral ugliness since everyone is sure that he is " honest." Cassio is too *likeable* — witness the lieutenancy.

by some designing villain like " honest " Iago, the
evidence they have to offer is, as might be expected,
eminently trustworthy. A special function is served,
on occasion, by the dignified representatives of
Church and State. Thus, as Professor W. W. Lawrence has pointed out, an ecclesiastic — Friar
Laurence, for instance, or Friar Francis in *Much
Ado* — is sometimes employed to give " confidence
and sanction to the execution of a ruse " ; and when
things are to be straightened out at the end of a
comedy it is likely to be a good duke who straightens
them.* The Archbishop of Canterbury does more
than explain Henry the Fifth's claim to the French
throne: he solemnly vouches for its authenticity, and
takes the whole war upon his own conscience.†
Somewhat similarly, the fact that Don Pedro has
given credence to the accusation against Hero, in
Much Ado, helps to make Claudio's behavior in the
church scene understandable. Even Leonato is
staggered by what he hears:

> Would the two princes lie? and Claudio lie,
> Who lov'd her so, that, speaking of her foulness,
> Wash'd it with tears?   Hence from her! let her die.
>
> (IV, 1, 154)

When, however, the good characters speak of
themselves, they are sometimes taken to task for call-

* *Shakespeare's Problem Comedies*, 93, 103. The testimony of ex-
perts, like the Doctor in *Lear*, has the same value.
† *H. V*, 1, 2. Note especially lines 29–32 and 97 ff.

ing attention to their own merits. We must be on our guard against making rash inferences here. Shakespeare, when all is said, lived three generations, and more, before Addison's ideas about good form had gained currency; and what seems to us an offense against reticence may not, in every instance, have seemed such to the Elizabethans.* It must be admitted, also, that at moments Shakespeare the poet is not wholly reconcilable with Shakespeare the dramatist. When Helena, in *A Midsummer Night's Dream*, speaks of herself and her friend as

> Two lovely berries moulded on one stem,

she is not to be judged by standards of prose.†

As we have seen in the case of the villains, it is easy to cite as examples of the primitiveness of Shakespeare's art passages which on closer scrutiny may prove to be perfectly justifiable in themselves. Early in *King Lear*, Cordelia explains, in two important asides, that she dearly loves her father though she shall be unable to say so when it is time for her to speak. Later, when France expresses a fear, natural, under the circumstances, that Cordelia has been guilty of some monstrous crime, she turns for justice on this point to Lear:

---

* The unwritten code of the English public schools was, again, a late influence. Stoll should be heard, on the other side (*Shakespeare Studies*, 70 ff.; *cf*. Schücking, p. 40).

† III, 2, 211.

> I yet beseech your majesty —
> If for *I want that glib and oily art*
> *To speak and purpose not; since what I well intend,*
> *I 'll do't before I speak* — that you make known
> It is no vicious blot nor other foulness,
> No unchaste action, or dishonour'd step,
> That hath depriv'd me of your grace and favour,
> *But even for want of that for which I am richer,*
> *A still-soliciting eye, and such a tongue*
> *That I am glad I have not,* though not to have it
> Hath lost me in your liking.   (i, 1, 226)

Professor Schücking holds that if we take the itali-
cized lines literally — which he refuses to do —
Cordelia's " air of knowing perfectly well what she
is doing in presenting her advantages in their true
light strikes a false note in the infinite harmony of
her being." * But if the lines are taken in their context, they are by no means out of character. Cordelia is without vanity. She is not abject, either.
" I yet beseech your majesty. . . ." Though she has
been terribly wronged, she asks only that the measure of injustice shall not run over. The hypocrisy
of her sisters — those " jewels of our father " — is,
yet, apparent to her, and she speaks with some
natural bitterness. At least, she says, I am not, nor
would I be, like them. Similarly, Brutus has been
thought to speak out of character when he refers to
himself as " arm'd so strong in honesty " that the
threats of Cassius pass by him like " the idle wind " ;

* *Character Problems*, 38, 39.

and when, again, he says that Octavius could not
" die more honourable " than at his hands.* But
the first phrase is wrung from him in the heat of
anger; while the second is not self-characterization
but part of the formal preliminaries — not, to be
sure, wholly realistic — to an Elizabethan stage
battle.†

But, surely, Caesar himself brags most thrasoni-
cally? I think not. As Shakespeare planned it,
Caesar was to be killed off when the play was a little
less than half over; then, as a ghost, was to reappear,
and avenge his own murder; and, meanwhile,
Brutus was to be, at least technically, the hero. In
practice, Caesar stood in danger of becoming either
too interesting or not interesting enough. Shakespeare attempted to humanize him — as, later, he
tried to make Macbeth " sympathetic " ‡ — intro-
ducing, or emphasizing, such minor defects in him
as his susceptibility to skilful flattery, his ill-health
and superstitiousness, and what may be a hint of
tragic infatuation. This last trait, which Calphurnia seems to notice —

> Alas! my lord,
> Your wisdom is consum'd in confidence — §

---

* *Jul. C.*, IV, 3, 67; V, 1, 59; Schücking, p. 39.

† On I, 2, 84–89, see Granville-Barker, *Prefaces*, 1st Series,
55, 56.

‡ As a result, paradoxically enough, Macbeth is often accused
of having too much goodness, and Caesar, too little greatness.

§ II, 2, 48.

is, perhaps, the real explanation of his manner of speech. On the other hand, as MacCallum points out, "the impression he makes on the unsophisticated mind, on average audiences and the elder school of critics, is undoubtedly an heroic one." * And if, as might be contended, this impression is due, in part, to our preconceptions in favor of the character, the Elizabethans had their preconceptions, too, as no doubt Shakespeare recognized. To many of those who first saw the play, Caesar's grandiloquent phrases would, I take it, have seemed "pompous" in their sense of the word rather than in ours. Others would have said that this was the old, Marlowe way of writing, which gave grandeur, as it were, directly reflected in speech. "I Scilla," says Pompey in Lodge's *Wounds of Civil War*,

> these are words of mickle worth,
> Fit for the master of so great a minde.†

Caesar, after all, was no mere English Harry Monmouth of yesterday, but a great worthy of antiquity — " the noblest man / That ever lived in the tide of times " (III, 1, 256). Even Cassius says nothing of his boasting.‡ His pride was another matter.

---

* *Shakespeare's Roman Plays and their Background*, 226. On Caesar, I am in substantial agreement with Schücking, pp. 40–52.

† Ed. J. Dover Wilson, line 407.

‡ For the testimony of Cassius, see pages 308, 309, below. He does refer, with derision, to the echoing " Caesars " of the first scene (I, 2, 141–147).

Two famous soliloquies by good characters —
Prince Hal's " I know you all " and Hamlet's
" Now might I do it pat " — remain to be considered. The first is now pretty generally accepted
as a sort of " choral interlude." If Hal should be
taken at his word — if, that is, there was design in
his sowing of wild oats — he would be in truth,
what Sir Arthur Quiller-Couch is tempted to call
him, " a prig of a rake." * Clearly, he is no such
monster. Shakespeare had been in trouble over Sir
John Oldcastle (*alias* Falstaff), and probably was
disinclined to run risks. Knowing perfectly well
that he was violating dramatic propriety by doing
so, he marched his prince down-stage, and made
him assure those persons in the audience who might
need assurance that he (the future Henry V) intended to reform, when the right moment came, and
that the world would admire him all the more because of the contrast with his youthful indiscretions.†
The true Hal comes out, happily enough, in a subsequent conversation with Poins:

I am now of all humours that have show'd themselves
humours since the old days of goodman Adam to the pupil age
of this present twelve o'clock at midnight. . . . What 's o'clock,
Francis?   (ii, 4, 105)

The reasons which Hamlet advances for not kill-

* *Shakespeare's Workmanship*, 121.
† *1 H. IV*, 1, 2, 217 ff. That Shakespeare did not quite drop the
fiction is suggested by *H. V*, 1, 2, 266–268; ii, 4, 36–40.

ing the King while he is praying are likely to be accepted as satisfactory reasons by those who absolve
the hero from the charge of unduly delaying his
revenge.* The idea that vengeance, to be complete,
must include the damning of your enemy's soul as
well as the taking of his life was a familiar one to the
Elizabethan audience. They would not have forgotten, we may be sure, the crowning horror of the
Ghost's narration:

> Thus was I, sleeping, by a brother's hand,
> Of life, of crown, of queen, at once dispatch'd;
> Cut off even in the blossoms of my sin,
> Unhousel'd, disappointed, unanel'd,
> No reckoning made, but sent to my account
> With all my imperfections on my head:
> O, horrible! O, horrible! most horrible! †

Nor does Hamlet forget it. He means, therefore,
exactly what he says. On the other hand, it is possible to hold that Hamlet did not procrastinate, and
yet refuse to take this soliloquy literally. For the
hero to pounce upon Claudius, there and then —
for him to kill a defenceless man who has just
awakened our sympathy in a very great soliloquy of
his own — would be unbecoming, as a tragic ending. In any case, it was not the ending that Shakespeare had in mind. He must, accordingly, find excuses, satisfactory to the audience, for Hamlet's
inaction; Hamlet must find excuses, satisfactory to

---

* See especially Stoll, *Hamlet*, 51 ff.
† I, 5, 74; *cf.* also I, 2, 182; V, 2, 47.

his sense of obligation, for not doing what, in point of fact, his whole nature forbids him to do.* Finally, there are those who believe that the hero was unequal to his task. They point with confidence to the Ghost's rebuke, in the next scene, and ask how " Hamlet's purpose " could " be ' almost blunted ' if in reality he was fiercely seeking a ' more horrid ' revenge." † They find significance, also, in the couplet spoken by Claudius after Hamlet's exit:

> My words fly up, my thoughts remain below:
> Words without thoughts never to heaven go.
>
> (III, 3, 97)

Thus, they assure us, Shakespeare " condemns Hamlet's refusal of the pat opportunity " ‡ — but the King's lines need not be so construed. It remains true that we cannot take *both* Hamlet's soliloquy and the Ghost's rebuke at quite their face value.

* This explanation is Professor Kittredge's.
† J. Q. Adams, ed., *Hamlet*, Boston, 1929, p. 277; and see pages 189 ff., above.
‡ Adams, *ibid.*; Bradley, 171 and note.

Chapter IX

ALLOWANCE FOR MOTIVE AND PREJUDICE

The Death of Ophelia — Misstatements about Known
Facts — About Known Characters — And Unknown
Characters — Some Problems not Problems to Elizabethan Audience — Misstatements about Facts which
lie Outside our Knowledge — Hamlet's Delay.

MORE than once, in the preceding pages, it
has been necessary to explain in terms of
the speaker's character some passage which, at first
sight, appeared to be purely expository. Where are
we to look for impartial judgments if not in the
speech of dismissal and reconciliation which closes
an Elizabethan tragedy? Yet it will be remembered
that Malcolm, at the end of *Macbeth*, is not in the
least impartial, calling Macbeth a " dead butcher "
and Lady Macbeth a "fiend-like queen." The
convention of the final speech was a useful one, as
Shakespeare knew, but to have followed it with
Malcolm in *Macbeth* would not have been to follow
life.*

By following life, Shakespeare is continually
brushing aside the technical formulas of his critics.
Thus Professor Schücking maintains, quite plausibly, that we should prefer the Queen's explanation

* See page 131, above.

of Ophelia's death to the Grave-digger's. " The report of the Queen is the first," he notes, " that
brings the event to the spectator's knowledge " ;
and the Grave-digger is merely a low comedian
whose opinions would not be " taken seriously by
anybody." * But Schücking forgets the Priest (or,
as Professor Dover Wilson would have it, the Doctor
of Divinity), who is a very dignified witness indeed:

> Her obsequies have been as far enlarg'd
> As we have warrantise: her death was doubtful,
> And, but that great command o'ersways the order,
> She should in ground unsanctified have lodg'd
> Till the last trumpet.   (v, 1, 248)

If we believe with Gertrude that Ophelia's death
was accidental, we are to suppose that the Priest
represents a special point of view — that of " the
rigid ecclesiastical authorities " who have not been
satisfied by what they have heard.† If, on the other
hand, we hold with the Priest that Ophelia probably took her own life, we may assume that Gertrude's story was colored by her pity, or that new
facts have come to light, meanwhile. In other
words, we cannot treat *both* accounts as if they were
retailed by the classical Messenger or by a First and
Second Gentleman. " Shakspere," writes Dow-

---

* *Character Problems*, 85, 86; *cf.* Feuillerat's review in *Litteris*,
III (1926), 24, 25.
† J. Dover Wilson, ed., *Hamlet*, 238 (Wilson would have Hora-
tio's " accidental judgments "— v, 2, 396 — refer to the death of
Ophelia).

den, " sees the fact " of Ophelia's death " from the
Queen's point of view, and from Hamlet's; from the
priest's and from the grave-digger's points of view.
That is to say, he sees the fact in the round; and the
pathos of Ophelia's death is in the drama as real as
it would be if the occurrence became actual." *

Sometimes, on the good old Bartley principle, a
misstatement of facts known to the audience is
labelled for what it is, and the motives which
prompted the speaker to depart from the truth are
carefully set forth. An example occurs near the end
of the *First Part of Henry IV*. Worcester, who has
been sent to parley with the King, is told by him
that if Hotspur and the rebels will " take the offer
of our grace " their offences will be forgotten:

> Both he and they and you, yea, every man
> Shall be my friend again, and I 'll be his.
>
> (v, 1, 107)

Next we see Worcester talking with Vernon:

> *Worcester.* O, no! my nephew must not know, Sir Richard,
> The liberal kind offer of the king.
> *Vernon.* 'T were best he did.
> *Worcester.*   Then are we all undone.
> It is not possible, it cannot be,
> The king should keep his word in loving us.
>
> (v, 2, 1)

Hotspur may be forgiven, he admits, but Northumberland, and Worcester himself, will never be. So,

* *Shakspere,* 316.

in the scene that follows, the King's attitude is deliberately misrepresented. Hotspur is killed at Shrewsbury. Worcester is taken prisoner. Before he is led away to be executed, he is blamed by the King for what has happened:

> Ill-spirited Worcester! did we not send grace,
> Pardon, and terms of love to all of you?
> And wouldst thou turn our offers contrary? . . .

Worcester. What I have done my safety urg'd me to.*

Usually, however, a misstatement of facts known to the audience goes unlabelled. No one, I take it, is perplexed by the bland falsehoods of Petruchio when, in the second act, he assures the company that Katharina really loves him:

> 'T is bargain'd 'twixt us twain, being alone,
> That she shall still be curst in company.
> I tell you, 't is incredible to believe
> How much she loves me: O! the kindest Kate.
> She hung about my neck. . . .
> (*Tam. Shr.*, II, 1, 298)

We have just seen them together, and Kate certainly did not hang about his neck; but Petruchio is Petruchio, we say, and by this time we know pretty well what his game is. Shakespeare, to put it another way, was turning to account the advantages of preparation as against surprise.

After the scuffle between Kent and Oswald by moonlight, each talks about what has happened,

* v, 5, 2; *cf.* also 2 *G. Ver.*, 1, 3, 45 ff.

both speak in character, and neither tells the truth.*
Oswald pretends that he " spar'd " Kent " at suit
of his grey beard," and perceptibly distorts the circumstances of their earlier encounter. Kent implies that the mere sight of Oswald's face infuriated
him, and suppresses the real cause of his hate —
Oswald's studied impudence toward Lear. Kent
himself is not over-considerate of Cornwall's feelings
— having, as he says, ' seen better faces in his time '
— and Cornwall coolly sums him up for the benefit
of the others:

> This is some fellow,
> Who, having been prais'd for bluntness, doth affect
> A saucy roughness. . . .
>
> These kind of knaves I know, which in this plainness
> Harbour more craft and more corrupter ends
> Than twenty silly-ducking observants,
> That stretch their duties nicely.   (II, 2, 101)

The acuteness of the description is remarkable, but
Kent is already the darling of the audience, and it
does him no harm with them, and Cornwall no
good.†

Once, indeed, we have made up our minds about
a character, we change them — at least in the popular theatre — somewhat grudgingly. Shakespeare
counted on this; counted, also, on our ability to

---

* *Lear*, II, 2, 55 ff.
† *Cf.* Granville-Barker, *Prefaces*, 1st Series, 193. Cornwall is, as
yet, practically unknown.

recognize obvious motives and obvious prejudices. So Octavius may call Antony an " old ruffian," Angelo maintain that his real reason for rejecting Mariana was that " her reputation was disvalu'd / In levity," and Falstaff confide to Mrs. Tearsheet that the Prince was a " shallow young fellow " who "would have made a good pantler" — in every case, we know better, and make the necessary allowances.* Even Berowne, the chorus character in *Love's Labor's Lost*, starts aside from the truth, when he is vexed, and roundly abuses Boyet:

> Some carry-tale, some please-man, some slight zany,
> Some mumble-news, some trencher-knight, some Dick,
> That smiles his cheek in years, and knows the trick
> To make my lady laugh when she 's dispos'd,
> Told our intents before. . . .
>
> You put our page out: go, you are allow'd;
> Die when you will, a smock shall be your shroud.†

Boyet has been a principal instrument in the discomfiture of Berowne and his companions; and, as the only male among their tormentors, he must bear the brunt of their annoyance.‡

> Here comes Boyet, and mirth is in his face,

---

* *A. & C.*, IV, 1, 4; *Meas.*, V, 1, 214 (*cf.* III, 1, 215 ff.); *2 H. IV*, II, 4, 257.
† V, 2, 464; *cf.* 316 ff.
‡ Similarly, Belleur, after being teased by Rosalura, in *The Wild-Goose Chase*, vents his anger on the two unknown Gentlemen (III, 1).

the Princess had noted, earlier in the same scene; and, at the end, Berowne is reconciled with him, despite himself — " Well said, old mocker: I must needs be friends with thee." * That, we feel, is as it should be, for we like them both.

But misstatements about known characters may be one thing, and misstatements about unknown characters quite another. Shakespeare habitually takes the audience into his confidence from the outset, though, as we have seen, he allows Iago to begin *Othello*. Early in *Cymbeline*, Iachimo and a Frenchman talk disparagingly of Posthumus. He has been admired, they grant, but that is because he is Imogen's husband:

Iachimo. This matter of marrying his king's daughter, — wherein he must be weighed rather by her value than his own, — words him, I doubt not, a great deal from the matter.
Frenchman. And then, his banishment.   (I, 4, 15)

And they ask Philario how this " beggar " crept into his acquaintance. Now it is true that we have not seen much of Posthumus thus far, but he was introduced as favorably as possible by the two expository Gentlemen, his brief scene of parting with Imogen is moving, and his successful skirmish with Cloten is designed to win our approbation. Iachimo and the Frenchman do not inspire confidence, in any case. And if, by any chance, we are disturbed by their insinuations, it is only for a moment. The

* v, 2, 79, 550.

next thing we hear is the account of a chivalrous challenge issued by an English gentleman in honor of his lady. After that, Posthumus is safe with us.

Shakespeare, once more, is not to be interpreted by means of formulas. If there is one thing which this study of his technique shows clearly, it is that. So it is well to recognize that a dramatist who usually avoids surprise — who, as we have seen, works *with* his audience, habitually — will be unlikely to introduce misstatements about the principal character at the beginning of a play. But when it comes to converting this likelihood (or rather, unlikelihood) into a fixed rule, we should grow suspicious. The first mention of Hamlet's love for Ophelia comes from Laertes, who instructs her, with fraternal gravity, to

> Hold it a fashion and a toy in blood,

and bids her " be wary." * Now English criticism has never doubted that Hamlet loved Ophelia, and there is no need, I think, to labor the point.† It was natural for the sensitive Laertes to warn his sister, and natural for Shakespeare to introduce upon such an occasion the subject of Hamlet's love. Ophelia's smiling reply suggests how her brother's admonition should be taken. And if, after the play is over, we

* I, 3, 6.
† Schücking does not accept the traditional view (*Character Problems*, 67 ff.)

recall his words, they will not be found wanting in irony. For Hamlet did break Ophelia's heart, and it was an ill thing for her that she loved him.

Yet in a play the sequence of the speeches matters greatly, and *where* a passage occurs may imply how it is to be understood. At the end of the first scene of *King Lear*, Goneril and Regan are alone on the stage:

Goneril. I think our father will hence to-night.

Regan. That 's most certain, and with you; next month with us.

Goneril. You see how full of changes his age is; the observation we have made of it hath not been little: he always loved our sister most; and with what poor judgment he hath now cast her off appears too grossly.

Regan. 'T is the infirmity of his age; yet he hath ever but slenderly known himself.

Goneril. The best and soundest of his time hath been but rash; then, must we look to receive from his age, not alone the imperfections of long-engraffed condition, but, therewithal the unruly waywardness that infirm and choleric years bring with them.

Regan. Such unconstant starts are we like to have from him as this of Kent's banishment.

They must " hit together," they say, or Lear's abdication " will but offend " them.

Regan. We shall further think on 't.

Goneril. We must do something, and i' the heat.

Obviously, the speeches look forward. The wicked sisters have combined against their father. They will discover, in his conduct, pretexts for their own inhumanity. But the speeches look back, as well. Though Goneril and Regan are hostile to Lear, they

tell us what is substantially the truth about him.
" The observation we have made . . . hath not
been little " — it is almost undramatic, almost a
label. This first discussion of him is in prose, not
verse. It is cruelly dispassionate. Lear was wrong
in casting off Cordelia, and wrong in banishing
Kent. He is rash, and violent, and old. The " in-
tellects " of the speakers " are not at fault if their
hearts are." *

It remains to say something about a last group of
misstatements — those which have to do with facts,
or events, lying outside the knowledge of the audience. But first, it must be suggested that many
matters which we find puzzling today would not
have seemed so when Shakespeare's plays were put
on at Blackfriars or the Globe. *Then* the spectators,
knowing beyond a peradventure what Octavia
looked like — had they not seen her on the boards,
only a moment before? — could enjoy the shifts of
Cleopatra's Messenger as he suited his story to the
desires of his listener.[†] They had seen Claudius, too,
and were not taken in, as some of the commenta-
tors have been, by what Hamlet says of him. Of
course, Claudius may have looked like Richard III
without his hump.[‡] But there is no evidence that
he did. If we are to believe Hamlet when he likens

* Miss Fansler, *The Evolution of Technic in Elizabethan Tragedy*, 189.
    † *A. & C.*, III, 3; *cf.* II, 2, 134, 249, and Hazlitt, *Shakespeare's Library*, pt. I, vol. III, p. 384.
    ‡ *Cf.* J. Q. Adams, ed., *Hamlet*, 182.

his uncle to " a mildew'd ear," we ought to believe
Hamlet, also, when he calls him " a vice of kings "
and a " king of shreds and patches," which plainly
he is not.* The audience, I repeat, had seen Claudius; and they were quite capable of allowing for
prejudice.

When, in the same play, Gertrude is telling Claudius about the death of Polonius she is asked where
Hamlet has gone.

> *Queen.* To draw apart the body he hath kill'd;
>   O'er whom his very madness, like some ore
>   Among a mineral of metals base,
>   Shows itself pure: he weeps for what is done.
>
> (IV, 1, 24)

Some of the critics have believed her.† But when
we last saw Hamlet he was far from weeping.

> I 'll lug the guts into the neighbour room,

he had said grimly. And the same strain of sardonic merriment is continued in the scene that follows. What is more, the Queen is palpably desirous
of shielding her son. Hamlet did not hear " something stir " behind the arras, as she now asserts he
did: he heard a man's voice calling for help.‡ Slight
as it is, the deviation from truth is significant. In
another tragedy, Cassius hates Caesar, and tells dis-

---

* III, 4, 64, 98, 102. It is good to hear Saintsbury, in a characteristic parenthesis, call Hamlet's " abusive description " of Claudius
" 'not evidence,' if ever anything was not " (*Shakespeare*, 79).

† Dowden, *Shakspere*, 130; Schücking, *Character Problems*, 225.

‡ Bradley, *Shakespearean Tragedy*, 104, note.

creditable stories about him to Brutus. Presumably, these stories were not made up for the occasion. There is no reason to suppose that Caesar may not have contended in swimming, and lost, or that he may not have suffered from fever, and called for drink. It is the emotional coloring of the account — the "coward lips," the crying to Titinius like "a sick girl" — that is false.* Shakespeare trusts his audience to suspend judgment for a little: presently they will hear Caesar on Cassius. In *Lear*, finally, Goneril has been thought to have a case against the King in the riotous behavior of his knights.† A sufficient answer to this charge is found in the brief scene between Goneril and Oswald, just before Lear's return from hunting. Goneril begins with fact: Lear has struck one of her gentlemen " for chiding of his fool." He 'flashes' into 'gross crimes,' she says (as if that were one!), and " his knights grow riotous."

> Put on what weary negligence you please,
> You and your fellows; I 'd have it come to question:
> If he distaste it, let him to my sister.   (I, 3, 13)

Then she takes Oswald into her confidence, telling him that Regan is at one with her about Lear:

> Old fools are babes again, and must be us'd
> With checks as flatteries, when they are seen abus'd.
> Remember what I have said.

---

* I, 2, 98 ff.; see also Schücking, 66, 67.
† Miss Lily Campbell, *Shakespeare's Tragic Heroes*, 190–192.

Oswald.   Well, madam.
Goneril.   And let his knights have colder looks among you;
              What grows of it, no matter; advise your fellows so:
              I would breed from hence occasions, and I shall,
              That I may speak: I 'll write straight to my sister
              To hold my very course.

The pretext, which Regan adopts in her turn, is here tagged and docketed for what it is. Lear gives Goneril the lie direct:

> My train are men of choice and rarest parts,
> That all particulars of duty know

(men, in other words, like Edgar and the well-behaved Knight whom we have just seen).* No one in the theatre would doubt which to believe.†

At moments, however, it is difficult to know whether we should allow for prejudice on the part of a witness or not. And that brings us back to *Hamlet*. How are we to understand the soliloquies in which the hero blames himself for his inaction? Is he, in effect, prejudiced? He must wait, say some of the critics, and while he waits is it not perfectly natural that he should expostulate with himself, kick against the pricks, and search his own heart, desperately, for what is not there? And, again, would not the audience recognize that he was doing

---

* I, 4, 287; II, 1, 96.
† Nor would anyone in the theatre believe, with Professor Stoll, that what Othello tells Desdemona about the handkerchief (III, 4) was " a tale made up for the occasion to scare the poor lady into betraying her guilt " (*Othello*, p. 25, note).

this? * Yet it is precisely to the same soliloquies that
other critics point confidently for evidence that
Hamlet was at fault! The existence of such major
differences among acknowledged authorities is a
little dispiriting; but, at least, it is assumed by both
sides that Shakespeare wrote for the Elizabethan
stage and for the Elizabethan audience. . . . That
he wrote, also, to please himself has been suggested
more than once in the course of the present inquiry.

* Professor Spencer makes the interesting point that in Better-
ton's time, when the *Hamlet* tradition seems still to have been alive,
the soliloquies were drastically abridged in performance (" Seven-
teenth-Century Cuts in Hamlet's Soliloquies," *Review of English
Studies*, IX [1933], pp. 257–265).

INDEXES

Index of Shakespearean Plays

General Index

223